Something Borrowed, Something Learned?

SOMETHING BORROWED, SOMETHING LEARNED?

The Transatlantic Market in Education and Training Reform

David Finegold
Laurel McFarland
William Richardson

The Brookings Institution
Washington, D.C.

379.41
S696

About Brookings

The Brookings Institution is a private nonprofit organization devoted to research, education, and publication on important issues of domestic and foreign policy. Its principal purpose is to bring knowledge to bear on current and emerging policy problems.

The Institution was founded on December 8, 1927, to merge the activities of the Institute for Government Research, founded in 1916, the Institute of Economics, founded in 1922, and the Robert Brookings Graduate School of Economics, founded in 1924.

The Institution maintains a position of neutrality on issues of public policy. Interpretations or conclusions in Brookings publications should be understood to be solely those of the authors.

Copyright © 1993
THE BROOKINGS INSTITUTION
1775 Massachusetts Avenue, N.W., Washington, D.C. 20036

All rights reserved

Library of Congress Cataloging-in-Publication data

Something borrowed, something learned? : the transatlantic market in education and training reform / [edited by] David Finegold, Laurel McFarland, William Richardson.
    p. cm.
Includes bibliographical references (p.)
IBSN 0-8157-2804-2 (cl) -- ISBN 0-8157-2803-4 (pa) :
1. Education and state--Great Britain--Cross--cultural studies.
2. Education and state--United States--Cross--cultural studies.
3. Educational change--Great Britain--Cross-cultural studies.
4. Educational change--United States--Cross-cultural studies.
5. Education--International cooperation. I. Finegold, David.
II. McFarland, Laurel.   III. Richardson, William.
LC93G7.S66   1993   93-28640
379.41--dc20   CIP

9 8 7 6 5 4 3 2 1

The paper used in this publication meets the minimum requirements of the American National Standard for Information Sciences--Permanence of paper for Printed Library Materials, ANSI Z39.48-1984

Contents

University Libraries
Carnegie Mellon University
Pittsburgh PA 15213-3890

Part 1

Introduction

DAVID FINEGOLD, LAUREL McFARLAND, AND WILLIAM
RICHARDSON

A distinct pattern emerged in the British education and training reform
process in the latter half of the 1980s. A government minister or a team of
policy experts would pay a brief study visit to the United States, and a short
time later a new initiative that bore a close resemblance to a U.S. program
would be announced. Among the U.K. reforms that appear to have been at
least partially inspired by U.S. experience are magnet schools and city
technology colleges, training and enterprise councils (TECs),
education-business compacts, community colleges, student loans for higher
education, licensed teachers, and employment training. In some cases, the
borrowing process involved the transfer of personnel rather than the flow of
ideas across the Atlantic. The U.K. Department of Employment, for
example, acquired an aide from former governor Michael Dukakis's office in
Massachusetts to help in the development of TECs and, later, compacts,
based on her experience working with U.S. private industry councils (PICs).

More recently, the flow of policy ideas across the Atlantic appears to
have reversed directions. American commentators are beginning to show
keen interest in reforms introduced by the Thatcher government in two
policy areas. In relation to schools the combined elements of the Education
Reform Act (national curriculum and assessment, local management of
schools, opting out) constitute a far more comprehensive move toward an
educational marketplace than scattered U.S. experiments (Chira 1992a).
American interest is also noticeable in the area of industrial training, where
British initiatives in the 1980s to create clearly defined occupational
standards (National Vocational Qualifications) and a national foundation
skills program for school leavers (the Youth Training Scheme and its

The volume is based on the proceedings of a July 1990 conference organized by
David Finegold and William Richardson of the University of Warwick's Vocational
Education and Training Forum in conjunction with Laurel McFarland of the
Brookings Institution, Washington, DC.

replacements) may provide valuable lessons for the United States in the decade to come.

Education reforms in the two countries have also developed along similar lines during the 1980s and early 1990s without direct policy transfer occurring. These reforms include the movement to increase parental school choice, and hence consumer power in education, greater pressures for accountability among education professionals, debates over "workfare," and attempts to better equip young people for the work world and to motivate underachievers by bridging the academic-vocational divide.

Although the volume of recent education and training policy traffic between the United States and United Kingdom is new and unusual, the more general phenomenon of appropriating other nations' policies is not. As David Phillips observes, there is a long history of policymakers importing foreign solutions to domestic problems and of academics pointing to the difficulties of transferring policies into different national contexts. In a similar vein, David Brian Robertson and Jerold L. Waltman draw from the political science literature to focus specifically on the politics and politicians involved in international borrowing. They argue that the likelihood of borrowing increases when possible solutions from recent domestic history have been tried and have failed.

In spite of the problems associated with transplanting one nation's policies into another country's historical and institutional setting, the process of transnational borrowing is likely to become more common in the years ahead. This is not a comment on convergence between the political economies of the United States and United Kingdom, but rather on the general internationalization of the world's academic and policy communities. As the cost of sending people and information between countries has fallen, it has become more practical to include other nations' experiences in the domestic policy equation. And with the growing interdependence between industrialized economies, the pressure is likely to increase on those nations trailing in the competitive race to emulate their more successful rivals.

The concentration of numerous cases of British appropriation of U.S. education and training (ET) policies in a brief time period—the final years (1986–90) of the Thatcher government—provides a unique opportunity to improve our understanding of the ET reform process and the role that international comparisons can play in shaping the domestic ET policy agenda.

This book develops a three-tiered approach to the comparative analysis of ET. In part 1, Phillips and Robertson and Waltman draw from various social science resources to create an analytical framework for the study of ET policy borrowing. Part 2 examines the specific context in which the transfer of policies has occurred, asking why Britain looked to America for ET policy inspiration in the latter half of the 1980s? This section explores those similarities in the two countries' political idealogies, economic systems, and ET problems that made borrowing attractive and the differences in culture and institutional structures that may produce unintended policy consequences. Part 3 examines individual cases of ET reforms in the United States and United Kingdom and attempts to distill lessons about the process of transferring ET reforms from one nation to another. The case studies also provide description and evaluation of U.S. programs that may serve as a useful guide to how the borrowed policies will evolve in Britain and the problems they may encounter.

Why the United States and United Kingdom? The Economic and Political Context

Many American ET experts have been surprised and confused to learn that Margaret Thatcher looked to their country for policy ideas. They are surprised because they tend to view the British education and training system as relatively successful; they are confused because, in the United States, the ET system is widely considered to be in such a state of crisis that no nation would want to emulate it. For observers of the British scene, these American problems will seem familiar: significantly lower levels of attainment in reading, math, and science compared to its main international competitors; high drop-out rates in secondary schools, particularly in the inner cities; and growing skills shortages in specific industrial sectors. Ironically, it is the common institutional setting of these problems, rather than any record of success, that may explain the affinity between the two countries' policymakers.

To understand the reasons for ET policy convergence between the United States and United Kingdom, including cases of direct policy borrowing, part 2 examines the broader economic and political context of ET policies in America and Britain in the late 1980s. David Finegold suggests that common economic forces have been driving ET reform in all the industrialized countries during the last decade. The rapid changes in technology and the internationalization of capital place the efficiency of nations' ET systems and the adequacy of their skills base under the political microscope. Within this general trend, he and Sarah Cleveland point to the shared characteristics of U.S. and U.K. political economies to explain why ET policy converged in these two countries.

Not only do the United States and United Kingdom display common symptoms, such as declining competitiveness in world markets and low skill demands from many employers, but they also appear to be suffering from the same underlying ailments: the short-term bias imparted to managers by the stock market and a lack of cooperative mechanisms to share the cost and knowledge needed to pursue high-skill strategies. Hong Tan and Christine Peterson emphasize the key role the market plays in allocating training in employment in the two countries, while David Raffe and Russell Rumberger examine the common problem of low participation levels in post-compulsory education and its dual manifestation: high drop-out rates in the United

States and low staying-on rates in the United Kingdom. As Cleveland points out, however, analyses of the low skills deficiencies in both countries suggest that policy borrowing from each other may be the least appropriate source of inspiration.

Not only have the U.S. and U.K. governments faced common problems, but they have also shared a similar interpretation of the state's proper role in solving these problems. The Anglo-American emphasis on voluntarism, or leaving training to the market, combined with the weakness of corporatist arrangements, has served to separate the United States and United Kingdom from western Europe and Asia.

The historical linkages between the two nations' languages, cultures, and state structures, however, were strengthened in the 1980s by the political ideologies of Margaret Thatcher and Ronald Reagan. Each stressed the need to release market forces, cut taxes, and reduce the power of trade unions. Indeed, as the close personal relationship between Reagan and Thatcher developed, they became joint leaders in the worldwide spread of "new right" ideas (Smith 1990). Such ideas in New Zealand Australia, Spain, and eastern Europe have not been confined to right-wing parties.

A number of the chapters in this volume refer to broad political and institutional issues that arise from the release of market forces promoted by the new right. For example, problems of accountability of British agencies removed from traditional forms of local government control are discussed in the context of TECs and education-business compacts (Bailey and Richardson). Tan and Peterson analyze the self-regulation of the training markets in both countries, and the tension between the centralization and decentralization of policy is raised in the cases on magnet schools and compacts (Richardson and Green).

In the specific education and training policy context, new right ideas in the United States and United Kingdom have also closely resembled each other. Anthony Green and William Boyd for example, discuss the central concept of choice and the stress on market mechanisms in school provision evident in recent United States and United Kingdom school reform. Allied to this trend is an emphasis, in both countries, on further reducing the role of the state. In part 3 Thomas Bailey, William Richardson, and Laurel McFarland assess a private sector intervention in the context of employer-led training policy, in school management, and in the financing of higher education.

Nevertheless, the similarities that may appear to make U.S.-U.K. policy emulation irresistible should not be overemphasized. There are major differences between the ET and economic systems in the two countries. For instance, in the United States higher education is treated as an investment for which individuals and their families are prepared to pay, while in the United Kingdom it has traditionally been seen as a right, or consumption good, where the state covers the full tuition costs for the much smaller group who qualifiy (McFarland). At the other end of the educational spectrum, the scale of the underclass, and the public policy problems this creates, are far greater in the United States than in Britain (Green). In the school context, Cleveland and Green refer to the different American and British interpretations of and expectations for "comprehensive" education, and Boyd comments on the strikingly polarized and politicized nature of education reform literature in the United Kingdom compared to that of the United States before reviewing evidence of the divergent experiences in the two countries of the operation of open enrollment. With regard to post-compulsory ET, Raffe and Rumberger assess important differences in the two countries' institutional structures, social demographics, and labor markets, while Tan and Peterson examine the different experiences of young workers in training.

Perhaps the most significant difference between the two countries in the ET context is the much stronger role that central government can play in reforming the ET system in Britain than in the United States. Educational reform in the United States requires the active involvement of federal, state, and local government. The examples of education-business partnerships and compacts (Richardson) show clearly the U.K. Department of Employment's capacity to take an initiative that was begun locally in America and replicate it across Great Britain. In contrast, a wave of skepticism accompanied President Bush's National Goals for Education with commentators pointing to the inability of the U.S. federal government to ensure that its proposals would be adopted at the state level.

Such differences between the U.S. and U.K. ET systems certainly complicate the transfer of policy across countries and may be the main cause of unintended consequences in the process. And, as Raffe and Rumberger point out, the greater the differences between features of national systems, the greater the level of abstraction required when attempting such policy transfers.

The Borrowing Process: Lessons from the Case Studies

The final set of questions that arises from our consideration of British policy-borrowing of U.S. ET initiatives surrounds the borrowing process itself. What is the effect of differing social, economic, and political contexts on transplanted policies. Can a particular program, like a donor organ, work in isolation from the ET system that created it? What problems have been encountered as transplanted policies are put into practice? How have the British policies, once borrowed and implemented, differed from their American counterparts? Raffe and Rumberger suggest that policy borrowing can arise from heightened self-awareness of the domestic system generated by comparative analysis, the identification of both positive and negative features in the foreign example that are absent at home, and a recognition of the functional equivalence in contrasting systems (that is, the need to differentiate the stages of a foreign system from the age groups in them).

Complimenting this perspective, the case studies in this volume provide new insights into the borrowing process, with perspectives on the likelihood of unintended consequences, the effects of borrowing at different levels within the political system, and the importance of borrowing agents.

Unintended consequences may yet have considerable effects on two U.S. policies now operating in Britain. Bailey's analysis of PICs and TECs shows how the mechanism of employer-led training was borrowed from the United States, in the face of evidence that employers have not made a significant contribution to PIC effectiveness, and how demands made on employers will be much greater in the British version. McFarland highlights a similar issue concerning student loans where it seems highly unlikely that the U.S. model favored by the British government can fulfill its aim of reducing public funding of higher education. As TECs and student loans develop, it will be a test of effective borrowing to see if U.K. policymakers use comparative research evidence to anticipate unintended consequences of policy borrowing. Early in the student loans case, for example, the British government suffered the embarrassment of the collapse of the bank consortium set up to run the system.

The speed with which borrowing can take place is illustrated in Richardson's analysis of compacts. The Boston model was replicated in both countries ahead of either a clear understanding of the operation of incentives in the youth labor market or the determinants of the Boston compact's early "success." Several British commentaries have criticized a U.S. tendency to place social policy replication before understanding its effect (Johnstone 1988; Walker 1990) while, in the British case, compact replication satisfied Thatcher's need to act speedily on inner-city policy after promises made on election night 1987. Richardson's analysis also highlights the question of the costs of borrowing: the low cost to the British government of compact replication and the high cost, in terms of effectiveness, when borrowed policy is introduced into a changed economic environment.

That borrowing occurs at various political and institutional levels is shown in several of the case studies. Richardson shows how the Thatcher government took credit for compact policy-borrowing when this had been pioneered by local education-business leaders in London, and Anthony Green shows the difference between the incentives of local and national British policymakers in emulating U.S. magnet schools: local Conservative councils saw them as a way of alleviating falling rolls, while the Conservative government stressed the new right idea of consumer choice in schooling. Even at the local level, however, the attraction of borrowing differed. Head teachers and the Chief Education Officer of Wandsworth returned from the United States divided over the merits of magnet schools.

Each of the case studies points to the importance of the borrowing agent. Government ministers, seconded advisers, local government politicians, private sector companies, traveling fellowship programs and the managers of education institutions all play their part (see figure 1). In the

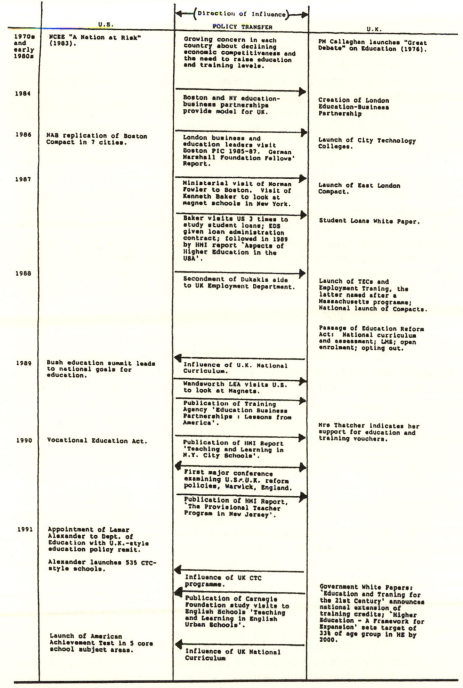

Figure 1. US/UK ET policy borrowing.

Sources: Chapters in this volume; New York Times (1991).

controversy over the local and central control of compacts (Richardson), the British education press specifically citicized the role of U.S. adviser Catherine Stratton, brought from Massachusetts to advise the secretary of state, while praising the "brilliant initiative" in Boston.

The cases also throw light on other borrowing processes. McFarland points to elements in the U.K. political environment after 1987 likely to encourage borrowing: a weak opposition party and strong prior beliefs among Conservative ministers, coupled with the closed, secretive nature of British government.

On the question of transplanting policies from one system to another, the case evidence is varied (Richardson, McFarland, and Green). Compact replication has satisfied the need to act swiftly, although Richardson suggests that specific social, educational, and economic benefits are likely to be increasingly difficult to demonstrate. The original policy context (U.S. desegregation and ethnic quotas) of Green's magnet school case has been transformed in Britain into a new right, choice policy. In the student loans case, McFarland suggests that British economic and political variables—government cost reduction goals, national income distribution, the tax system, and private sector risk assessment—will make policy transplantation very difficult. On perhaps the biggest policy gamble of all, the devolution of more than £2 billion in training programs to the TECs, there is still insufficient evidence to make a judgment (Bailey). While the British government has made a conscious attempt to learn lessons from the PICs, rather than simply duplicate the program, there are signs that TECs are encountering some of the same difficulties—for example, design of performance indicators—that bedeviled the PICs' training efforts in the United States.

Conclusion

John Major's replacement of Margaret Thatcher as leader of the Conservative Party in November 1990 appeared to end this particular episode of concentrated British borrowing of U.S. ET policy. While the new prime minister has continued to foster the "special relationship" across the Atlantic, he has been more open than his predecessor to policy interchange with European countries. The influence of the European Community over British education and training is also likely to increase in the years ahead when this policy area becomes subject to majority voting following the December 1991 Maastricht summit.

While the sources of policy borrowing are likely to be broader in the 1990s, the close linguistic, cultural, and institutional ties between the United States and United Kingdom suggest that the two countries will continue to look to each other for policy ideas. British Conservatives remain covetous of the U.S. labor market's capacity to create jobs and convince individuals to invest in their own education and training. At the same time, in the early

1990s, the United States has become increasingly interested in Britain's experience with national assessment, school-to-work transition programs, and experiments to expand parents' choice over their children's schooling. Though America's weaker central government limits its ability to introduce any of these programs broadly or quickly, the prospect of borrowing from British experience has become front-page national news (Chira 1992b).

Ultimately, Britain's closer integration with Europe will place the questions addressed in this volume in an even broader context: do the U.S. models that have been appropriated in the past decade offer a more successful or appropriate model for the United Kingdom to draw on than that of other industrial countries such as Germany, Sweden, or Japan? International policy borrowing shows no signs of abating in the future. With the pressures to improve educational performance and the declining cost of global communications, an education or training strategy that appears to be effective on the other side of the world can now be rapidly and relatively cheaply replicated. The New Zealand reading program that was borrowed by both the state of Ohio and a British local authority is a reminder of this global trend (Strickland 1992). As governments become more internationally strategic in their educational policy-making, borrowing may soon become the norm rather than the exception. Becoming more self-conscious about why and how policy is borrowed from abroad may have limited influence on actual policy-making, but at the very least it injects some caution into the proceedings, and at best it offers significant enlightenment to enacting better education and training policy.

This book is designed to enhance our understanding of ET policy convergence by providing a comprehensive examination of the politics, processes, and consequences of policy borrowing, by sythesizing and interpreting the literature relevant to the international transfer of policy and by analyzing a set of studies focused on the U.K.-U.S. experience in the 1980s.

It is hoped that this volume will provoke further research on policy borrowing around the world. Future researchers may elect to treat cases of policy borrowing and policy convergence as a subset of the broader areas of comparative public policy. Political scientists can shed light on how different state structures function by examining how and why one country's program changes as it passes through another country's political process. Scholars in comparative studies can use the introduction of similar policies in different countries to compare the reform process or policy effectiveness in a variety of cultural and institutional settings. The questions raised by this volume's work, including why and how nations borrow from overseas, are truly global concerns.

References

Chira, Susan (1992a) "Schools Vie in a Marketplace: More 'Choice' Can Mean Less; Lessons from Britain," New York Times, January 7, p. 1.

Chira, Susan (1992b) "A National Curriculum: Fairness in Uniformity?: Lessons from Britain," New York Times, January 9, p. 1.

Johnstone, D (1988) Enterprise USA: Employment and Training through British Eyes, The Planning Exchange, Glasgow.

Smith, G (1990) Thatcher or Reagan, Bodley Head.

Strickland, S. (1992) "Parties Clash over Cost of Schools Reading Scheme," The Independent, January 4, p. 1.

Walker, Gary, "Foreword" in DeLone, Richard (1990) Replication: Strategy to Improve the Delivery of Education and Job Training Programs, Public/Private Ventures, Philadelphia.

Borrowing Educational Policy

DAVID PHILLIPS

A Frenchman, an Englishman, and a German, were commissioned, it is said, to give the world the benefit of their views on that interesting animal the Camel. Away goes the Frenchman to the Jardin des Plantes, spends an hour there in rapid investigation, returns, and writes a feuilleton, in which there is no phrase the Academy can blame, but also no phrase which adds to the general knowledge. He is perfectly satisfied, however, and says, Le voilà, le chameau! The Englishman packs up his tea-caddy and a magazine of comforts; pitches his tent in the East; remains there two years studying the Camel in its habits; and returns with a thick volume of facts, arranged without order, expounded without philosophy, but serving as valuable materials for all who come after him. The German, despising the frivolity of the Frenchman, and the unphilosophic matter-of-factness of the Englishman, retires to his study, there to construct the Idea of a Camel from out of the depths of his Moral Consciousness. And he is still at it.

I begin with this quotation from Lewes's *Life of Goethe* (Lewes, 1864, pp. 396-97) not because it could be taken to characterise approaches to education in the three countries concerned (though it *might*), but to reinforce at the outset what must be the most important notion to bear in mind when considering the possibilities for educational 'borrowing', namely that cultural imperatives are of fundamental significance in determining approaches to education in particular nations. It is the socio-cultural setting that keeps policies in place and that provides resistance to the implanting of ideas from other systems. A French education minister is reported to have responded, when confronted with research evidence throwing doubt on the practice of *redoublement* (grade repetition): *Mais ... le redoublement, c'est une tradition de la France!* (Postlethwaite, 1984, p. 196).

The concept of 'educational borrowing' has a long history, and we are often rightly reminded that the notion can be traced back as far as Plato. But it was only in the early nineteenth century that the concept of educational borrowing began to be properly developed. In 1816-17 Marc-Antoine Jullien, held by many to be the modern father of comparative education, put together questionnaires designed to identify good educational practice and facilitate its transfer to other systems. The questions he proposed were systematic and exhaustive, and covered most aspects of educational provision; some of them have a familiar ring:

- Must primary school teachers give a report at specific times, of the condition of the classes they superintend, of the behaviour and progress of the children? When and under what form and particular relationships are these reports demanded? To whom are they addressed? What means are taken to verify correctness?
- Does one assign first place to the knowledge most important for *practical* life?
- Is the present organisation of secondary instruction established on a sufficiently broad, solid, and complete basis to supply children of the intermediate and middle class with all the knowledge indispensable to them, and to exercise and develop their faculties? (Fraser, 1964)

Jullien's questions marked the starting point for a long tradition of examination of, and borrowing from, foreign models of provision in education; at times these processes have been systematic, at others random, most of the suggestions for borrowing being highly selective and reflecting the perceived needs of the moment in particular countries.

Noah & Eckstein, in their important book *Toward a Science of Comparative Education*, provide an account of the nineteenth-century educationalists who travelled in search of ideas to be borrowed. Their approaches were largely unsystematic. Horace Mann, for example, was 'prepared to report on whatever happened to catch his eye'; as Noah & Eckstein put it:

> The a priori assumption was blithely made that institutions, even whole systems, could be reproduced at will on foreign soil, given only that their existence was available, and that somehow or other the ground at home was prepared for their reception. (Noah & Eckstein, 1969, p. 32)

This naivety of approach, forgiveable because understandable as far as the pioneer comparativists were concerned, often still characterises the use to which data about other systems are put. I shall return to some recent examples, but first it is necessary to rehearse the warnings against education policy borrowing.

Michael Sadler directed the Office of Special Inquiries and Reports of the English Board of Education from 1895 to 1903 and in that time was responsible for a vast output of detailed information about aspects of education in other countries which was made available in order to inform the debate about provision at home. Some countries – Germany principally – received exhaustive attention, and there was at the time a widespread view that much could be learnt from practice abroad. As one of Trollope's characters (in *Barchester Towers*) had expressed it some fifty years earlier: 'You'll have those universities of yours about your ears soon, if you don't consent to take a lesson from Germany'. There were indeed many lessons to be learnt: German universities led the world in scholarship; Prussia had had compulsory schooling for a hundred years or so; teaching approaches in some subjects – foreign languages, to take just one example – were widely admired; great advances had been made in vocational training, which was to become compulsory by the end of the First World War. But while the reports produced by his office reflected interest in all of these advances, Sadler was always careful to warn against the too easy emulation of foreign models:

> In studying foreign systems of education we should not forget that the things outside the schools matter even more than the things inside the schools, and govern and interpret the things inside. We cannot wander at pleasure among the educational systems of the world, like a child strolling through a garden, and pick off a flower from one bush and some leaves from another, and then expect that if we stick what we have gathered into the soil at home, we shall have a living plant. A national system of education is a living thing, the outcome of forgotten struggles and 'of battles long ago'. It has in it some of the secret workings of national life. (Sadler, 1900, p. 49)

That warning has become one of the classic statements on the value and limitation of comparative studies. Its message, that education systems are, for all their imperfections, part and parcel of the fabric of their society, and that those who would understand them must take into account their historical, political, social and cultural settings, is all too often forgotten by the policy-maker who sees in a particular country's organisational arrangements a quick solution to a perceived problem at home.

We must also consider what is in effect the corollary of borrowing, namely the testing of a potential solution to an educational problem by looking at how it works in another country where it has long been the practice. Torsten Husen has recently reminded us that the Swedish comprehensive school was investigated by foreign observers in the 1960s in order both to argue for implementing a similar type of school at home and to warn against the model adopted by the Swedes – it was 'exemplary both ways', as he puts it (Husén, 1989, pp. 345-55). Elsewhere in this volume (Robertson and Waltman) we are reminded that 'supporters will characterise a borrowed policy in ways that make it appear effective while opponents will make it appear to have uncertain or negative consequences', and reference is made to current (positively motivated) observations about the superiority of other countries' vocational training provision over that in the US or Britain, while pointing to the negative 'guilt by association' verdicts that might be made on seemingly superior provision in nations enjoying disfavour, albeit for temporary periods. It is doubtful, for example, whether the record of the German Democratic Republic in pre-school provision will ever be properly recognised.

Those arguing for national testing of all pupils at various stages of their learning would do well to examine American experience with the SAT; the disadvantages of particular approaches to continuous assessment are clear from a close investigation of experience in the Federal Republic of Germany; some countries with rigid central control of a national curriculum will provide instances of how such control can stifle curricular initiative; the pressures on Japanese schoolchildren demonstrate at what expense high levels of measurable performance may be reached. Often those looking at the measured outcomes of particular systems quite fail to consider the *processes*, some of them highly questionable, that have produced them.

Let me return to some recent instances of what I have called 'cross-national attraction' (Phillips, 1989, pp. 267-74). (The term 'borrowing' is, incidentally, curiously inappropriate for the processes it describes; 'borrowing' implies a temporary *loan* of something, the understanding being that it will be returned at a future stage. Some would argue that the return of 'borrowed' policies might be a just reward for 'lender' systems . . .). Mention of other systems of education has become almost *de rigueur* when making the case for educational change and development. Both Sir Keith Joseph and Kenneth Baker, during their respective terms of office as British Secretary of State for Education and Science, would frequently hold up the example of West Germany when defending the notion of a national curriculum (even though, as it happens, Germany has centrally agreed curricula within each of the *Länder*, rather than a *national* curriculum as such). So great was the interest in the German system that the Department of Education and Science produced a special report by Her Majesty's Inspectors on aspects of curriculum and assessment in that country – the first report of its kind to be published on another country since Sadler's day. That report has been followed by others, covering *inter alia* aspects of education in The Netherlands, France, Denmark and the United States, the latter case being the subject of no fewer than three studies – on higher education, on the 'Provisional Teacher Program' in New Jersey, and on New York City schools. Each of these reports contains elements which could support policy developments at home, but, since they have been produced by the independent Inspectorate, they also take a critical view of some of the issues in question. In the United States the substantial degree of interest in the Japanese achievement in education has found expression in the US Department of Education report of 1987, *Japanese Education Today*; some quarter of a century earlier it was the Sputnik shock that had stimulated an interest in the Soviet example, an interest encapsulated in the title of Arthur Trace's book *What Ivan Knows that Johnny Doesn't*.

Much media attention has been devoted to the lessons to be learnt from studies such as those undertaken by Sig Prais on Germany and Japan (Prais, 1987; Prais and Wagner, 1985). Findings which say that 'over half of all German pupils, compared with only just over a quarter of all pupils in England, attain a standard above or equivalent to a broadly-based set of O-level passes' and that 'attainments in mathematics by those in the lower half of the ability-range in England appear to lag by the equivalent of about two years' schooling behind the corresponding section of pupils in Germany' are bound to excite interest in how it is that the Germans are apparently getting it right. Newspaper headlines confirm the tendency to try to learn from the foreign example: 'Why England is to be found sitting in the dunce's corner'; 'How a maths test left the Japanese number one'; 'Lessons of hope for our crumbling classrooms'; 'German-style traineeships floated'; 'Poor education puts Britain on the skids'.[1] There is little doubt, as far as the UK is concerned, that attention in the media has considerably reinforced the notion that much can be learnt from selected foreign models of educational provision, and that this notion is firmly established in the minds of policy-makers.

There is, then, a clear interest in what foreign models might teach us; that interest is potentially of enormous value provided a tenet of Michael Sadler's is borne in mind:

> The practical value of studying, in a right spirit and with scholarly accuracy, the working of foreign systems of education is that it will result in our being better fitted to study and to understand our own. (Sadler, 1900, p.49)

Robertson and Waltman (next chapter) outline some of the processes involved in policy borrowing of various kinds. Three particular points they make are of considerable importance in the context of *educational* policy borrowing in particular. The first is their description of the short- and long-term motives that guide policy-makers: 'Elected officials', they write, 'are more likely to be interested in a borrowed policy's political symbolism and in short-term benefits for which they can claim credit'. A British Secretary of State wishing to press the case for City Technology Colleges will make sure that the public is made aware of American 'magnet' schools, for example (see Green, this publication, Part 2); or if he wishes to argue for a compulsory curriculum, he will point to the West German example, remembering to remind his audience of the Federal Republic's economic success.

Secondly, there is the notion of the borrowing of techniques and tactics rather than strategy. Two simple examples will illustrate the possibilities. There is no doubting the success of foreign language teaching in many nations of Europe. If we look at the techniques used we find that it is *required* of language teachers in the Federal Republic of Germany, for example, to teach *through the medium* of the target language. This is the kind of technique or tactic that can be, and indeed is being, easily adopted from a foreign model, albeit under very different conditions, in the UK. Similarly, we are able without too much difficulty to adopt a notion such as that of the 'leaving certificate' which most children in continental Europe attain at the end of their compulsory schooling, while ensuring that such certificates and the processes that lead to them are not alien to the home system and its expectations. Robertson & Waltman's quotation from Woodrow Wilson points to what would otherwise have to be done – to adopt another country's certification procedures would necessitate their being 'anglicised' – 'radically, in thought, principle, and aim as well'.

Thirdly, there is the question of the politician seeking 'to borrow strategy without borrowing either the tactics or the contextual changes needed to make a strategy effective', and Robertson & Waltman cite in this context Margaret Thatcher's enthusiasm for entrepreneurial cultures and the increased use of centralised control to impose the market-oriented policies those cultures espouse. Such overarching strategy currently informs policy-making at all levels of British educational provision from school to university, but sufficient attention has not been given to the 'tactics and contextual changes' necessary – many of them implying a commitment to increased funding – to implement the strategy successfully, or at least with the support of the key participants.

Whatever we may make of these particular issues, it is refreshing to note a current awareness of the same kind of warnings about borrowing that Michael Sadler was formulating at the turn of the century. Robertson & Waltman rightly warn of the 'surprising and unintended results' that can ensue when a policy is 'torn from its native habitat of institutional structure and political culture' and urge that political caution should inform the kind of major educational changes that we in England and Wales are currently experiencing.

Note

[1] From *The Independent*, 15.1.87; *The Independent*, 5.2.87; *The Times*, 22.1.90; *The Sunday Times*, 11.2.90; *The Times Educational Supplement*, 16.3.90; *The Sunday Times*, 6.5.90.

Bibliography

Department of Education and Science (DES) (1986) Education in the Federal Republic of Germany: Aspects of Curriculum and Assessment, London (HMSO).

DES (1987) Aspects of Primary Education in the Netherlands, London (HMSO).

DES (1989a) The Provisional Teacher Program in New Jersey, London (HMSO).

DES (1989b) Aspects of Higher Education in the United States of America, London (HMSO).

DES (1989c) Initial Teacher Training in France: the training of secondary teachers in the Académie de Toulouse, London (HMSO).

DES (1989d) Education in Denmark: aspects of the work of the folkeskole, London (HMSO).

Fraser, Stuart (1964) Jullien's Plan for Comparative Education, 1816-1817, New York (Teachers College, Columbia University).

Husén, Torsten (1989) The Swedish School Reform – Exemplary Both Ways, Comparative Education, Vol.25, No.3.

Jullien, Marc Antoine (n.d.) Esquisse d'un ouvrage sur l'éducation comparée, Ann Arbor & London (University Microfilms).

Lewes, George Henry (1864) The Life of Goethe, London (George Routledge), second edition.

Noah, Harold J. & Eckstein, Max A. (1969) Toward a Science of Comparative Education, London (Macmillan).

Phillips, David (1989) Neither a Borrower Nor a Lender Be? The Problems of Cross-National Attraction in Education, Comparative Education, Vol.25, No.3.

Postlethwaite, T. Neville (1984) Research and Policy-making in Education: Some Possible Links, in : Educational Research and Policy – How Do they relate? Torsten Husén & Maurice Kogan (Eds), Oxford (Pergamon).

Prais, S.J. (1987) Educating for Productivity: Comparisons of Japanese and English Schooling and Vocational Preparation, National Institute Economic Review, February.

Prais, S.J. & Wagner, Karin (1985) Schooling Standards in England and Germany : some summary comparisons bearing on economic performance, National Institute Economic Review, May (also in Compare, 16, No.1, 1986).

Sadler, Michael (1900) How far can we learn anything of practical value from the study of foreign systems of education? Address of 20 October, in Selections from Michael Sadler, J.H. Higginson (Ed.), Liverpool (Dejall & Meyorre).

Trace, Arther S. (1961) What Ivan Knows That Johnny Doesn't, New York (Random House).

United States Department of Education (1987) Japanese Education Today, Washington (US Government Printing Office).

The Politics of Policy Borrowing

DAVID BRIAN ROBERTSON & JEROLD L. WALTMAN[1]

If any of the citizens desire to survey the doings of the outside world in a leisurely way, no law shall prevent them; for a State that is without experience of bad men and good would never be able (owing to its isolation) to become fully civilized and perfect, nor would it be able to safeguard its laws unless it grasped them, not by habit only, but also by conviction ... In search of these men it is always right for one who dwells in a well-ordered State to go forth on a voyage of enquiry by land and sea, if so be that he himself is incorruptible, so as to confirm thereby such of his native laws as are rightly enacted, and to amend any that are deficient. For without this inspection and enquiry a State will not permanently remain perfect, nor again if the inspection be badly conducted.

Plato, *Laws*, Book XII, p. 507.

Though modern policy makers often follow Plato's advice, the process of policy borrowing is much more disjointed and uncertain than he would have wished. In this chapter we review the modern politics of policy borrowing, examining conditions that lead governments to search for models of policy success in other jurisdictions. Policy borrowing encounters a special set of constraints, because democratic states deal with unavoidable and especially difficult problems and must adopt borrowed policy through an open, formal, and complex process.

Borrowers have greater incentives to import narrow policy instruments than encompassing policy strategies. But in practice, borrowing the elements of policy disconnected from their roots often results in unanticipated consequences. If those who borrow public policy reflect on the differences between their political system and the system that generates the 'solutions' they find attractive, they can better anticipate the limitations of achieving in one polity what is believed to have been achieved in another.

The Need to Borrow

In contrast to Plato's ideal state, most nations resort to copying others' solutions when easier alternatives are in short supply. In any organization, key decision makers cannot routinely invest the considerable time and energy that the development of new policy ideas entails. Organization theorists point out that habit, not innovation, is the norm in public as well as private organizations. Organizational decision-making rarely approximates the model of utility-maximizing 'rational choice' in which leaders rank all organizational goals, search extensively for alternatives, and select from a long list the optimal solution. Instead, decision-makers minimize effort by clinging to standard operating procedures (for example, see Sharkansky, 1970). They avoid disrupting established patterns of behavior unless compelled to do otherwise.

The search for innovative solutions to organizational problems usually is driven by the perception that an organization is performing unsatisfactorily (March and Simon, 1958, pp. 113-121, 182-186; see also Steinbrunner, 1974). The search for alternatives seldom is exhaustive. Decision-makers reduce the cost of problem solving by examining similar problems and the policies that address them. Often they simply borrow solutions to other problems and adapt these existing policies to their immediate needs (Cyert and March, 1963, pp. 114-127).

In the realm of policy, modest dissatisfaction leads to changes in the techniques used to bring about desired changes. Intense dissatisfaction with existing policy, as often accompanies major economic disruptions, can lead to more far-reaching changes in a government's policy strategy (that is, the overall goals and direction of policy). Successive changes in American and British employment policy through the mid-1970s reflected changed techniques that built upon existing programs (Franklin and Ripley, 1984; Moon, 1983). After the early 1970s stagflation and recession severely tested the industrial democracies and caused more critical assessments of existing social programs and expenditures. In the US and the UK, where economic growth and productivity have stagnated (see Finegold, Part 2), dissatisfaction with existing policy has been especially pronounced. Such factors contributed to the election of governments that questioned the basic goals of these existing policies and redirected policy consistent with their neo-laissez-faire principles.

The first source for policy inspiration is often an organization's past record. Sir Godfrey Ince in Britain and Eli Ginzberg in the United States both extrapolated from their experiences in meeting World War II manpower needs to mold new programs for peacetime labor market improvement (Perry, 1976, p. 76; Ginzberg, 1958). It is also common to adapt recent organizational successes in one area to problems in another. The principle of 'experience rating', originally included in American workers' compensation programs so that employers with a high accident rate would pay a higher premium to state insurance funds, later was imported into the design of other American social insurance plans. These included the Progressive-era public health insurance proposals and most of the state unemployment insurance programs enacted in the 1930s (Robertson, 1989).

Only when past remedies do not appear successful or feasible do policy-makers broaden their search for alternative solutions. Borrowing from other organizations or other governments is therefore most likely to occur when an organization is perceived to be performing poorly and when no past or present internal solution can rectify the situation. Under such circumstances borrowing the solutions of similar institutions can be an effective way for both public and private organizations to attempt to solve complex problems.

Uncertainty, Conflict and the Decision to Borrow Solutions

The perception of unsatisfactory performance may be driven by uncertainty or by conflict, or both. Each affects the decision to borrow. Whether in government or a private organization, the greater the conflict over goals and the greater the uncertainty about causal relationships, the more likely it is that organizational performance will be perceived to be unsatisfactory. Doubts about the effectiveness of current solutions or disagreements about how they ought to work fuel the sense that there is a problem that must be solved. These two dimensions of organizational decision-making – uncertainty and conflict – provide a framework for examining decisions to borrow policy. James D. Thompson distinguished four types of decision issues (Figure 1) based on two dimensions: agreement or disagreement about preferences regarding possible outcomes, and certainty or uncertainty about cause and effect relationships (Thompson, 1967, p. 134).

	Preferences Regarding Possible Outcomes	
	Consensus	Disagreement
Certain	Computation	Bargaining
Uncertain	Estimation	Inspiration

Beliefs About Cause / Effect Relationships

Figure 1. Four types of decision strategies. Adapted from James D. Thomson (1967) *Organizations in Action*, p. 134. New York: McGraw-Hill.

When cause-and-effect relationships are well understood and all participants agree on goals, then participants can arrive at an optimal solution with relative ease (some public engineering decisions have this quality). Policy borrowing under these conditions is a technical problem of technology transfer (or, under more dramatic circumstances, espionage). In the other three situations, uncertainty or conflict can make the problem seem less easy to solve, and can intensify the search for alternatives. When policy makers are uncertain about 'what causes what' and 'what works' (in such areas as welfare or education, where problems are especially complex and often individualized), they must search for additional information, including new ways to define the problem and new ways to solve it. When serious conflict erupts among policy makers (as in such labor market issues as wages, working conditions or the prerogatives of management and labor), they are likely to search for solutions that can achieve a consensus among the participants.

Combining uncertainty and controversy makes the borrowed innovation both more vulnerable to error and more politicized. For example, the public's dissatisfaction with the education system in the United States in the 1980s prompted a great deal of experimentation and international and interstate policy borrowing (Bowman and Kearney, 1986). It was not certain that some of the innovations, such as performance pay for teachers, would have the intended effects. The speed with which reforms spread across American states inevitably resulted in the adoption of some programs that were untested. Several proposed changes, such as a 'back to the basics' curriculum, standardized tests, and changes in the financing of public education, engendered intense disagreements and required extensive political bargaining before they could be enacted and implemented.

Because uncertainty and disagreement complicate collective decision-making and policy borrowing, many policy experts have an incentive to define problems in the most certain and uncontroversial manner, for example, by recommending more efficient budgeting or personnel techniques. For experts and institutions that must serve a wide range of partisan interests (such as the Organization for Economic Cooperation and Development or the US General Accounting Office), description and narrow, technical improvement mark a middle course between opponents and proponents of change. Such a course offers the only way for them to gain politically (or to avoid political loss) because it minimizes the chance that partisans will question their expertise or objectivity in order to undermine their recommendations. To the extent that experts can present incontestable information about self-evidently superior techniques, they provide a resource for coalition building among divided partisans because such techniques require less bargaining than far-reaching, divisive proposals. Thus the preponderance of expert analysis is likely to focus on whether a program can work rather than on whether it should be implemented

(Robertson, 1991). When policy borrowing is dominated by policy experts it tends to result in noncontroversial and technical innovations.

Policy borrowing tends to result in more far-reaching changes in policy direction when the process is dominated by ideological and political partisans. Partisans have incentives to use lessons from abroad to advance their policy agenda. Proponents of a particular ideological position can advocate that their polity emulate the programs of a polity in which their policy preferences prevail. Thus in the 1970s social democrats encouraged their governments to imitate Scandinavian social and economic policy. In the 1980s, free-market conservatives encouraged government to copy some of the policies of the Reagan administration in the United States and the Thatcher administration in Great Britain. Conservatives in Britain and the US in particular were attracted to some of each other's policy models (ibid.).

The degree to which partisans can borrow a program from a philosophically compatible state and implement it in a similar form depends on their political strength, the capacity of the government they can command, and the similarity of the context into which the borrowed program is interjected. At the helm of a parliamentary system in a relatively centralized state and facing a divided opposition, the Thatcher government could borrow policies from the Reagan administration and implement them more straightforwardly than in the original American attempt. When the Thatcher government borrowed the idea of Private Industry Councils from American job training, for example, it explicitly claimed to be taking a 'truly radical step' that would 'give leadership of the training system to employers, where it belongs' (Cm. 540, 1988, p. 43) and vested the British equivalents (Training and Enterprise Councils) with more authority and more resources than their American counterparts (*The Economist*, 1990, p. 63; Bailey, this publication, Part 3).

Even if policy makers successfully import an overseas policy, it does not necessarily follow that it will solve the targeted problem effectively. The more *inherently* uncertain and controversial the problem, the more likely that a borrowed policy will be proposed, even though claims that it makes a modest change with reasonably predictable effects cannot always be justified subsequently. Alternatively, in the originating society the program may be nested in a broader set of institutions that are indispensable for its success. Thus British efforts to copy elements of German or French vocational education and training policy may be seen to have ignored 'wider lessons about the social and economic contexts in which these systems operate, or about the general forces and principles that underpin their success' (Keep, 1991, p. 11).

The Unique Circumstances of Public Sector Borrowing

Competition and market change have prompted private enterprises to provide many of the best examples of borrowed techniques and strategies.[2]

Fundamental differences between the private and the public sector in terms of the nature of problems and the problem-solving process make it more difficult for governments to borrow policy.

The Nature of Public Problems

Public sector problems are normally harder to solve than private sector problems; it is always an attractive alternative to avoid a problem altogether. When technical difficulties or a lack of consumer response make problems too insurmountable for company managers, they often can abandon the problem voluntarily, by exiting from that particular market or, involuntarily, through business failure. But in the public sector, only occasionally can officials abandon the stubborn problems on their agenda. Bureaus with a statutory mission to enhance education cannot drop this function to enter a more profitable business.

To complicate matters, it is usually the most intractable social problems that are on the government's agenda. Some problems may not be amenable to solution by any available technique, or by any technique that yields measurable improvement. In the private sector, market share or profits provide a discrete and precise measure of organizational performance. Government, however, must assume responsibility for those larger and more diverse problems that the market cannot solve or that the market has created. Governments' agendas include, for example, the provision of public goods such as defence and investment in infrastructure. Citizens often hold government responsible for rectifying private sector externalities (such as pollution) and unacceptable consequences of market operations (such as 'sweated labor'). The least well understood and most difficult social problems of all are those that involve such intangibles as human behaviour, talents, and skills – matters which lie at the heart of education and training.

The inherent difficulties in the agenda of public organizations affect policy borrowing in two respects. First, these difficulties make the search for effective and politically advantageous models more imperative for those agencies where the standard for success is controversial. The Weberian model of routinized administration suggests that many bureaus oppose innovation as a threat to established relationships (for example, the FBI under the directorship of J. Edgar Hoover). But for bureaus with an uncertain power base and opaque goals (for example, labor ministries), a routine scan of counterparts abroad can provide critical lessons about improving the bureau's stock of political capital as well as its operations.

Second, the fact that public sector solutions are more likely to fall into Thompson's categories of 'estimation' and 'bargaining' decision strategies reduces the likelihood that decision-makers will find a consensual, effective solution to borrow. Agreement is likely only on relatively small-scale solutions that prompt less controversy and involve better-understood relationships, such as education or training programs that target a small, homogeneous, and tractable population, that have been proven effective in a variety of contexts, and that involve a relatively small commitment of resources.

A broad issue such as unemployment exemplifies a diverse, partially understood and intensely controversial problem that periodically causes governments to search widely for new policies. The search for remedies to unemployment has stimulated much cross-national dialogue about defining the problem (resulting in the identification of distinct 'cyclical', 'frictional', and 'structural' diagnoses of unemployment) and efforts to borrow from abroad. Often the solutions enacted combine incremental technical change (sometimes inspired by foreign practice) with rhetorical bombast and, public opinion willing, increased government expenditure. For example, program operators tend to select the most well-prepared and least-needy applicants ('creaming') in many education and training programs because such individuals have a relatively high probability of demonstrating success with or without government help (Robertson, 1987a, p. 73, in Waltman and Studlar).

The Process of Solving Public Problems

A second difference between the public sector and the private sector is that the public policy-making process is much more contentious and tortuous. When a business innovation fails (the Edsel or the 'new' Coke), consumer reaction quickly and unambiguously signals that a problem exists and corporate leaders can respond quickly to minimize their losses.[3] But public innovation must meet the test of political acceptability. Government actions tend to be universal and coercive, so that when a government innovation fails (such as the UK 'Poll Tax'), taxpayers, clients and other groups cannot exit a market or opt for other 'products' in the same way as consumers. Government cannot easily abandon the enterprise, and even the defeat of an incumbent political party necessarily has a limited policy impact. In these circumstances dissatisfaction takes the form of vocal opposition (Hirschman, 1970), which offers a very ambiguous and easily biased indicator of public preferences.

New policy initiatives in democratic nations are adopted through a process of forced public collaboration imposed by formal institutional arrangements, informal institutional mechanisms, and the publicity surrounding a decision-making process influenced by the mass media, political parties, and competing private interests. While organization theorists describe decision-making in the private sector in terms of 'bounded rationality', public policy scholars describe public sector decision-making as a disjointed 'garbage can' process in which agendas, alternatives, and problems develop somewhat independently of each other. Policy results when favorable mixes of problems, solutions, and political circumstances align. Problems emerge on the public agenda, while other problems disappear, sometimes to return in the future in a somewhat different guise. Participants engage and disengage themselves, or even change goals, during the process (March and Olsen, 1989, pp. 11-13; Kingdon, 1984).

Policy communities indispensably bridge the gap between complex public problems and potential solutions. Such communities involve 'specialists in a given policy area [who] are scattered through and outside of government' (Kingdon, 1984, p. 23). The education policy community includes among others: national and local administrators; teacher union staff; specialist academics; journalists; and various elected officials. These individuals have in common their concern with one area of policy problems. In addition they may 'know each other's ideas, proposals, and research, and often they know each other very well personally' (ibid, pp. 122-138). These policy communities keep abreast of the arsenal of possible solutions to public problems. They stand armed and ready to offer these solutions (sometimes borrowed from abroad) when a portentous alignment of problems and political circumstances comes about.

The evolution of American unemployment insurance and old age pension proposals exemplifies this process and the central role that policy communities play in the policy borrowing process. Beginning around 1910 a small group of elite policy experts thoroughly familiar with European social insurance practices advocated copying these nations' policies. But their borrowed ideas initially made little headway because very few political elites or citizens viewed unemployment and old age as matters calling for government action. The experts' political impotence did not, however, dampen their zeal, and when the Great Depression changed the political agenda they stood ready with an array of policy proposals. In the end, government produced a set of policies remarkably similar to the ideas imported before the First World War. The Social Security Act of 1935 depended simultaneously on the occurrence of the Depression, on a new definition of the problem of economic insecurity, on a new alignment of political forces in American government and on the availability of a policy solution, in this case borrowed from abroad. (Waltman, 1980, pp. 54-55; Nelson, 1969).

The public nature of this 'garbage can' borrowing process invites conflict over goals and facts, and often both. Thus the publicity surrounding government initiatives reduces the opportunity to apply Thompson's computation strategy to solve public problems even when it is relevant. At the same time, uncertainty and conflict make the search for alternatives more imperative. Indeed, the more contentious the problem, the more the proposed solution is likely to become caught in political conflict independent of its objective merits and consequences. In the United States, for example, the 'enterprise zone' concept, borrowed from the Thatcher government, became enmeshed in partisan, class, and racial enmities that eventually precluded its unmodified transfer to the American political agenda and its adoption by the national government.

Because 'problems are defined in politics to accomplish political goals – to mobilize support for one side in a conflict' (Stone, 1988, p. 183), public policy borrowing also can become infused with provocative symbolism. Supporters will advertise the borrowed policy in ways that highlight its supposed superiority. Opponents will make it appear to have uncertain or negative consequences. In both the United States and Britain proponents of vocational education, apprenticeship improvement and job training constantly refer to competitors abroad whose superior policies give (or threaten to give) them the upper hand in international economic competition. As American proponents of vocational education wrote in 1914, 'Our foreign commerce, and to some extent our domestic commerce, are being threatened by the commercial prestige which Germany has won, largely as a result of a policy of training its workers begun by the far-seeing Bismarck almost half a century ago' (Commission on National Aid to Vocational Education, 1914, p. 23). The lesson-drawing persists: '...Britain is second to West Germany in training stakes' (*The Times Educational Supplement*, 1983, p. 4). On the other hand, policies that resemble those in competitor nations frequently are doomed to guilt by association, as happened to American health insurance proposals that were linked unflatteringly to Germany in 1917 and to the Soviet Union during the Cold War.

The fact that elected officials are adopting a borrowed policy further complicates the process. Public policies ultimately tend to distribute benefits to a wide array of people, a consequence of the need to build a coalition in support of an innovative policy in the legislature. To the extent that government institutions depend on geographical representation, there is an incentive for government to distribute public benefits across a large number of jurisdictions. This is particularly true where political parties have very little capacity to discipline their members and thus to motivate them to make decisions with redistributive consequences, as in the United States. For example, advocates of the US Model Cities program originally conceived it as an experiment in concentrating federal resources in as few as five distressed cities. By the time the bill emerged from Congress, its watered-down benefits extended to 75 cities, and another 75 were added the following year (Robertson and Judd, 1989, pp. 310-312).

Political executives who are elected (or serve at the pleasure of elected officials) usually have different interests in policy borrowing than those of career administrators and outside specialists in the policy community. Concerns about long-term effectiveness and performance guide career civil servants and specialists, while officials dependent on the electoral cycle understandably are preoccupied with the short-term *perception* of success. Elected officials are more likely to be interested in a borrowed policy's political symbolism and in short-term benefits for which they can claim credit. These distinct interests may cause specialists whose ideas are borrowed to criticize elected officials during the policy implementation process, as Milton Friedman did in 1982 when he complained that monetarism was being used by the British government 'to cover anything that Mrs Thatcher at any time expressed as a desirable object of policy' (Riddell, 1983, p. 6).

The Policy Borrowing Process

The complex circumstances in which public policy borrowing occurs make the processes that accompany it inherently difficult to characterize and explain. An appropriate starting point is the literature on the diffusion of innovations. This literature describes both the intentional and the serendipitous spread of innovations.

'Policy diffusion' in the political science literature connotes a deliberate emulation of other states' policies. Leading diffusion scholar Everett Rogers observes that there are four elements in the process of the diffusion of any social innovation, a list which provides a useful way to organize the speculations about the process of public policy borrowing (Rogers, 1983): 1) someone must develop an innovative policy; 2) the innovation must be communicated to potential borrowers; 3) the borrowing occurs within an existing social system with established socioeconomic, political, and cultural characteristics that affect the outcomes; 4) the borrowed policy must be implemented.

Sources and Communication of Public Policy Innovations

A public policy innovation may be defined as 'a program or policy that is new to the country adopting it, no matter how old the program may be or how many other nations have adopted it' (Walker, 1969, p. 881). Unfortunately there is very little systematic research on how such borrowed policies originate. Case studies of specific new policies point to a multitude of sources of policy innovation, including political parties and interest groups, policy experts, administrators, and elected officials. It is not known (and likely unknowable) what circumstances favor a particular source, as reflected in the fact that Thompson could only label decisions marked by uncertainty and controversy as 'inspirational.' Yet many important public problems require such an inspired strategy.

The public nature of the policy process facilitates communication and the use of others' policies. No copyright or patent laws impede the communication of borrowed policy ideas. Elected officials benefit when they can give constituents evidence that their products succeed (or appear to succeed), and academics like John Maynard Keynes or Milton Friedman gain international credibility when others widely disseminate and adopt their ideas. Since one always can deny that other policy makers used the good idea the right way, the benefits of such credit claiming entail little cost or risk. The 'global village' brought about by high-technology communications makes information about problems and solutions available swiftly and universally. As a result of all these processes, information about public policy innovations has been spreading faster over time (Walker 1969, Savage 1985).

Policy communities exchange information about new policy ideas regularly and methodically. National policy networks detail other nations' policies in their specialized publications. US employment policy experts, for example, learned of developments abroad in the pages of the *American Labor Legislation Review* from the 1910s through the 1930s. *The Employment and Training Reporter* has played a similar role since the early 1970s. Private 'think tanks' such as the Brookings Institution, the American Enterprise Institute, and the Heritage Foundation in the United States or the Centre for Policy Studies or Adam Smith Institute in the United Kingdom facilitate shared information and exchanges between private and public sector specialists. International organizations such as the Organization for Economic Cooperation and Development explicitly publicize successful policy innovations through general publications (the *OECD Observer*) and specialized reports (for example, the OECD's *Manpower Policy* series published between 1963 and 1975). At the sub-national level in the United States, the interstate contacts of policy communities have become especially frequent and routine. The Council of State Governments now frequently publishes profiles of path-breaking state programs under the auspices of the Innovations Transfer Project (for example, Chi, 1986). International and interstate conferences further facilitate the exchange of ideas.

Government itself underwrites much of this communication by subsidizing conferences, special studies and investigations into the policies of other nations. Especially during the period of social activism in the 1960s and early 1970s, American policy makers took intensive interest in foreign experience, as evident in the series of Department of Labor studies and Congressional hearings on social policy abroad (Green, 1966; Hansen, 1967; Reubens 1970; National Commission for Manpower Policy, 1978; US Senate, 1974). Elected political leaders notice and legitimize foreign models, as did President Franklin Roosevelt when he took an active interest in Keynesian principles (Schlesinger, 1958, p. 219). Margaret Thatcher's government explicitly drew attention to apprenticeship training in Germany and France in its plans for overhauling British training policy (Cmnd. 8455, 1981; Cmnd. 9474, 1985, pp. 13-14; Cm. 540, 1988, pp. 28-29). In turn, some governments (such as Sweden's) have widely disseminated information about their programs.

The ferment surrounding education policy in the United States and Britain in the 1980s illustrates these points vividly. In each nation the professional policy communities and elected politicians became dissatisfied with policies of the immediate past. Lagging economic growth and perceptions of declining educational standards levels measured by national examinations partly triggered this dissatisfaction. Despite occasional glances toward and rhetoric about Japan and Germany, policy-makers in both countries most frequently looked to each other for problem definitions and solution. This is surely a testament to the strength of ingrained habits, established communication channels and the compatible neo-laissez-faire ideologies of the Thatcher and Reagan administrations (Waltman and Studlar 1987).

Predictably, throughout the last few years political leaders have wanted a 'quick fix' at minimal cost, while teachers and other professional groups have sought longer term changes (often calling for more authority and money for themselves). Should some of the recently borrowed policies produce at least enough success to lower the political pressure, or should things turn around independently, borrowing may subside for a while. If, though, the educational systems in the two countries continue to perform poorly, policy makers may have to look further afield. If so, it will almost certainly be the policy community that offers explicit proposals for policy innovation.

Borrowing and the Structure of Social Systems

Prospective borrowers must adapt programs developed in one context to their own unique socioeconomic, political, and cultural circumstances. Much of the research on policy diffusion focuses on the relationship between these circumstances and the timing and patterns of the spread of policy innovations.[4] Many studies conclude with Flora and Alber (1981) or Walker (1969) that the more affluent the polity, the sooner it will adopt a policy innovation. This finding corresponds to cross-national evidence that wealthy states are more likely to develop extensive public policies (Wilensky et al, 1985, p. 14). On the other hand, some studies have shown that these variables have weak or even negative correlations in some policy areas, such as land use policy (Savage, 1985; Scheb and Matheny, 1988).[5]

Critics of these studies point out that a focus on internal characteristics of policy borrowers risks 'Galton's problem' – that researchers will incorrectly infer that highly correlated variables (for example, industrialization, urbanization, and social welfare policy) are causally related when, in fact, they have diffused across polities simultaneously. They argue that different polities come under tremendous pressure to conform to policy examples set by other nations. Such emulation is likely to occur between geographically contiguous nations (such as the US and Canada), between economic rivals (such as Britain and Germany), and between nations with deep cultural bonds (such as the US and Britain). Bendix (1967) suggested that the most economically advanced nations provide policy models that are emulated by other nations at progressively less advanced stages of economic development. In a cross-national study of the spread of social security programs across 59 industrial nations, Collier and Messick (1975) have also shown that geographical proximity is an important element in policy borrowing. They argue that not only do factors within nations, such as socioeconomic development, lead to the adoption of innovations, but also that there are recognizable patterns both of hierarchical and spatial diffusion of these policies from central Europe to the European periphery and former British colonies, and finally to Latin America, the Middle East and Asia. Furthermore, the spread of many programs across American states and Canadian provinces provides evidence that physical proximity facilitates borrowing. Some states or provinces clearly seem to act as regional or national leaders, whose innovations are disproportionately copied by neighboring jurisdictions (Walker, 1969; Lutz, 1989).

Patterns of diffusion vary markedly from policy to policy. The United States lagged behind other nations in establishing unemployment, old age and health insurance programs, and this pattern continues in laws ranging from pre-notification of factory closure to family allowances. Yet the US has traditionally been a leader in education policy (Heidenheimer, Heclo, and Adams, 1990) and in other policy areas as diverse as civil rights, environmental protection and disclosure of public information. Among American states civil rights, education, and welfare policies each diffuse in a different pattern, with little correlation between these categories (Gray, 1973).

Many issues in the policy borrowing process remain open. In his aptly titled summary of the US state policy diffusion literature, *Confusion, Diffusion, and Innovation*, Robert Eyestone (1977) concluded that

> The diffusion of policy innovations ... is a complicated phenomenon for which several models provide partial explanations ... Some states are consistently among the leaders on a variety of policies, while others lag behind in nearly every area. Yet diffusion patterns may record the spread of necessity rather than the emulation of virtue: leaders may lead because they are also the first to suffer the undesirable side effects of urban and industrial growth which create demands for state policy responses.

This analysis leaves open the possibility that policies that ostensibly are copied would, in fact, have been implemented without the existence of a model to copy.

The emphasis in political science literature on policies that completely diffuse across a given set of governments also leaves open the issue of why some policies are borrowed and some are not. Programs which are not borrowed extensively are often the most uncertain or controversial. Such factors as different political ideologies, the relative strength of business and labor, and alternative political parties influence whether or not a specific policy will be adopted by another polity. For example, Swedes appear willing to tolerate higher taxes and more government activity than Americans; and among Americans, citizens of Wisconsin and New York are more supportive of government activism than those in many other states. Previous policy experiences and long-established programs also affect the propensity to borrow from other jurisdictions (See Heclo, 1974, Waltman, 1987).

Because the date of program adoption provides no information about the content or fate of the program that is borrowed, these studies also leave open the possibility that borrowed programs are transformed in the process of borrowing. Social insurance programs that spread across Europe and American states resembled each other in name and demonstrably were informed by other nations' models. But these programs evidently were transformed in the process because they varied widely in terms of coverage, financing, eligibility, and other details that are critical determinants of policy outcomes (Wilensky et al, 1985, p. 14). A superior level of government may counteract divergence of policy implementation by offering incentives to adopt a particular policy model and imposing costs for refusing to act. This is clearest in federal systems such as the US, where national government grants programs clearly affect the rate and nature of policy diffusion (Welch and Thompson, 1980). Grants and directives from the institutions of the European community are having a similar (if weaker) effect in Western Europe (Rose & Davies, forthcoming, ch. 2).

Thus policy may be borrowed intact, or may be borrowed in a transformed version. Even if conscious borrowing does not occur, separate national policies may converge in a common policy direction and settle upon nearly identical programs. Among the next logical steps in diffusion research are 'tracer' studies that focus on the generation and spread of specific policies addressing related problems. There is also a critical need for rich contextual analysis of the process of borrowing by particular polities (Waltman, 1980).

Implementing Borrowed Policy

Yet another possible outcome of the policy borrowing process exists: if borrowing is attempted, policy may fail to take root in the borrowing nation. Because organizations seek satisfactory rather than optimal performance, innovators have little incentive to develop perfect policy models. Borrowers have little incentive to borrow policy intact if there is a high risk of failure. In fact, most public policy borrowing appears to involve administrative techniques (such as budgeting or personnel systems) rather than a change of policy direction. Discrete, narrow policy techniques usually require less estimation and less bargaining than more far-reaching changes in policy strategy.

Policy borrowing in both Britain and the United States often entails importing a superior administrative method from another nation. In the 1930s American public administration experts exhaustively advocated emulating British personnel practice even though experts in Britain questioned whether or not British lessons could transfer to the United States (Finer, 1936). This pattern is even clearer in studies of policy diffusion across the American states. Walker (1969) explicitly limited himself to programs that spread to virtually all the states, and most of the initiatives he identified were technical advances and administrative reforms (such as the creation of new boards, commission, and agencies) that involved little public controversy and were reasonably well-understood.

Efforts to adopt policy techniques from one polity and import them into another often lead to unanticipated consequences. A prime example is the effort to import British and German administrative principles into the American bureaucracy. Under American conditions, the civil service became a tool in the struggle for party and institutional supremacy. During the rapid turnover of party administrations in the late nineteenth century, each president extended civil service protections to encompass the partisans appointed during his administration. Early in the twentieth century, Theodore Roosevelt extended the civil service to protect the executive branch of government from incursions by Congress, despite the fact that his party dominated the House, the Senate, and the executive branch (Skowronek, 1982).

Some appealing policy elements are so inseparable from a given political system that they are nearly impossible to copy despite widespread interest in their use. Two examples repeatedly discussed in Britain and in the United States are continental European labor market policy and the Japanese Ministry of Industry and Trade. Both Britain and the United States, however, lack a tradition of the kind of strong, centralized government and corporatist policy making that is a necessary condition for the success of industrial and labor market policy in these nations (Wilensky and Turner, 1987; Freeman, 1989; Keep, 1991).

A Typology of Policy Borrowing: Categorizing Reforms Undertaken by the Thatcher and Reagan Governments

Policy borrowing may result in several distinct outcomes. It may or may not be attempted even when governments regularly communicate about policy innovations and share kindred ideological biases. Even when borrowing takes place, national policies may not converge because borrowed programs may fail to take root, or they may be transformed in the borrowing process. Figure 2 lays out these alternatives.

Policy borrowing between the Thatcher and Reagan governments illustrates all these possibilities. Margaret Thatcher and Ronald Reagan imbued their administrations with a distrust of the public sector, an emphasis on market solutions to social problems, and a desire to renew the spirit of entrepreneurial capitalism in their nations. The American and British public had little confidence in the Democratic and Labour parties, respectively, and both publics showed a willingness to permit conservative leaders to experiment with market-oriented policy designs. During the first terms of Reagan and Thatcher, both economies experienced unemployment levels unprecedented since the 1930s. One would have expected British and American policy to converge during their synchronous terms in office.

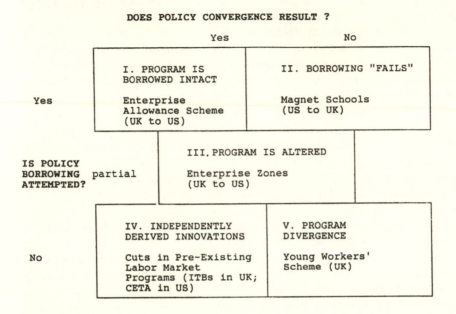

DOES POLICY CONVERGENCE RESULT ?

Figure 2. Types of policy borrowing outcomes, with illustrations from ET in the UK and US in the 1980s.

However, a number of forces counteracted these pressures and limited borrowing and convergence. Reagan and Thatcher inherited different social and economic policies from their predecessors, and this legacy of past commitments created different sets of institutional opportunities and constraints for the two leaders (Waltman, 1987). The leaders differed about the use of government. The American president eschewed active government as an evil to be limited, Mrs. Thatcher showed a willingness to use a strong state to recreate a 'free economy' and an entrepreneurial culture (Gamble, 1988). These leadership differences coincided with a contrast between the individualistic, laissez-faire political culture of United States and the government paternalism that infuses much of conservative political thought in Britain. Finally, Margaret Thatcher commanded a parliamentary government in a centralized political system, while Ronald Reagan presided over a more fragmented political system in which legislative support was much more uncertain and in which subnational governments enjoyed more autonomy.

In some cases, the expected convergence occurred (Figure 2, box I). William Richardson details one example in his paper on UK emulation of US city compacts (this publication, Part 3). Another example of clearly borrowed policy involves the US importation of the 1983 British Enterprise Allowance Scheme (itself inspired partially by a similar French program), which encouraged the use of unemployment insurance to fund the start-up of small businesses. Explicitly citing the British and French initiatives in a study in the mid-1980s, experts inside and outside the US Department of Labor debated the idea among themselves and in public editorials (US Department of Labor, 1986; Friedman and Jones, 1985; Steinbach, 1985; Bendick and Egan, 1987). In 1989 Congress authorized the establishment of demonstration projects in the states of Washington, Oregon, and Maryland. By the spring of 1990 these projects were receiving the favorable attention of the national press and were being incorporated into welfare policy. (US House of Representatives, 1988, pp 383-384; Kilborn, 1990; Hinds, 1990, p. 1).

The fact that these cases involved narrow innovations set within a broad consensus on appropriate policy responses clearly facilitated convergence. In both cases the proposed reform seemed a 'good idea' to experts and to policy makers across a wide range of the political spectrum. The fact that Sweden, Denmark and the Netherlands had adopted enterprise allowance programs legitimated them for liberals. Moreover, neither reform threatened the foundations of existing institutional prerogatives or seriously undermined the existing distribution of resources; instead, they offered new options that built on existing arrangements.

Even in these relatively staightforward examples of policy borrowing, the variables that limit borrowing and convergence perceptibly altered the outcome. The idea of using unemployment insurance for small business start-ups is being put to subtly different use in each nation because past social security and labor market policies differ. The British Enterprise Allowance Scheme constituted a small contribution to the Thatcher government's effort to steer the United Kingdom's labor market policies toward the development of entrepreneurship. The effort in the United States built on a long-established American tradition of policies aimed to wean welfare recipients from 'welfare dependency.' In 1990 the Enterprise Allowance Scheme seemed to replay on a smaller scale the experience of job training programs of the 1960s: part of labor market policy in the United Kingdom, and part of income maintenance policy in the United States (Robertson, 1987b; Kilborn, 1990).

In other cases, borrowing was attempted but the prospects for successful implementation were poor (Figure 2, box II). In these cases the economic, social, and political conditions in the two nations differed sufficiently to render the program less capable of taking root in the nation that borrowed. One example of such difficulties is the faltering of British efforts to transplant the US magnet schools concept (Green, this publication, Part 3).

In a second example, Rose (1990) points out that Mrs. Thatcher's efforts to import German vocational training ideas are unlikely to yield large, immediate benefits. New initiatives in the 1980s were implemented in the context of a labor market policy that, in contrast to Germany, had placed relatively little emphasis on vocational training in the past. The implementation of German vocational training in Britain did not result in immediate results in part because such a program would first have to alter existing institutions, such as the lack of qualified trainers or strong employer organizations.

In still other cases, the governments borrowed programs only in a significantly altered form (Figure 2, box III). Often these programs were more controversial than programs in boxes I and II, and different political constraints and opportunities intervened to alter their design as they were borrowed. Two notable examples are enterprise zones and the concept of local employer management of public training programs. American conservatives enthusiastically embraced the Thatcherite concept of enterprise zones that would turn blighted urban areas into dynamic entrepreneurial centers. One of the chief American popularizers of the concept of enterprise zones is Stuart Butler, associated with the conservative Heritage Foundation. Butler begins his book on the topic by outlining Sir Geoffrey Howe's 1978 speech in London's Isle of Dogs district in which Howe introduced the concept in Britain (1981). But while the British version included fairly drastic reductions in government regulation in the zones, the American proposal that Congress took most seriously in 1985 was completely shorn of efforts to reduce anti-discrimination, health, safety, a minimum wage, and working standards. By 1986 thirty-two American states had created such programs. Virtually all of these were variations on the ingrained American tradition of interstate competition designed to lure business investment through subsidies and tax incentives (Eisinger, 1988), rather than the more radical British plan to undo taxation, spending, and regulatory policies. (Barnekov, Boyle, and, Rich, 1989).

If American neo-conservatives found that they could borrow the policies of their British counterparts only in a diminished form, the Thatcher government's importation of local, employer-dominated job training councils illustrates the latitude enjoyed in Britain to implement much more ambitious forms of neo-conservative policy than those realized in the US (Bailey, this publication, Part 3).

A fourth kind of policy process arises in those situations where borrowing is not attempted but, given similar ideologies and roughly comparable economic and political circumstances, similar outcomes have sometimes occurred anyway (Figure 2, box IV). Both the Thatcher and Reagan governments severely cut existing public labor market programs and overhauled job training policy soon after they took office. Although there is little evidence that they copied each others' strategies for doing so, in both cases job training institutions established in the 1960s (Industrial Training

Boards in the UK, and 'community-based' organizations in the US) were given a vastly diminished role in the job training system. In response to high unemployment rates unprecedented in the previous forty years both governments also permitted the creation of public jobs despite their shared ideological reservations (Robertson, 1987).

Finally, in many cases the divergent political cultures, structures, and long-established programs inherited by the two governments propelled their policies along divergent paths (Figure 1, box V; Waltman, 1987). Margaret Thatcher took the helm of a unitary state with a parliamentary system that provided relatively little opportunity for her opponents to check her plans. While she expressed admiration for entrepreneurial cultures such as the United States and Hong Kong, her attempts to instill market-oriented solutions and an entrepreneurial work ethic in Britain ironically have involved the use of increased central government power to impose a national curriculum and the prosecution of a conservative version of an active labor market policy.

The Youth Training Scheme (see Raffe & Rumberger, pp. 126-7) exemplifies the Thatcher government's divergence from the Reagan strategy of labor market detachment. The YTS subsidized employers for providing low-paid jobs to employees under the age of 18. Not until George Bush was in the White House did Congress enact a distantly related initiative in the form of a sub-minimum wage for 16 to 19 year old workers. Unlike the YTS scheme, however, the American sub-minimum wage involved no subsidy and was limited to a three month period.

Policy Borrowing and Political Caution

Plato's advocacy of policy-borrowing seems to have taken hold in the modern world, although certainly not by direct inspiration. This suggests that no national political system is unique and that all can draw valuable lessons from other polities. The flow across political boundaries – particularly in areas dominated by policy communities whose members communicate extensively – satisfies one of the necessary conditions of borrowing. Although it seems that seldom is there a direct 'demonstration effect', except in the most technical and non-controversial realms of government, policy is affected by the desire to import. Realizing borrowed policy requires disruption of the routines of a political system by the appearance of a daunting problem and a serious search for solutions.

The problems of policy borrowing show that no system is perfectly open to any policy borrowed from any source (Rose & Davies, forthcoming). The process of policy borrowing is especially difficult, messy and uncertain in democratic polities. Seldom will every political interest view a policy import in the same light, and struggles will ensue to alter the distribution of its costs and benefits. Furthermore, even if the policy is adopted in a semblance of its original form, it may produce surprising and unintended results when torn from its native habitat of institutional structure and political culture.

In the uncertain world of public policy a solution that works anywhere has much to recommend it. But even a policy that fails or yields ambiguous results provides valuable lessons on which counterparts abroad may draw. For that reason, a judicious seeking and tracking down of other nations' policies is part of the essence of political wisdom. Thus one should not conclude that a policy-maker should 'neither a borrower nor a lender be.' One must be a politically cautious policy borrower who is cognizant of the prerequisites of innovation, the political benefits and liabilities of a foreign model, and the opportunity and risks of importing policy solutions.

Notes

[1] The authors thank David Finegold, David Phillips, and Richard Rose for helpful comments on earlier versions of this argument. David Robertson acknowledges the valuable support provided by the Public Policy Research Centers at the University of Missouri–St. Louis.

[2] Hagedoorn (1989) reviews some of the literature on the diffusion of business innovations, while Chandler (1977) discusses cases of the diffusion of business tactics and strategies, such as the spread of vertical integration and of mail-order retailing.

[3] Government frequently winds up with the responsibility to clean up the "externalities," as with margin stock purchases in the 1920s or savings and loans in the 1990s.

[4] The dominant question in political science studies of policy diffusion involves the internal characteristics of the polities that borrow relatively quickly and those that borrow relatively late. This research is especially extensive in studies of the American states (McVoy, 1940; Walker, 1969; Gray, 1973; Eyestone, 1977; Savage, 1985; for Canadian provinces, see Lutz, 1989). These studies assume that the adoption of a novel policy indicates a government's policy effort, and is a measure of policy effort that is superior to expenditure. Such research focuses on aggregate data on the date of policy adoption, not on cases of policy innovation. Most cross-national studies focus on the adoption of social insurance laws in the industrialized democracies over the last century (see Flora and Alber, 1981). Walker (1969) examined the diffusion of 88 public policies across the American states, and Savage (1978) used a similar approach in a study of a more diverse set of 207 policies. These studies usually developed a measure of innovativeness and examined it as a dependent variable, arriving at conclusions remarkably similar to those reached by diffusion scholars in entirely different fields (Rogers, 1983)

[5] In aggregate data studies, other contextual variables also have yielded mixed results (Savage, 1985). A more politically mobilized working class seems to contribute to the adoption of national social insurance programs (Flora and Alber, 1981; Korpi, 1989). Studies that examine the effect of political structures, such as the intensity of political party competition and the extent of legislative and administrative professionalism, show inconclusive results in borrowing among US states. Cultural factors, such as individualism or, curiously, a tradition of innovativeness, also have proved to be uncertain predictors of whether a polity will adopt or reject a borrowed policy.

[6] Based on research on U.S. state education, lobbying, and revenue programs that diffused across most states, Jill Clark (1985) concluded that the group of states that adopted the programs earliest and the group of states that adopted the programs last adopted the programs with the broadest options (such as 100% testing of students in education, rather than a smaller proportion). Borrowers in the middle of the diffusion process seem to adopt innovations with narrower scope. She ascribes this pattern to the fact that, for the borrowers in the middle, a new policy remains somewhat experimental, information on political and technical feasibility is less reliable, and increased internal demands for such a new policy may not have developed fully. For the last states adopting the policy, cause-effect relationships are better understood and political conflict over the proposal is less intense, so that the scope of the policy is likely to be broad relative to middle adopters.

References

Bendick, M., and Egan, M. (1987) "Transfer Payments for Small Business Development: The British and French Experience", Industrial and Labor Relations Review, 40, 4, pp. 528-542.

Bendix, R. (1967) "Tradition and Modernity Reconsidered," Comparative Studies in Society and History 9, pp. 292-346.

Bowman, A.O., and Kearney, R.C. (1986) The Resurgence of the States, Englewood Cliffs, NJ, Prentice-Hall.

Barnekov, T., Boyle, R., and Rich, D. (1989) Privatism and Urban Policy in Britain and the United States, Oxford, Oxford University Press.

Butler, S.M. (1981) Enterprise Zones: Greenlining the Inner Cities, New York, Universe Books.

Chandler, A. (1977) The Visible Hand: The Managerial Revolution in American Business, Cambridge, MA, Belknap.

Chapman, R.A. (1973) "The Fulton Committee on the Civil Service," in Chapman, R.A. (ed.), The Role of Commissions in Policy-Making, London, Allen and Unwin.

Chi, K.S. (1986) "House Arrest: Florida's Community Control Program," Innovations, RM-764, Lexington, KY, Council of State Governments.

Clark, J. (1985) "Policy Diffusion Research and Program Scope: Research Directions," Publius 15, 4, pp. 61-70.

Collier, D., and Messick, R.E. (1975) "Prerequisites versus Diffusion: Testing Alternative Explanations for Social Security Adoption," American Political Science Review, 69, 4, pp. 1299-1315.

Cmnd. 8455 (1981) A New Training Initiative, London, HMSO.

Cmnd. 9474 (1985) Employment: Challenge for the Nation, London, HMSO.

Cm 540 (1988) Employment for the 1990s, London, HMSO.

Commission on National Aid to Vocational Education (1914) Report of the Commission on National Aid to Vocational Education, House Doc. 1004, 63rd Cong., 2nd sess., Washington, GPO.

Congressional Record (1982) "Conference Report on S. 2036," pp. H7686-H7726.

Cyert, R.M., and March, J.G. (1963) A Behavioral Theory of the Firm, Englewood Cliffs, NJ, Prentice-Hall.

Economist (1990) "The Training Trap," April 21, pp. 63-64.

Eisinger, P.K. (1988) The Rise of the Entrepreneurial State: State and Local Economic Development Policy in the United States, Madison, University of Wisconsin Press.

Eyestone, R. (1977) "Confusion, Diffusion, and Innovation," American Political Science Review 71, 2, pp. 441-447.

Finer, H. (1936) "Better Government Personnel: America's Next Frontier," Political Science Quarterly 51, 4, pp. 569-599.

Flora, P., and Alber, J. (1981) "Mobilization, Democratization, and the Development of Welfare States in Western Europe," in Flora, P., and Heidenheimer, A.J. (eds) The Development of Welfare States in Europe and America, New Brunswick, NJ, Transaction Books.

Franklin, G.A., and R.A. Ripley, (1984) CETA: Politics and Policy, 1974-1982, Knoxville, University of Tennessee Press.

Freeman, J.R. (1989) Democracy and Markets: The Politics of Mixed Economies, Ithaca, Cornell University Press.

Friedman, R., and Jones, M. (1985) "Pay the Unemployed to Create New Jobs," New York Times, September 8, p. 2F.

Gamble, A. (1988) The Free Economy and the Strong State: The Politics of Thatcherism, Durham, Duke University Press.

Ginzberg, E. (1958) Human Resources: The Wealth of Nations, New York, Simon and Schuster.

Gray, V. (1973) "Innovation in the States: A Diffusion Study," American Political Science Review 67, 4, pp. 1174-1185.

Green, A.L. (1966) Manpower and the Public Employment Service in Europe, Washington, GPO. "

Guttman, B. (1981) Memorandum to Kitty Higgins and Kris Iverson, re "Specifications for 'Training for Jobs' Bill," December 16.

Hagedoorn, J. (1989) The Dynamic Analysis of Innovation and Diffusion: A Study in Process Control, London, Pinter.

Hansen, G.B. (1967) Britain's Industrial Training Act: Its History, Development, and Implications for America, Washington, National Manpower Policy Task Force.

Heclo, H. (1974) Modern Social Politics in Britain and Sweden, New Haven, Yale University Press.

Heidenheimer, A.J., Heclo, H., and Adams, C.T. (1990) Comparative Public Policy: The Politics of Social Choice in America, Europe, and Japan, 3rd edn, New York: St. Martin's.

Hinds, M.D. (1990) "Door to a Business of One's Own Can Be Good Exit From Welfare," New York Times, June 3, p. 1.

Hirshman, A.O. (1970) Exit, Voice, and Loyalty, Cambridge, MA, Harvard University Press.

Keep, E. (1991) "The Grass Looked Greener – Some Thoughts on the Influence of Comparative Vocational Training Research on the UK Policy Debate," in Ryan, P (ed.) International Comparisons of Vocational Education and Training for Intermediate Skills, London, Falmer Press.

Kilborn, P.T. (1990) "Novel Program for Jobless Aims to Create Entrepreneurs," New York Times, May 16, p. 1.

Kingdon, J.W. (1984) Agendas, Alternatives, and Public Policies, Boston, Little, Brown.

Korpi, W. (1989) "Power, Politics, and State Autonomy in the Development of Social Citizenship: Social Rights During Sickness in Eighteen OECD Countries Since 1930," American Sociological Review 54, 3, pp. 309-328.

Lutz, J.M. (1989) "Emulation and Policy Adoptions in the Canadian Provinces," Canadian Journal of Political Science 22, 1, pp. 147-154.

McVoy, E.C. (1940) "Patterns of Diffusion in the United States," American Sociological Review 5, 2, pp. 219-227.

March, J.G., and Simon, H.A. (1958) Organizations, New York, John Wiley.

March, J.G., and Olsen, J.P. (1989) Rediscovering Institutions: The Organizational Basis of Politics, New York, Free Press.

Moon, J. (1983) "Policy Change in Direct Government Responses to UK Unemployment," Journal of Public Policy 3, 3, pp. 301-330.

National Commission for Manpower Policy (1978) European Labor Market Policies, Staff Report 27, Washington, NCMP.

Nelson, D.J. (1969) Unemployment Insurance: The American Experience, 1915-1935, Madison, University of Wisconsin Press.

Perry, P.J.C. (1976) The Evolution of British Manpower Policy From the Statute of Artificers 1563 to the Industrial Training Act 1964, London, BACIE.

Plato (1926) Laws, tr. R.G. Bury, London, William Heineman.

Reubens, B.G. (1970) The Hard-To-Employ: European Programs, New York, Columbia University Press.

Riddell, P. (1983) The Thatcher Government, Oxford, Martin Robertson.

Robertson, D.B. (1987a) "Labor Market Surgery, Labor Market Abandonment: The Thatcher and Reagan Unemployment Remedies," in Waltman, J.L. and Studlar, D.T. (eds), Political Economy: Public Policies in the United States and Britain, Jackson, University Press of Mississippi.

Robertson, D.B. (1987b) "Mrs. Thatcher's Employment Prescription: An Active Neo-Liberal Labor Market Policy," Journal of Public Policy, 6, 3, pp. 275-296.

Robertson, D.B. (1989) "The Bias of American Federalism: The Limits of Welfare-State Development in the Progressive Era," Journal of Policy History 1, 3, pp. 261-291.

Robertson, D.B. and Judd, D.R. (1989) The Development of American Public Policy: The Structure of Policy Restraint, Glenview, IL, Scott, Foresman/Little, Brown.

Robertson, D.B. (1991), "Political Conflict and Lesson Drawing," Journal of Public Policy, IL, 1, pp. 57-78.

Rogers, E.M. (1983) The Diffusion of Innovations, 3rd Ed, New York, Free Press.

Rose, R. (1990) "Prospective Evaluation Through Comparative Analysis: Youth Training in a Time-Space Perspective," Studies in Public Policy Number 182, Strathclyde, Centre for the Study of Public Policy.

Rose, R. and Davies, P.L. (forthcoming) Inheritance Before Choice in Public Policy. Chatham, N.J., Chatham House.

Rudd, R., and Davenport, P. (1989) " £3bn Scheme to Train Workers for 21st Century," The Times, March 11, p. 5.

Savage, R.L. (1978) "Policy Innovativeness as a Trait of American States," Journal of Politics, 40, 2, pp. 212-224.

Savage, R.L. (1985) "Diffusion Research Traditions and the Spread of Policy Innovations in a Federal System," Publius: The Journal of Federalism 15, 1, pp. 1-27.

Scheb, J., and Matheny, A. (1988) "Judicial Reform and Rationalization: The Diffusion of Court Reform Policies Among the American States," Law and Policy, 10, 1, pp. 25-42.

Schlesinger, A. (1958) The Coming of the New Deal, Boston, Houghton Mifflin.

Sharkansky, I. (1970) The Routines of Politics, New York, Van Nostrand Reinhold.

Skowronek, S. (1982) Building a New American State: The Expansion of National Administrative Capacities, Cambridge, Cambridge University Press.

Steinbach, C. (1985) "Europeans are Giving Unemployed an Opportunity to Become Entrepreneurs," National Journal 17, 10, March 9, pp. 527-529.

Steinbrunner, J.D. (1974) The Cybernetic Theory of Decision: New Dimensions of Political Analysis, Princeton, Princeton University Press.

Stone, D. (1988) Policy Paradox and Political Reason, Glenview, IL, Scott, Foresman / Little, Brown.

Thompson, J.D. (1967) Organizations in Action, New York, McGraw-Hill.

Times Higher Education Supplement (1983) "Britain is Second to West Germany in Training Stakes," September 2, p. 4.

US Department of Labor (1986) Alternative Uses of Unemployment Insurance, Washington, GPO.

US House of Representatives (Committee on Ways and Means, Subcommittee on Public Assistance and Unemployment Compensation) (1988) Federal-State Unemployment Compensation System, WCMP 100-39, Washington, GPO.

US Senate (Subcommittee on Employment, Poverty, and Migratory Labor, Committee on Labor and the Public Welfare) (1974) Hearings on Labor Market Policy in Sweden, Washington, GPO.

Walker, J.L. (1969) "The Diffusion of Innovations Among the American States," American Political Science Review 67, 3, pp. 880-899.

Waltman, J.L. (1980) Copying Other Nations' Policies: Two American Case Studies, Cambridge, MA, Schenkman.

Waltman, J.L. (1987) "The Strength of Policy Inheritance," in Waltman, J.L. and Studlar, D.T. (eds), Political Economy: Public Policies in the United States and Britain, Jackson, University Press of Mississippi, pp. 259-269.

Welch, S. and Thompson, K. (1980) "The Impact of Federal Incentives on State Policy Innovation," American Journal of Political Science 24, 4, pp. 715-729.

Wilensky, H.L., and Turner, L. (1987) Democratic Corporatism and Policy Linkages: The Independence of Industrial, Labor-Market, Incomes, and Social Policies in Eight Countries, Berkeley, Institute of International Studies, University of California.

Wilensky, H.L., Luebbert, G.M., Hahn, S.R., and Jamieson, A.M. (1985) Comparative Social Policy: Theories, Methods, and Findings, Berkeley, Institute of International Studies, University of California.

Williams, S. (1981) Youth Without Work: Three Countries Approach to the Problem, Paris, OECD.

Wilson, W. (1887) "The Study of Administration," Political Science Quarterly 2, 2, pp. 197-222.

Wright, D. (1989) "LENs in the Light of TECs," Personnel Management 21, 5, pp. 42-45

Part 2

The Changing International Economy and Its Impact on Education and Training

DAVID FINEGOLD

In the late 1980s, education and training (ET) policy in America and Great Britain converged. At the same time, both countries seemed to become more reliant on programs transplanted from the other. An examination of the economic context in which policy has developed in the two countries can explain these recent episodes of policy convergence and transplantation.

This paper divides the discussion of the economic context into two parts: firstly, how economic change has been the driving force behind ET reform in all advanced industrial countries, including the US and UK, since the mid-1970s. The integration of world markets, technological change, and the increasing uncertainty are particularly significant hallmarks of recent economic change. The second part will demonstrate that the British and American experiences can be distinguished from that of their main competitors by their shared context of relative economic decline. Part of the decline stems from structural features of the US and UK economies that have discouraged key decision makers from adopting high-skill strategies; the US and UK are less able to adapt to changes in the international economy due to their institutional structures and low levels of education and training. While the emphasis will be on institutional factors that separate Britain and the US from the more successful industrialized countries, the section will also explore critical differences between the US and UK that give America significant advantages in creating and sustaining high skill enterprises.

Economic Change Drives ET Reform

Since the mid-1970s, ET reform has emerged as a major political issue in most of the advanced industrial countries. In Britain, the origins of the dramatic changes to the ET system, which have flowed almost continuously over the last decade, are generally traced back to then Prime Minister James Callaghan's speech at Ruskin College in October, 1976, during which he criticized the ET system for failing to meet the needs of British industry

(Callaghan, 1976). The publication of *A Nation at Risk* sparked off a similar educational debate in the US, with the warning:

> Our once unchallenged preeminence in commerce, industry, science, and technological innovation is being overtaken by competitors throughout the world .... If an unfriendly foreign power had attempted to impose on America the mediocre educational performance that exists today, we might have viewed it as an act of war. As it stands, we have allowed this to happen to ourselves .... We have, in effect, been committing an act of unthinking, unilateral educational disarmament. (NCEE, 1983, p. 5).

The variety of ET reforms that followed at state level were given added impetus by the Hudson Institute's *Workforce 2000* reports (Johnston and Packer, 1987; Packer, 1990) and *Investing in People* (US Department of Labor, 1989) which pointed to the gap between the growing skill demands of a rapidly changing economy and the quality and quantity of the outputs of the ET system. The reform movements in the US and UK had a particular urgency because of the two nations' shared experience of relatively declining prosperity.

Across Europe the push for educational change has been equally apparent. Under the Mitterrand Government, education has become one of France's top priorities, as a country which had the same relatively low participation rates in post-compulsory education as England in the 1960s strives toward the ambitious target of having 80 percent of school leavers pass the baccalaureate by the end of the 1990s (White, 1989). In Germany, education and training reforms are proceeding in tandem, with educational institutions struggling to cope with a near doubling of the numbers staying-on through university, while the already well-respected apprenticeship system is being redesigned to accommodate significant shifts in the occupational structure (Diepold, 1988).

Even in the economic success stories of the 1980s, education reform has been a major political issue. In Japan, the Nakasone Government responded to fears that the education system was not fostering the individual creativity essential if the nation was to retain its leadership role in the international economy by launching two high profile education commissions; although the consensus required for significant changes has thus far failed to emerge, education retains a prominent place on the political agenda (Schoppa, 1990). In nearby South Korea, there is widespread support for continued educational expansion, which is viewed as the foundation on which the nation's rapidly developing industrial economy has been built. The system already provides nearly universal secondary education and higher education for more than 36 percent of the population, but demand is far from satisfied; a 1987 survey revealed that 84.5 percent of Korean parents want to provide their children with a college level education (Economic Planning Board, 1987 in Porter, 1990).

All of these reform initiatives have been triggered, to some extent, by the perceived need to adapt ET systems to the economic and technological changes that have taken place during the last two decades. These shifts differentiate the competitive climate in the 1990s from the sustained period of economic growth and relative stability that ran from the end of World War II through to the 1973 oil shock, often referred to as 'the Golden Age of Fordism' (Glyn et al., 1990).[1]

Integration of World Markets

One of the most striking features of the new economic context is the growing interdependence of national economies. In the US, for example, the value of imports and exports accounted for just over ten percent of GNP in 1965; by 1980, the importance of international trade to the economy had more than doubled to nearly one quarter of GNP (US Survey of Current Business, 1965, 1980). There have been significant, though less dramatic, increases in the relative importance of international trade to all the major industrialized countries (Piore and Sabel, 1984, p.185). The expansion has been most apparent in trade between the developed countries, including a large rise in international competition in services (Porter, 1990, Ch. 6).

Official trade figures, however, capture only one strand of the expanding web of connections that bind the advanced industrial countries together. Multinational corporations, in search of lower wage costs and new markets, have dispersed their facilities throughout the world, often generating products or services that are sold locally and thus not included in trade statistics. Another sign of international interdependence is the growth in joint ventures among large companies which accelerated in the early 1980s (Ohmae, 1989). In just a three year period, Cooke (1988) recorded more than 400 strategic alliances between American and European corporations, 150 between European and Japanese firms and more than 200 between Japanese and US companies. The internationalization of capital has been given further impetus by new developments in computer and fibre optic technology, as the instantaneous availability of information and the unprecedented speed with which it can be processed have linked the world's financial markets into a single network. The high profile initiative to create a single market for the twelve members of the European Community by the end of 1992 and the signing of the North American Free Trade Agreement are the latest and most extensive steps in the trend toward increasing integration of world markets.

One upshot of the move toward a global marketplace is that it has become increasingly difficult to speak of national companies. Ohmae (1987) has traced the developmental stages of the multinational corporation, arguing that there is a gradual shift underway from export-driven, nationally-centered companies – which the Far East has been very successful in creating – to a new phase of international competition, dominated by truly global corporations, where all aspects of a company's operations are located in those areas that offer the best source of comparative advantage. Following this logic, Robert Reich asks: "Which company is more American, more vital to the success of the US economy and the welfare of its work force – Company A, with headquarters in the US and a predominantly American ownership, but with most of its manufacturing facilities located abroad, or Company B, that is run and financially controlled by members of another country, yet has large manufacturing and research facilities in the US that supply not only American markets, but also generate substantial export dollars?" (Reich in Morris, 1990).

The greater integration of the advanced industrial economies has taken place at the same time that major new competitors have joined the battle for the world's capital and consumer goods markets. The most notable new economic superpower is, of course, Japan, whose share of international sales of manufactures rose from just 3.4 percent in 1950 to 13.1 percent in 1973 (Matthews et al. 1982, p. 435). Japan's share continued to rise in the last decade as it outperformed all the industrialized nations in the largest and fastest growing sectors of world trade (Porter, 1990, p. 418). Following closely behind Japan were its newly industrialized Asian neighbours: Hong Kong, Singapore, Taiwan and South Korea. Between 1968 and 1976 their share of world exports doubled (Piore and Sabel, 1984, p.178) and by 1987 they had accumulated a trade surplus with the US of more than \$30 billion (Magaziner and Patinkin, 1989, p.19). Not only are these countries capturing a greater quantity of international trade in manufactured goods, but they are also moving rapidly into higher quality, higher value-added market segments once dominated by the US and Western Europe.

The imperative for ET reform created by the internationalization of capital and the advent of these new competitors is spelled out clearly by Reich (1988): as the major factors of production (capital, technology and raw materials) move more freely and quickly across national boundaries, labor, the least mobile factor, becomes a more central component in firms' search for competitive advantage. Since the advanced industrial countries cannot compete with developing countries on the basis of labor cost, the survival of their manufacturing base – and the vast array of services which supports it – depends upon superior labor quality and hence the skills of current and future employees.

Technological Change

A second key factor which has shaped the new economic context is the rapid spread of microelectronics and information technologies (OECD, 1988). Technological innovations have transformed both what is sold – giving birth to new industries, such as personal computers, information databases and a dramatic expansion of financial services – and how these goods and services are produced (Northcott and Walling, 1988). In the manufacturing sector, some see the introduction of computer numerically controlled (CNC) machine tools and computer-aided design as making possible a return to the artisanal relationship between machine and man (Leborgne and Lipietz, 1988); workers can use computers to reassume control over the tasks they perform, rather than simply feeding material to a machine dedicated to a single function. These new technologies allow companies to respond quickly to shifts in customer demand through rapid reprogramming, thereby minimizing the economies of scale advantages of the old assembly line structure and opening the way for new ways of organizing manufacturing (Freeman, 1987; Senker, 1988).

Numerous studies have attempted to measure the effects of these new technologies on the organization of production and skill levels (Rajan and Pearson, 1986; Wood, 1989; Jaikumar, 1986; Rumberger and Levin, 1989; US Department of Labor, 1989). Among the problems which this research faces is the extent to which changes in the nature of work are often hidden in broad occupational categories. Many jobs – such as secretaries or bank clerks – have retained the same title they held a generation ago, while the tasks and skills involved have been transformed (Noyelle, 1989). Another difficulty is how to cope with the pace of change. There is a danger of portraying recent economic history as divided into two eras – old technology and new technology or Fordist and post-Fordist – when in fact there have been several distinct phases of technological change in just the last few decades (Bailey, 1989).[2] As companies move into later stages of automation, shifting from isolated, computer-based work stations to integrated, flexible manufacturing systems, the number of manual workers required is reduced and the costs of any error or downtime in production are multiplied, thereby placing a premium on the skills of the remaining employees (Walton, 1985).

While the results of the 'up-skilling' versus 'de-skilling' debate remain unresolved on both sides of the Atlantic, some of the most optimistic early claims for the adaptability of the new technologies and their potential to make the Fordist assembly line obsolete have been rejected. Not only are CNC machine tools more time consuming to reconfigure than some of their more enthusiastic proponents suggest (Williams et al., 1987), but the high cost of installing the new equipment has tended to limit its use in all of the major industrial countries to the largest enterprises (e.g. McCormick, 1988; OECD, 1989; Campbell et al., 1989).

One clear conclusion that does emerge from the research on technological change is that the impact of computers and other new machines is not deterministic (Walton, 1988; Dertouzos et al., 1989). While they contain the potential to remove low skilled work and broaden job definitions, they do not dictate that companies follow this path, leaving open the alternative of reducing the skill level of labor and increasing managerial control. As the next section will show, managers must decide, after evaluating their firm's strategic needs and its organizational capacity for meeting them, which course to follow.

David Finegold

Divergent Paths to Flexibility

The integration of international markets and spread of new technologies are two of the major factors that destabilized the world economy in the 1970s.[3] With the loss of its dominant postwar position in international trade, the US could no longer afford to underwrite the stability of world financial markets, leading to its decision to abandon the Breton Woods Agreement. This triggered a marked increase in exchange rate volatility, which was in turn amplified by the linking of the world's financial centers by computers, satellites and fiber-optic cable in a 24-hour trading network. An event across the globe could now cause an immediate shift in the value of a country's currency or a company's shares. The result is that firms have been forced to adapt to far greater rates of change and uncertainty.

Alongside these long-term, structural shifts in the economic order came exogenous shocks which added to the instability of the international system.[4] The oil crises of 1973 and 1980 led to deep recessions and the new phenomenon of stagflation: simultaneous increases in unemployment and inflation.

To survive in this turbulent competitive climate all of the industrialized economies have been compelled to restructure. One of the main objectives of restructuring has been to create greater 'flexibility,' both among individuals and firms (for critical reviews of the 'flexibility' literature see Wood, 1989; Pollert, 1988). Policy makers called on ET systems to enhance individuals' abilities to adapt to the new environment in a number of ways: by providing alternative transitions from school to work for large numbers of the young unemployed (OECD, 1985); by equipping individuals with the new skills (e.g. problem solving, computer literacy) they require in the workplace (Freeman, 1987; OECD, 1989); and by creating opportunities for those already in the workforce, particularly individuals who have been made redundant, to update their skills or acquire new ones.[5] Among companies in the advanced industrial countries restructuring took place across sectors – with significant shifts from traditional manufacturing to services and high technology sectors – and within individual firms. In all industries managers sought to improve their companies' response to external changes by cutting both the length of time required to adjust their existing production system and to turn a new idea into a finished product. This entailed abandoning production systems with a large number of semi-skilled workers each performing a narrow array of tasks on dedicated machinery, the hallmarks of Fordism; this form of work organization had evolved to satisfy large, stable demand for mass-produced goods and was ill-suited to serving more specialized, rapidly changing niche markets (Fonda and Hayes, 1988; Piore and Sabel, 1984).[6]

In place of Fordist strategies, companies have looked for more flexible management models, often taking their inspiration from the East. It was Japanese firms which pioneered the development of just-in-time production systems, achieving substantial savings in inventories and unprecedented levels of market responsiveness by making goods to order using carefully coordinated supply chains and constant monitoring of customer demand (Sayer, 1986). Likewise leading Western firms studied their Japanese rivals to learn ways of reducing product development times by conducting the many operations this process entails in tandem, with research and design staff working together with the engineers responsible for creating the new manufacturing system (Sayer, 1986). Corning Glass, for example, has maintained its dominant position in the fiber optic cable industry by constructing five new generations of factories in just eight years (Magaziner and Patinkin, 1989, pp. 294-295).

But while companies in all the advanced industrial countries have sought ways to shorten response times, the types of flexibility strategy they have adopted and the skill levels associated with these strategies have differed significantly. Some have concentrated on cutting fixed costs, reducing the permanent workforce in favor of part-time or temporary workers and linking wages more directly to individual or firm performance through such devices as profit-sharing, bonuses, ESOPs, etc. (Atkinson, 1984; Harrison, forthcoming). Others have focused on improving the flexibility of their existing organization and employees, by devolving control over the work process to the lowest levels of a flattened managerial hierarchy, where multi-skilled workers take charge of monitoring quality and reconfiguring production (Brusco, 1982; *Society and Space*, 1988). Multi-skilling, however, must be contrasted with multi-tasking (Jones, 1989a), with the latter involving a number of operations all at the same skill level (job intensification), while the former connotes increased worker responsibility and higher-level skills (job enrichment).

Managers deciding between the various forms of flexibility will evaluate the costs and benefits of each strategy for their particular business. The low skill flexibility approach has the attraction of curtailing costs, by relying on relatively cheap labor and reducing the risk of excess capacity. In some sectors, such as fast food and mass retailing, minimizing skill requirements may be an advantage since it enables the work system to be transferred relatively easily within and between countries (Porter, 1990, Ch. 6). For companies seeking to compete in high value-added markets in the current, rapidly changing economic climate, however, there are a number of distinct advantages to high skill flexibility strategies including: enhanced quality of goods or services; reductions in downtime in capital-intensive work systems (Walton, 1988); and, most importantly, improved capability for continuous innovation in both products and the production process (Fonda and Hayes, 1988).[7]

All firms will not be in an equal position to adopt high-skill strategies, however. The capacity of firms to make successful high-skill investments will be determined, in part, by the countries in which their companies operate.[8] To understand why this is the case it is essential to grasp the interdependence between corporate/product strategy, competence requirements and the ET system (Campbell et al., 1989). Managers may desire a high-skill work system but be unable to put it into effect because of the absence of the required skills either in their existing workforce or in the external labor market. Likewise, individuals will be less likely to invest in their own ET if they receive signals from the labor market – through the jobs and wages on offer – that companies are organized in ways which do not reward skills. In each country, therefore, a vicious or virtuous circle may develop between the ET system and economic organization, where choices by managers and individuals regarding skills are influenced by the preexisting levels of ET and the institutional environment in which these decisions are taken.

The inexorable link between the supply and demand for skills can be demonstrated by examining what happens to firm flexibility strategies when the average ET attainment level is raised. The result will be greater incentives for managers to opt for high-skill forms of work organization by making it easier to recruit skilled manpower and reducing the need for remedial or basic skills training, thus freeing companies to concentrate on building firm- or job-specific skills. In the German case, Streeck (1989) has described how a high quality ET system can act as a driving force for innovation within companies, by reversing the traditional 'poaching' argument: managers realize that they must design strategies and organize the work process in ways that offer their employees continuous opportunities to learn and utilize their skills or risk losing their best performers to their competitors.

The remainder of this paper will focus on institutional structures in the British and American economies that have discouraged ET investment and hence made it less likely that firms within them will adopt high-skill strategies. In the UK case, I have described the network of institutional factors that stifles both the supply and demand for skills as a "low skill equilibrium" (Finegold and Soskice, 1988). While the mass higher education system and heavy individual spending on ET enable a larger sector of the US economy to escape from a low skill equilibrium, it shares common institutional features with the British system that dissuade a substantial number of individuals and firms from investing in skills and help explain the similarities in the two countries' government policy and managerial responses to the new competitive climate.

The broad contrast between the US and UK and the structure of more successful advanced industrial countries – Japan, Germany and regions of Northern Italy – is not intended to obscure significant variations in company organization and skill levels within each country. Among the factors which cut across national boundaries and affect skill requirements are: firm size; the nature of the production process (e.g. continuous flow, mass or batch production); and the type of business or product market (high versus low quality goods or services) (Jones, 1989a; Sabel, 1989). Even in those countries that have progressed farthest down the high-skill flexibility path there remain periphery sectors of low-wage, low-skill labor or dual labor markets (Piore, 1986). In Japan, successful multinational companies are underpinned by tiers of subcontracting firms, often stretching down to home-based, family enterprises, that provide less job security and lower pay than the large corporations (Sako, 1988), while in Germany a core sector of highly trained, heavily unionized workers with well protected jobs coexists alongside a migrant labor force that can be easily removed during economic downturns (Casey, 1986). Conversely, in the US and UK there are a number of firms which have overcome institutional obstacles to pursue successful high-skill strategies (Best, 1989; Porter, 1990).

Evidence of the Low Skill Equilibrium

When controlling for these intranational variations, there remain significant differences in the supply and demand for skills among the advanced industrial countries. Although it is difficult to obtain good comparative data on ET levels, the evidence which does exist suggests that in Britain and the US the majority of individuals leave the compulsory education system with a relatively low level of attainment. Signs of this failure are provided by the performance of average British and American students on standardized achievement tests in such basic subjects as mathematics and science, where they consistently rank at or near the bottom relative to their peers in the other industrialized countries (Postlethwaite, 1988). While these international exams have been criticized on methodological grounds and for an overemphasis on rote learning (Walberg, 1989; NCES, 1990), their general results have been confirmed in more detailed case studies of mathematical achievement: Lee and Stigler (in Bishop, 1989) found that the best of the 20 elementary school classrooms that they sampled in Minneapolis, Minnesota was outperformed by every one of comparable groups they studied in Sendai, Japan and 19 of the 20 examined in Taipei, Taiwan, while Prais and Wagner (1983) administered a series of tests in West German and English secondary schools which revealed that the lower half of the ability range in Germany scored higher than the average pupil in England.

In England, the problem of low levels of achievement in schooling is compounded by the low staying-on rates in post-compulsory ET.[9] Whereas 85-95 percent of 16-18 year olds participate in full-time education or high quality training in Japan and the northern European countries, in England in 1989, only a third of this age group stayed-on in school or college and less than 18% went on into higher education.

In the US, the problem is not primarily participation rates. Nationally, the vast majority of students (87% in 1982, according to the Department of Education) stay on in school until 18, with roughly half the age cohort continuing into some form of higher education; the high school dropout problem is concentrated in the inner cities and poorest states, with estimates of the number failing to obtain a diploma varying significantly (Haggstrom et al., 1991). Public and employer concern over dropouts began to increase along with the scale of the problem in the 1970s, and more recent attention has focused on demographic trends which indicate that the main supply of new entrants to the labor force in the 1990s will be those groups – blacks and hispanics – historically at greatest risk of dropping out (McKinsey, 1987). The main problem confronting the US, however, is what is achieved by those remaining in the ET system (Bishop, 1989). In contrast with other industrial nations, the US basic qualification – the high school diploma – is a leaving certificate that includes no externally-assessed standards. For the majority of individuals who do not go on to get a degree, there are few clearly defined routes to technical or vocational qualifications.

The result of these trends is that employers in the US and UK are worried that a large portion of the existing work force and the young people now leaving school lack the basic literacy and numeracy skills which are necessary to function in a modern economy and provide the essential foundation from which to build higher-level competencies (Johnston and Packer, 1987; US Department of Labor, 1989; MacLeod, 1990; Cassels, 1990). In 1987, for example, a US telephone company had to test 57,100 people in order to find 2,000 with the skills needed to fill the relatively undemanding posts of telephone operator and repair technician (Rachman, 1989). This is simply one case in a broader trend, as the Hudson Institute estimates that only 22 percent of the new entrants to the US labor force in the next decade will have the 'level 3' skills – i.e. the ability to read safety instructions and write a simple report – that will be required for the majority of all new jobs (*Business Week*, 1988). In Britain, skill shortages have been a persistent problem, with approximately one quarter of all manufacturing companies reporting that lack of skilled workers had restricted output in 1989 (Training Agency, 1989). Public sector professions such as teaching and nursing are experiencing similar difficulties in recruiting from the limited pool of candidates with the necessary qualifications, a situation likely to worsen as the number of young people declines in the first half of the 1990s (Bernstein, 1988).

Skill shortages, however, seriously underestimate the scale of the problem which the US and UK face. Even if every vacancy were filled, Britain and America would still lag behind their main competitors because employers' skill demands for the average worker are lower than in rival industrial nations. In the British case, this has been clearly demonstrated in a number of studies, most notably the work of Sig Prais and his colleagues at the National Institute for Social and Economic Research (NIESR, 1990;

Hirst and Zeitlin, 1989; Sorge et al., 1983; Campbell et al., 1989). The NIESR has conducted a series of matched firm comparisons in industrial sectors ranging from metal working and construction to retailing and hotels, showing how British companies consistently provide poorer quality goods or services and attain lower levels of productivity than comparable enterprises in Germany, France and the Netherlands. They trace the British failure to forms of work organization that rely on poorly trained managers and workers. Perhaps the most striking finding came in their study of small and medium-sized hotels, where West German establishments' labor productivity was 65 percent higher than their British counterparts, a difference directly related to the greater quality and quantity of training of German front-line staff and supervisors (NIESR, 1990). While no such body of comparative research exists for the US, a number of recent studies have pointed to the relatively low levels of skill which American firms expect from their employees (Cleveland, this volume; Dertouzos et al., 1989; Kazis, 1989).

Further evidence of US and UK firms' inclination toward low-skill strategies comes from the ways in which they have introduced new technologies. The UK and US were pioneers in the development of flexible manufacturing systems (FMS), with Britain establishing the world's first prototype FMS factory in the 1960s (Jones, 1989b), but as with many major scientific and technological breakthroughs they failed to capitalize on their early lead. British and American firms have typically bought FMS as complete packages from outside vendors, using them to solidify managerial control over the production process by transferring skilled tasks from line workers to white collar programmers (Sorge et al., 1983; Jones, 1989a; Katz and Sabel, 1985; Scarborough, 1986; Lane, 1988; Brady, 1984; Campbell et al. 1989; Jaikumar, 1986). A study which I conducted in 1985 in the telecommunications sector showed how US companies have utilized new technologies to reduce the skill level of already relatively low-skilled jobs (Finegold, 1985). A new computer system responsible for regulating the flow of incoming calls was designed without consulting the operators, creating problems during the implementation phase and increasing job dissatisfaction and turnover rates. The computers monitored the time required to handle each call to the tenth of a second, compelling operators to rush through the most difficult customer problems and forcing them to raise their hands if they wanted to go to the bathroom. In this case, as with the introduction of most forms of automation in the US and UK, managers' primary justification for the investment was reduced costs and improved efficiency. The chairman of the UK's Department of Trade and Industry Committee on New Production Techniques summarized the situation: "[British companies are using] very high technology to manufacture low technology products cheaper than the rest of the world" (Jones, 1989b, p. 116).

This Anglo-American approach to new technologies can be contrasted with the higher skill flexibility strategies many companies have adopted in Japan, Germany and Sweden. These have avoided some of the problems US and UK firms encountered by customizing FMS to their particular needs and turning greater control over the machines to front-line workers, who can spot and repair difficulties as well as reprogram the computers in response to changing demand (Shirai, 1983; Sayer, 1986; Jones, 1989b; Aguren et al., 1984).

Institutional Disincentives for High-Skill Investment

Why should the supply and demand for skills be lower in Britain and America than in their main competitors? And why should these two countries look to each other for policy inspiration when they both suffer from relatively poor ET and economic records? Of all the industrialized countries, the US and UK are the strongest proponents of free markets, including lack of state regulation over ET (Hall, 1986). As Streeck (1989, p.15) observes, however, "the skills needed for industrial modernization have peculiar collective good properties [such that] firms acting 'rationally' in a liberal political economy" will not produce them in sufficient quantities, nor can "they be generated by unilateral state provision." Streeck's concern, and the main focus of this chapter, is not with the research and scientific manpower – who are educated in universities in all the industrialized countries – but rather with the skills of the average worker and their managers who are responsible for turning research breakthroughs into successful products and services.

In order to analyse the 'properties' of the skills investment decision and the specific characteristics of markets in Britain and the US that have discouraged key actors from investing in high levels of ET I have constructed an analytical framework (for a fuller explanation see Finegold, 1991). It consists of three players – company managers, government policy makers and individuals – representing the three principal investors in ET. The players decide whether to spend their time and money on ET based on the institutional situation in which they are placed. The framework is designed to move beyond the specifics of national or local cases to look at the underlying rationale of skills investment and the incentives which govern players' decisions. As with economists' formal game theory models, each player's moves will be affected by the moves of the others, highlighting the interdependence of ET investment decisions. By treating ET investment as a game, it is possible to avoid an overdetermined perspective by introducing an element of chance or probability into the model. Countries will contain a wide spectrum of companies and individuals, who will respond differently to the same set of incentives; the institutional setting in a particular case can be seen as setting the odds that any one set of players will invest in higher level skills. Though the analysis here will focus on national institutions, a similar framework could be applied at sectoral, regional or local level to explain some of the variations in skill investment within countries.

The framework focuses on two integral characteristics of higher level skills – their long payback period and the externalities associated with this investment. For each factor it will analyse a set of political and economic structures in the US and UK that lead the players to make a relative under-investment in ET and hence make high-skill flexibility strategies less attractive.

Short-Term Outlook

Education and training can serve a variety of economic functions, from induction to company practices and the preparation of workers for specific tasks to the development of general skills that enable individuals to adapt to changes in the organization of work and technology or progress within a company hierarchy. Each of these forms of ET will have different costs and payback periods. The high cost and deferred nature of returns to the development of higher level, transferable skills means that players are far more likely to invest in building these competencies if they have a long-run, strategic perspective. There are a series of structural characteristics in the British and American economies, however, that make it more likely that the three players, most critically the company manager, will adopt a short-term outlook when making ET decisions.

For *top management*, the critical institutional factor determining their investment time frame is the relationship between financial and industrial capital (Moorhouse, 1989). American and British companies are far more reliant on capital markets as a source for long-term investment than their Japanese or European counterparts who look to banks rather than the stock market as the primary source of finance (Zysman, 1983, p. 124).[10] In part, the evolution of capital rather than credit-based systems of finance is dictated by securities law in the US and UK, where commercial banks are prohibited from taking ownership stakes in industrial corporations. The inevitable information disparities or insider-outsider problems that arise in capital markets create a tendency toward short-termism, as financial analysts tend to focus on those measures of company performance – such as quarterly earnings and revenue – that are easiest to predict.[11] This in turn affects the priorities of company managers, as a survey of more than 500 executives of US and Japanese corporations revealed: US managers placed 'share price increase' second to 'return on investment' in their ranking of ten corporate objectives, while Japanese managers' main objective was improved 'market share' with 'share price' receiving by far the least attention (Abegglen and Stalk, 1985, p. 177 in Dertouzos et al, 1989).

The significant expansion in the size and number of hostile takeovers in the US and UK in the 1980s – a practice virtually unheard of in Japan or West Germany due to government regulations and structures of ownership – further sharpened the focus on short-term results and maximizing shareholder value, as chief executives of even the largest corporations feared that a drop in the share price could attract corporate raiders. This short-term perspective is transmitted down to lower level managers who are responsible for most training decisions through budgeting systems and the criteria used to evaluate and reward managerial performance. The organization of firms into cost and profit centers along with a heavy reliance on traditional accounting techniques that fail to measure the less tangible benefits of upgrading skills (e.g. lower turnover rates, enhanced product quality or improved customer satisfaction) combine to make training a low managerial priority in most US and UK corporations (Coopers and Lybrand, 1985; Dertouzos, 1989, Campbell and Warner, 1991). These structural factors, along with the finance orientation of much British and American management and the absence of high status, well-trained trainers equivalent to the German 'meisters' (Rose and Wignanek, 1990), combine to make training within US and UK firms vulnerable to cuts during a recession or through the pressure to meet short-term profit targets.[12] In contrast, Japanese and German firms have made skills development an integral part of their corporate structures and use economic downturns as an opportunity to increase training so that they will be in a position to take full advantage of the recovery (MSC/NEDO, 1984).

The capacity of *individuals* to view their own ET from a long-term perspective is a product of two stages of institutional incentives: those affecting decisions during full-time education and those which link further ET decisions with labor market outcomes. Although the specific institutional reasons differ, the British and American education systems share the common problem of failing to provide the majority of students with an incentive to invest their time and effort in ET. As Bishop (1989, p. 11) argues convincingly, in the US "students who do not aspire to attend-selective colleges benefit very little from working hard while in high school" because

> ...the labor market fails to reward effort and achievement in high school. The peer group actively discourages academic effort; [and] admission to selective colleges is not based on an absolute or external standard of achievement in high school subjects.

In England, the problem stems from a historically elitist examination structure designed for the small number of individuals who go on to higher education while branding the vast majority of students as failures (IPPR, 1990). Although the introduction of the National Curriculum and the General Certificate of Secondary Education (GCSE) should improve the incentives within the ET system for average students to work hard until sixteen – by introducing continuous assessment and clear stages of progression in a unified system – these reform efforts have, thus far, not been extended successfully into the post-compulsory phase (beyond the age of 18); the advanced (A) level examination, the high status option which promises entry to HE or a good job, is designed so that only roughly twenty percent of each age cohort will pass. For the rest, the labor market may actually create an incentive to leave school or college, since employers attach little reward to education-based vocational qualifications and recruitment to the best apprenticeships is often restricted to 16 year olds (Raffe, 1987). Again this situation stands in sharp contrast with Germany and Japan, where students of all abilities have clear incentives to work hard during compulsory schooling because their performance is clearly related to their future career prospects.

Once individuals have left school, the structure of labor market rewards will be the primary factor determining their willingness to invest in further ET. The ease with which British and American companies can hire and fire workers has hindered the development of strong internal labor markets that give individuals an incentive to invest in training. The US and UK lack institutional structures – such as German labor law or the Japanese 'lifetime employment' model – which encourage firms to tie job security to skills acquisition by employees (Stern, 1982). Thus, in Britain and America the external labor market is the main driver of individuals' ET decisions.

It is at this point that the US enjoys a major advantage over Britain in the creation of skilled manpower. The US system contains powerful incentives for individuals to invest in general ET after compulsory schooling. The high value attached to degrees by employers and relatively open access to HE encourage a greater percentage of over-18s to continue in education than in any advanced industrial country. In Britain, by contrast, individuals have traditionally treated HE as a consumption good, with the number of places rationed by central government through the examination system. For the vast majority unable to obtain a place in HE, there is little incentive to invest in further ET because of the relatively low wage differentials between skilled and unskilled labor (Jones, 1988). With regard to technical training, however, both countries have suffered from the failure to develop a clearly defined, high status structure of vocational qualifications – as exists in Germany – that could encourage individuals to invest in their own skills development (Maurice, Sellier, and Silvestre, 1986; Perlman, 1988).

The inability of *government policy makers* in the US and UK to adopt a long-term perspective toward skills creation is largely a product of the institutional situation in which they are placed.[13] The time scale for reforms needed to elevate ET levels does not synchronize with the short-term political demands created by the electoral cycle.[14] Britain made an attempt to distance ET policy from short-term pressures with the creation of the Manpower Services Commission, a tripartite quango, in 1974. The politicization of this body and its subsequent abolition left the government without an effective institutional mechanism for long-term ET planning (Dale, 1989). The US Federal Government has never developed such a strategic capacity, with most educational powers continuing to rest with the states despite the creation of the Department of Education in the 1970s.

While the national government has played a larger role in training policy, its initiatives have focused on aiding the disadvantaged rather than developing higher level skills (Osterman, 1988). The short-term nature of the ET policy process in the US and UK is well illustrated by many of the case studies in Part 2 of this publication, where British reforms were designed and implemented at breakneck speed after ministerial study visits to America (Keep, 1991).

Absence of Cooperation within a Competitive Environment

A second factor which interacts with short-term perspectives to deter key actors in the US and UK from pursuing high-skill strategies is the relative absence of institutional mechanisms for cooperation. The importance of cooperation for ET stems from the externalities or collective good problems associated with the factors necessary for successful high-skill enterprises. This applies not only to training, but also to a number of other investments – such as research and development, introduction of the latest technologies and export marketing – that may be beyond the means of any one player to finance, but to their mutual benefit if they share the costs and the risks involved. Cooperation can take two forms within the game scenario: first, the creation of institutions for coordinating the activities of the same type of player – e.g. company managers – to prevent firms from free riding on the system, and second, the development of mechanisms for sharing information or joint action between players, such as cooperation between government and industry or individuals and employers.

The benefits of cooperation for managers seeking to create high-skill companies are demonstrated by the fact that in a wide range of the most advanced manufacturing and service industries the world leaders tend to be clustered in small geographical areas or 'industrial districts' (Sabel, 1989; *Society and Space*, 1988; Hirst and Zeitlin, 1989). Companies located in clusters such as those found in the Northern Italian areas specializing in advanced ceramics and high-quality textiles and apparel, or the machine tool and metal working regions of Smaland, Sweden, and Sakaki, Japan, are often small and medium sized enterprises. They compete fiercely to introduce the latest, most sophisticated product and develop new means of improving the production process; at the same time, however, they have developed means of cooperating – such as jointly financed training institutes – which give them a competitive advantage in international markets.[15]

Although Britain and America have some thriving examples of such industrial clusters (notably the financial centers of Wall Street and the City of London and the high tech agglomerations around Route 128, Silicon Valley and the M4 Corridor), they have, on the whole, been less successful in creating and maintaining them than their main competitors, with several once prosperous industrial districts slipping into decline.[16] In his study of ten industrialized countries, Porter (1990, p. 154) found: "mechanisms that facilitate interchange within clusters are generally strongest in Japan, Sweden, and Italy and generally weakest in the United Kingdom and United States."

One of the most effective mechanisms for cooperation among *managers* is strong employer associations, such as the chambers of trade and commerce found in France or West Germany.[17] These organizations have the membership (often compulsory) and sanctions necessary to insure that companies in a local economy or industrial sector devote sufficient resources to training, rather than 'poaching' their rivals' skilled workers. While Britain and America have a plethora of employer groups, whose ranks have swelled recently thanks to government initiatives creating Private Industry Councils and Training and Enterprise Councils (see Bailey, this publication, Part 3), these rarely have the regulatory backing or resources necessary to overcome free riders. Those few British or American employer organizations that do possess such powers, as in the construction industry, have been able to maintain at least a minimum level of transferable skills in their sector (Lusterman, 1985; Rainbird, 1990).

Cooperation between *managers and policy makers* is also essential to create the types of ET required for successful high-skill flexibility strategies. These skills are characterized by an inseparable blend of firm-specific and transferable competencies and a rapid rate of obsolescence (Kern and Schumann, 1989). Companies operating in isolation within a market environment will tend to over-emphasize job-specific training at the expense of general skills, while state ET institutions will find it difficult, if not impossible, to keep pace with changes in technology or simulate the process of workplace socialization that is an integral part of skills acquisition (Streeck, 1989, p.95). The shared Anglo-American institutional bias toward 'voluntarism' – the government leaving training decisions to managers and their employees – has mitigated against the close interchange between the state and key producer groups that is critical to fostering ET investment in transferable skills (Reich, 1983; Magaziner and Patinkin, 1989; Streeck and Schmitter, 1985). When Wilensky and Turner (1987) studied the structure of the government, trade unions and employer associations and the connections among them in the eight largest capitalist economies, they concluded that the US and Britain ranked last in their ability to operate effective active labor market and industrial policies.

The degree of cooperation between *managers and individual employees* or their representatives, the trade unions, will also have a major impact on what type of flexibility strategy companies pursue. The industrial relations structures in the US and UK have, for very different reasons, tended to discourage managers from following a high skill route (Lash and Bagguley, 1988). In Britain, the historical legacy of craft unionism, with one plant sometimes containing a dozen or more different unions, has hindered the reorganization of work and investment in new technologies needed to make a high skill flexible strategy work.[18] In America, by contrast, the general weakness of organized labor and absence of legislation to protect employees' rights found in many European countries, has allowed managers to dictate the terms of corporate restructuring with often little or no consideration given to the effects on skill levels.[19]

As with relationships between firms, management and labor can work together in areas of mutual interest, such as training and the introduction of new technologies, while continuing to compete or bargain over other issues – e.g. wages, benefits and hours. This is clearly illustrated in the German and Japanese cases, where unions have actively supported the introduction of advanced technologies and shared in the benefits of enhanced productivity that have resulted (Shirai, 1983; Porter, 1990). The role of organized labor in decisions over new technology and the oversight of training standards in these two countries is enshrined in institutional structures, such as German works councils, that are absent in the US and UK.

Competition is thus an essential complement to cooperation in encouraging high-skill investment. Without the sustained pressure to innovate generated by rivals in domestic and international markets, there is a danger that long-term perspectives and cooperative relationships will become a recipe for bloated bureaucracies and stagnation. In many business areas, particularly in the non-tradable sector, British and American companies have suffered due to the lack of pressure to keep pace with the world's leading companies (Rose, 1989). In the US case, the vast size of the domestic market and historically low levels of dependence on exports meant that firms in many sectors – such as automobiles, machine tools, steel, consumer electronics, etc. – were slow to adapt to changes in world competition. Britain, thanks to the legacy of its trading empire, is far more integrated into world markets, but conducts a relatively high percentage of its trade with developing, rather than industrialized, countries, thereby lessening the pressure to upgrade product quality. In addition, the dominance of one or two large firms in many industries (furthered in the 1960s and 1970s by the Labour Party's policy of nationalization) and the insularity of many sectors – like the London garment industry or Sheffield cutlery manufacturing – has contributed to economic decline (Zeitlin and Totterdill, 1989). Avoiding competition, however, is no longer an option for companies in either nation; a decade of market-oriented policies, such as privatization and deregulation, combined with the increasing integration of world markets means that they must match or better their high-skill international rivals if they are to survive.

Conclusion

Faced with the external pressures for reform that have swept all the advanced industrial countries and with a common set of deeply rooted institutional structures, it is far from surprising that the US and UK have responded with similar ET policies during the last decade. While the US starts from a higher base of general education, both countries' governments have acknowledged the urgent the need to improve their ET systems. Their desire for change, however, may not match their capacity to bring it about. Even if the respective British and American initiatives should succeed in significantly raising attainment levels of the majority of pupils, the implications of the game framework are that ET reform, by itself, will not succeed in creating a high skill economy. In both countries, ET has been but one part of the market-oriented thrust of the conservative administrations' industrial and labor market policies. By encouraging short- rather than long-term perspectives and competition at the expense of cooperation, these policies have reinforced rather than redressed the institutional disincentives that have discouraged key actors in the US and UK from investing in higher level skills.

Notes

[1] For a full explanation of 'Fordism' – a reference to Henry Ford's assembly line and its development into an international economic order centered around mass-produced consumer durables – see the French Regulation School (e.g. Leborgne and Lipietz, 1988).

[2] It is possible to identify at least four distinct phases in the literature on technological change and skill levels: Bell (1974) argued that the advanced industrial countries were moving toward a high-skill, "post-industrial society"; Braverman (1974) spawned a series of studies on the de-skilling effects of automation; Piore and Sabel (1984) and their followers countered that new programmable technologies were making possible a return to an artisan economy with clusters of high skill, small firms in industrial districts; and finally, the current phase features a more complex up-skilling versus de-skilling debate.

[3] Boyer (1988) provides a far more nuanced account of the factors which led to the decline of Fordism and the ensuing economic crisis than space allows for here.

[4] Evidence of the structural origins of the crisis of the 1970s and early 1980s can be found in the dramatic fall in profits experienced by companies in the advanced industrial countries in the mid-1960s. In the UK, for instance, the average rate of profits (excluding North Sea oil companies) shrank from 12 percent in 1964 to under five percent by 1976 (Metcalf, 1989, p.47).

[5] The demand for retraining was driven by the accelerating pace of technological change, which has dramatically reduced the 'half-life' of skills – the time required for an individual's skills to become obsolete (Walton, 1988).

[6] Piore and Sabel (1984) argue that changes in firm strategy have been driven by the saturation of domestic demand for mass produced consumer goods combined with the emergence of a new professional class with large disposable incomes and a taste for higher quality goods and services. Their emphasis on an exogenous shift in consumption as a principal driver of economic change has proved extremely controversial. While most authors concede that there has been a decline in product life cycles and a proliferation of new goods and services, it is difficult to measure whether this represents a major break with past practice or simply an extension of oligopolists' product differentiation strategies, like that used by GM in the 1930s to overtake Ford in the US car market.

[7] For a more complete discussion of the advantages of high- over low-skill flexibility for individuals and government policy makers as well as managers see Finegold, 1991.

[8] A problem with a large section of the post-Fordism literature, common to both its supporters and critics, is the neglect of national divergence; there is a tendency to pick a few key examples – Emilia Romagna, Baden-Wurttemberg as proof of the success of flexible specialization or the US and Great Britain as cases of failure – and over-generalize from them.

[9] It is important to distinguish Scotland from England at this point, since Scotland with a fully comprehensive system, a less specialized examination structure and different rules governing the leaving age has a significantly higher staying-on rate than south of the border (Raffe, 1984).

[10] In the US, the total value of bonds and equities exceeds the Gross Domestic Product (GDP) and in the UK it equals 84% of GDP compared with France and Germany where securities amount to 27 and 43% of GDP, respectively (Vittas, 1978, p. 30, in Zysman, 1983).

[11] See Soskice (1990) for a more detailed explanation of why capital markets tend to promote short-term decision-making.

[12] The US enjoys a significant advantage over Britain in the levels of management education. This may help account for why some US firms have realized the error of the short-term approach to skills formation, avoiding cutbacks in their training departments in the last recession (Lusterman, 1985) and introducing new cost accounting systems that attach a higher value to quality and training (Business Week, 1988).

[13] Zysman (1983, p. 300-1) argues that the state's capacity to act strategically is the product of three institutional variables: the method by which it recruits the national civil service, the extent to which its power is centralized, and its degree of autonomy from the legislature. On the basis of these factors, he finds that Japan and France have structures which favour state intervention, while the US and UK do not.

[14] Japan's system of one-party government shields ET policy makers from short-term electoral pressures, while in Germany, power over ET programmes and standards is centered in an independent, well funded research institute.

[15] Some authors (e.g. Sabel, 1989) focus on the cooperative dimensions of these industrial districts, stressing the product specialization that occurs between closely related firms, while others (Porter, 1990, pp.143-44) place greater emphasis on the role of 'domestic rivalry' in propelling innovation by generating new spin off companies and upgrading and stimulating domestic demand.

[16] Prominent examples of US and UK industrial clusters that have or are disintegrating include: the Detroit auto industry, shipbuilding in Glasgow and Sunderland, textiles in Lancashire and New England and cutlery in Sheffield.

[17] The Japanese have developed the world's most extensive network of cooperative relationships among employers, extending from the hierarchy of subcontracting relationships to the 'guruku', where several multinationals from different sectors join with a large bank in a complex web of mutual ownership and finance agreements (Dore, 1986). These arrangements foster a long-term perspective by preventing hostile takeovers, insuring plentiful supplies of capital and encouraging innovation through the exchange of information and expertise.

[18] In the last decade the combination of Thatcher's industrial relations reforms and structural changes in the economy have led to a significant weakening of trade union power and consequent reduction in restrictive work practices.

[19] There have been some qualified exceptions to this general rule, notably in the automobile and telecommunications industries. In the US, unions such as the United Auto Workers and Communication Workers of America have taken a leading role in negotiating agreements that combine flexible work practices with large investments in retraining to prepare workers for new jobs within the company or outside it (Kochan and Katz, 1984); in Britain, the Electricians have pushed for single union agreements and established their own training college, while Ford UK has worked with its unions to set up a pioneering further education program which has used a company subsidy to attract nearly half of its employees onto courses in their free time.

References

Abegglen, J. and Stalk, G. (1985) Kaisha: The Japanese Corporation, New York, Basic Books.

Aguren (1986) "Volvo Kalmar Revisited," Stockholm, Efficiency and Participation Development Council.

Atkinson, J. (1984) "Manpower Strategies for Flexible Organizations", Personnel Management, August.

Bailey, T. (1989) "Changes in the Nature and Structure of Work: Implications for Skills and Skill Formation," report for Conservation of Human Resources, Columbia University, November.

Bell, D. (1974) The Coming of Post-Industrial Society, London, Heinemann.

Bernstein, A. (1988) "Where the Jobs Are Is Where the Skills Aren't," Business Week, 19 September, pp. 104-106.

Best, M. (1989) "Sector Strategies and Industrial Policy: The Furniture Industry and the Greater London Enterprise Board,' in Hirst and Zeitlin.

Bishop, J. (1989) "Incentives for Learning: Why American High School Students Compare So Poorly to Their Counterparts Overseas," in Commission on Workforce Quality and Labor Market Efficiency [Investing in People], Washington, D.C., US Department of Labor, Vol. 1, pp. 1-84.

Boyer, R. (1988) The Search for Labour Market Flexibility, Oxford, Clarendon Press.

Brady, T. (1984) "New Technology and Skills in British Industry", Brighton, Sussex University, Science Policy Research Unit.

Braverman, H. (1974) Labor and Monopoly Capital, New York, Monthly Review Press.

Brusco, S. (1982) "The Emilian Model: Productive Decentralization and Social Integration," Cambridge Journal of Economics, 6, 2.

Business Week (1988) "How the New Math of Productivity Adds Up", 6 June, pp. 49-55.

Callaghan, J. (1976) "Ruskin College Speech", The Times Educational Supplement, p. 72.

Campbell, A. and Warner, M. (1991) 'Training Strategies and Microelectronics in the Engineering Industries in the UK and Germany', in P. Ryan (ed.) International Comparisons of Vocational Education and Training for Intermediate Skills, London, Falmer.

Campbell, A., Sorge, A. and Warner, M. (1989) Microelectronic Product Applications in Great Britain and West Germany, Avebury, WZB-Publications.

Casey, B. (1986) "The Dual Apprenticeship System and the Recruitment and Retention of Young Persons in West Germany", British Journal of Industrial Relations, 24, 1, March, pp. 64-80.

Cassels, J. (1990) "Britain's Real Skills Shortage", London: PSI.

Cooke, P. (1988) "Flexible Integration, Scope Economies and Strategic Alliances: Social and Spatial Mediations:, Society and Space, 6, 3, pp. 281-300.

Coopers and Lybrand (1985) A Challenge to Complacency, MSC/NEDO, Sheffield.

Dale, R. (1989) The State and Education Policy, Milton Keynes, Open University Press.

Dertouzos, M., Lester, R. and Solow, R. (1989) Made in America: Regaining the Productive Edge, Cambridge, MIT Press.

Diepold, P. (1988) "A New Concept of Vocational Education and Training," presented at "Strategic Occupational Training: German Experience of a Systems Approach,' London, The Prospect Centre, November.

Dore, R. (1986) Flexible Rigidities, Palo Alto Stanford University Press.

Economic Planning Board (1987) Social Indicators in Korea, Seoul.

Finegold, D. (1992) "An Institutional Analysis of Britain's Education and Training Failure", Oxford University, DPhil Dissertation.

Finegold, D. (1991) "Institutional Incentives and Skills Creation", in Ryan, P. (ed.) International Comparisons of Vocational Education and Training for Intermediate Skills, Basingstoke, Falmer.

Finegold, D. and Soskice, D. (1988) "The Failure of British Training: Analysis and Prescription," Oxford Review of Economic Policy, 4, 3, Autumn, pp. 21-53.

Finegold, D. (1985) Quality of Worklife at AT&T, Cambridge, MA, Harvard University undergraduate thesis.

Fiske, E. (1989) "Growing Gap in Worker Skills Alarms Corporate America," International Herald Tribune, 26 September, p. 3.

Fonda, N. and Hayes, C. (1988) "Education, Training and Business Performance." Oxford Review of Economic Policy, 4, 3, Autumn, pp. 108-119.

Freeman, C. (1987) Technical Change and Full Employment, Oxford, Basil Blackwell.

Freeman, R. (1976) The Overeducated American, New York, Academic Press..

Glyn, A., Hughes, A., Lipietz, A. and Singh, A. (1990) "The Rise and Fall of the Golden Age,' in Marglin, S., and Schor, J. (eds.) The End of the Golden Age, Oxford, Oxford University Press.

Guthrie, J. and Koppich, J. (1988) "Exploring the Political Economy of National Education Reform,' in Boyd, W.L. and Kerchner, C. (eds.) The Politics of Excellence and Choice in Education, New York, Falmer Press.

Haggstrom, G., Blaschke, T., and Shavelson, R. (1991) After High School, Then What? : A Look at the Postsecondary Sorting-Out Process for American Youth, Rand, pp.10-11

Hall, P. (1986) Governing the Economy, Oxford: Polity Press.

Harrison, B. (forthcoming) After the Crisis? The Struggle for Economic Dominance in the Age of Flexibility , MIT, working paper.

Hirst, P. and Zeitlin, J. (Eds.) (1989) Reversing Industrial Decline?, Oxford, Berg.

Hyman, R. and Streeck, W. (Eds.) (1988) New Technology and Industrial Relations, Oxford, Basil Blackwell.

Institute for Public Policy Research (1990) "The British Baccalaureate : Proposals for a Unified System of Education and Training," London, IPPR, July.

International Association for the Evaluation of Educational Achievement (IEA) (1987) The Underachieving Curriculum: Assessing US School Mathematics from an International Perspective, Champaign, IL, Stipes Publishing Co.

Jaikumar, R. (1986) "Postindustrial Manufacturing," Harvard Business Review, November-December.

Jensen, M. (1989) "Eclipse of the Public Corporation," Harvard Business Review, September-October, 68, 5, pp. 61-74.

Johnston, W. and Packer, A. (1987) Workforce 2000 Indianapolis, Hudson Institute.

Jones, B. (1989a) 'Technology, Jobs and Flexible Production Strategies,' paper presented at CLES Summer School, Barnsley, July.

Jones, B. (1989b) 'Flexible Automation and Factory Politics: The United Kingdom in Comparative Perspective," in Hirst, P. and Zeitlin, J. (eds.) Reversing Industrial Decline? Oxford, Berg.

Jones, I. (1988) "An Evaluation of YTS", Oxford Review of Economic Policy, 4, 3, pp. 54-71.

Katz, H. and Sabel, C. (1985) "Industrial Relations and Industrial Adjustment in the Car Industry,' Industrial Relations, 24.

Katzenstein, P. (1985) Small States in World Markets, Ithaca, Cornell University Press.

Kazis, R. (1988) 'The Relationship Between Education and Productivity,' Cambridge, MIT, Dept. of Political Science M.A.

Keep, E. (1991) "The Grass Looked Greener" in Ryan, P. (ed.) International Comparisons of Vocational Education and Training for Intermediate Skills, Basingstoke, Falmer.

Kern, M. and Schumann, M. (1989) "New Concepts of Production in West German Plants,' in Peter Katzenstein (ed.) Industry and Politics in West Germany, Ithaca, Cornell University Press, pp. 87-112.

Kochan, T. and Katz, H. (1984) Worker Participation and American Unions: Threat or Opportunity? Kalamazoo, MI, W.E. Upjohn Institute for Employment Research.

Lane, C. (1988) "The Pursuit of Flexible Specialisation in Britain and West Germany", Work, Employment and Society, 2, 2, pp. 141168.

Lash, S. and Bagguley, P. (1988) "Labour Relations in Disorganized Capitalism: a five-nation comparison," Society and Space, 6, 3, pp. 321-338.

Leborgne, D. and A. Lipietz (1988) "New Technologies, New Modes of Regulation: Some Spatial Implications," Society and Space, 6, 3, pp. 263-280.

Lillard, L. and Tan, H. (1986) 'Private Sector Training,' Santa Monica, Rand Corporation.

Lusterman, S. (1985) "Trends in Corporate Education and Training," report for The Conference Board..

MacLeod, D. (1990) "Warning on Literacy Problems among Young,' The Independent, 24 May, p. 6.

Magaziner, I. and Reich, R. (1982) Minding America's Business, New York, Harcourt Brace Jovanovich.

Magaziner, I. and Patinkin, M. (1989) The Silent War, New York, Random House.

Manpower Services Commission/NEDC (1984) 'Competence and Competition: Training and Education in the Federal Republic of Germany, the United States and Japan,' London, MSC.

Matthews, R. et al (1982) British Economic Growth, 1856-1973, Palo Alto, Stanford University Press.

Maurice, M., Sellier, F. and Silvestre, J.J. (1986) The Social Foundations of Industrial Power, Cambridge: MIT Press.

McCormick, K. (1988) 'Small Firms, New Technology and the Division of Labour in Japan,' New Technology, Work and Employment, 3, 2.

McKinsey and Co. (1987) "Data on the Dropout Crisis," Internal Report, 8 December.

Metcalf, D. (1989) 'Water Notes Dry Up,' British Journal of Industrial Relations, Spring.

Mishel, Lawrence and Teixeira, Ruy (1990) 'The Myth of the Coming Labor Shortage: Jobs, Skills and Incomes of America's Workforce 2000,' Economic Policy Institute, Washington, DC.

Moorhouse, H.F. (1989) "No Mean City? The Financial Sector and the Decline of Manufacturing in Britain–Review Article,' Work, Employment and Society, 3. 1, pp. 105-118.

Morris, B. (1990) 'America Finds Itself with an Identity Crisis,' The Independent on Sunday, 25 March, Business section, p. 14.

National Centre for Educational Statistics (NCES) (1990) Condition of Education 1990, Vol. 1, Washington D.C.

National Commission on Excellence in Education (NCEE) (1983) A Nation at Risk, Washington D.C., US Government Printing Office.

NIES (1990) Productivity, Education and Training, London, NIESR.

Northcott, J. and Walling, A. (1988) Micro-Electronics: Promise and Performance, London, Policy Studies Institute.

Noyelle, T. "Skills, Skill Formation, Productivity and Competitiveness: A Cross-National Comparison of Banks and Insurance Carriers in Five Advanced Economies," New York, Columbia University Institute on Education and the Economy working paper, February.

Ohmae, K. (1989) 'The Global Logic of Strategic Alliances,' Harvard Business Review, March, April, pp. 143-154.

Ohmae, K. (1987) "Companies without Countries," The McKinsey Quarterly, Autumn, pp. 49-63.

OECD (1989) Education and the Economy in a Changing Society, Paris, OECD.

OECD (1988) New Technologies in the 1990s, Paris, OECD.

OECD (1985) Education and Training After Basic Schooling, Paris, OECD.

Osterman, Paul (1988) Employment Futures: reorganization, dislocation and public policy, Oxford University Press.

Packer, (1990) "Preparing for Work in the Next Century: A Workforce 2000 Report," The Hudson Institute.

Perlman, R. (1988) 'Education and Training: An American Perspective,' Oxford Review of Economic Policy, 4, 3, pp. 94-107.

Piore, M. (1986) "Perspectives on Labour Market Flexibility", Industrial Relations, 25, 2, April.

Piore, M. and Sabel, C. (1984) The Second Industrial Divide, New York, Basic Books.

Pollert, A. (1988) 'Dismantling Flexibility,' Capital and Class, 34, Spring, pp. 42-75.

Porter, M. (1990) The Competitive Advantage of Nations, Macmillan, London.

Postlethwaite, N. (1988) "English Last in Science,' Guardian, 1 March.

Prais, S. and Wagner, K. (1983) Schooling Standards in Britain and Germany, NIESR Discussion Paper No. 60, London.

Rachman, G. (1989) "Schools Set Bush his Toughest Test,' Sunday Correspondent, 1 October, p. 13.

Raffe, D. (1987) "The Context of the Youth Training Scheme: an analysis of its strategy and development", British Journal of Education and Work, 1, p. 1-31.

Raffe, D. (1984) Fourteen to Eighteen, Aberdeen University Press.

Rainbird, H. (1990) "Labour Force Fragmentation and Skills Supply in the British Construction Industry," in Rainbird, H. and Syben, G. (eds) Restructuring a Traditional Industry, Oxford, Berg.

Rajan, A. and Pearson, R. (eds.) (1986) UK Occupational and Employment Trends, London, IMS, Butterworths.

Reich, R. (1988) Education and the Next Economy, Washington D.C., National Education-Association.

Reich, R. (1983) The Next American Frontier, Middlesex, Penguin.

Roderick, G. and Stephens, M. (eds.) (1984) The British Malaise, Basingstoke, Falmer.

Rose, R. (1989) What's New in Youth Unemployment? University of Strathclyde, Studies in Public Policy, No. 177.

Rose, R. and Wignanek, G. (1990) Training Without Trainers? London, Anglo-German Foundation.

Rumberger, R. and Levin, H. (1989) 'Schooling for the Modern Workplace,' Investing in People, Vol. 1, US Department of Labor.

Sabel, C. (1989) "Flexible Specialisation and the Re-emergence of Regional Economies," in Hirst and Zeitlin, pp. 17-69.

Sako, M. (1988) "Partnership Between Small and Large Firms: The Case of Japan," in European Community, Directorate for Enterprise, London, Graham & Trotman.

Sayer, A. (1986) 'New Developments in Manufacturing: the Just-in-Time System,' Capital and Class, 30, pp. 43-72.

Scarborough, H. (1986) 'The Politics of Technological Change at BL,' in Jacobi, 0. et al (eds.) Technological Change, Rationalisation and Industrial Relations, London, Croom Helm.

Schoppa, L. (1990) Education Reform in Japan, London, Routledge.

Senker, P. (1988) "International Competition, Technical Change and Training,' University of Sussex, SPRU Papers in Science, Technology and Public Policy No. 17.

Shirai, T. (ed.) (1983) Contemporary Industrial Relations in Japan, Madison, University of Wisconsin Press.

Society and Space (1988) Environment and Planning, Vol 6 (3) Sept.

Sorge, A. et al (1983) Microelectronics and Manpower in Manufacturing, Aldershot, Gower.

Soskice, D. (1990) 'Reinterpreting Corporatism and Explaining Unemployment: Coordinated and Non-Coordinated Market Economies,' in Brunetta, R. and dell'Aringa, C. (eds) Markets, Institutions and Cooperation: Labour Relations and Economic Performance, London, Macmillan.

Steedman, H. And Wagner, K. (1989) 'Productivity, Machinery and Skills: Clothing Manufacture in Britain and Germany," National Institute Economic Review, May, pp. 40-57.

Stern, D. (1982), Managing Human Resources: The Art of Full Employment, Boston, MA.

Streeck, W. and P. Schmitter (1985) Private Interest Government: Beyond Market and State, Beverly Hills, Sage.

Streeck, W. (1989) 'Skills and the Limits of Neo-Liberalism: The Enterprise of the Future as a Place of Learning,' Work Employment and Society, 3, 1, pp. 89-104.

Training Agency (1989) Labour Market Quarterly Report. May, p. 1.

Training Agency and Department of Employment (1989) Training in Britain, Sheffield, Training Agency.

US Survey of Current Business (various), Economic Statistics, Washington, DC.

US Department of Labor (1989) Investing in People, Report by the Commission on Workforce Quality and Labor Market Efficiency, Washington, DC, September.

Walberg, H. (1989) "Science, Mathematics and National Welfare: Retrospective and Prospective Achievements," in International Comparisons in Educational Reform, Alan Purvis (ed), Alexandria, Va., pp.99-111.

Walton, R. (1985) 'From Control to Commitment in the Workplace,' Harvard Business Review, 64, 2, pp. 76-84.

Walton, R. et al. (1988) Innovating to Compete: Lessons for Diffusing and Managing Change in the Workplace, San Francisco, Jossey-Bass.

White, M. (1989) 'Motivating Education and Training,' Policy Studies 10, 1, pp. 29-40.

Wilensky, H. and Turner, L. (1987) Democratic Corporatism and Policy Linkages, Berkeley, Institute of International Studies.

Williams, K., Cutler, T, Williams, J. and Haslam, C. (1987) "The End of Mass Production?", Economy and Society, 16, 3.

Wood, S. (1989) The Transformation of Work? Skill, flexibility and the labour process, London, Unwin Hyman.

Zeitlin, J. and Totterdill, P. (1989) "Markets, Technology and Local Intervention: The Case of Clothing," in Hirst and Zeitlin.

Zysman, J. (1983) Governments, Markets and Growth, Ithaca, NY, Cornell University Press.

Postschool Training of British and American Youth

HONG W. TAN & CHRISTINE PETERSON[1]

Technological change, rising international competition, and changing demographics have stimulated policy interest in education and training issues in many countries, including the United States and Britain. Policymakers in both countries have raised concerns about inadequate levels of skills investments – in schools and in the workplace – and have proposed wide-ranging strategies to reform the educational system, including the encouragement of greater employer provision of training (in the US, see Commission on Workforce Quality and Labor Market Efficiency, 1989; Department of Labor, 1989; Office of Technology Assessment, 1990). Much of this policy debate, especially about job-training within firms, has been limited by a paucity of reliable information, not only about how much training goes on in the country, but also about how this training compares to that of other countries.[2]

This paper examines the relationship between economic change and the private sector's provision of training to young male workers in the US and UK. We use the National Longitudinal Survey of Young Men (NLS) for the US, and the male sample of the National Child Development Study (NCDS4) for Britain to compare the post-school training experiences of young men in the two countries.[3] Though the surveys refer to the late 1960s and 1970s, they possess several attractive features. Both surveys elicited broadly similar kinds of information – on educational attainment, participation in formal training programs, wages, job attributes, and unemployment – as well as panel data on the variables of interest. We use these data to document and compare the incidence of youth-training in each country, not only at labor market entry, but over the early work career. We consider training from several sources – from employers and from off-the-job sources such as business and technical institutes, industry training-centers, and schools. Each training source is different, and important insights are lost when training from all sources is aggregated. We explore several hypotheses about the most important determinants of training from each source, and

73

study their impact on labor-market outcomes such as wages and the likelihood of experiencing unemployment.

In these analyses, we will be interested in addressing several broad questions. First, are education and work-related training complementary or substitute forms of skill investments? This issue is of policy interest because of the insights it gives into the question of whether youth 'make up' for low schooling attainment with more job training or, instead, are penalized in terms of access to future job-training opportunities. Second, what role does technology play in shaping educational and skill needs in the workplace? The kinds of training strategy employers adopt in response to technological change will have important implications for productivity growth, for innovation, and for competitiveness. Third, do unions inhibit job training? High union wages and restrictive work-rules are thought to reduce incentives for employers to provide training, especially in Britain where union coverage-rates are high. Finally, there are lessons for this volume's discussion of policy borrowing: how do patterns of training in the US and Britain compare? What policy lessons can be gained from analyzing the similarities and differences in the youth-training experiences of the two countries? What roles should the government and the private sector play in the provision of training?

Section 2 describes the NLS and NCDS4 surveys and presents summary information on the incidence of youth training in the two countries. Section 3 discusses the research hypotheses and main findings about the correlates of post-school training in the two countries. Section 4 focuses on the effects of training on weekly wages and the likelihood of unemployment. Section 5 summarizes the results of the cross-national comparisons and their implications for education and training policy in the United States and Britain.

Data and Overview

The US data come from NLS, a longitudinal survey of about 5,000 young men, age 14-24 years in 1966, who were followed over 14 years (until 1980) at one or two-year intervals. The NCDS4 is a retrospective survey conducted in 1981 of one cohort of British youth – born in 1958 – who were thus 24 years old at the time of the fourth wave. To make the two datasets comparable, the NCDS4 monthly calendar and date information were used to restructure the NCDS4 as a longitudinal dataset with one record for each 12 month period. For NCDS4 respondents joining the labor market at the minimum school-leaving age of 16, we observe a panel of up to 8 years; for those completing a first degree, we observe a shorter panel of only 3 years. We restrict our analysis to the NCDS4 sample of about 6,250 males.

The Training Data

Respondents in both surveys reported their participation in two broad kinds of formal training programs – company training, and training from various outside sources. Company training is unambiguously defined in both surveys as taking place in the firm. The 'outside' category varies in how finely the training source is identified. In the NLS, outside sources include (1) business-technical institutes, (2) school-based course-work, and (3) 'other' sources such as government training-programs and correspondence-courses. In the NCDS4, this outside category is of two types: (1) job-related training taken off-the-job in Industry Training Centers and Government Skill Centers, and (2) school-based course work for a higher qualification. One major drawback of these data is that they refer only to formal training; we thus miss potentially sizable investments in informal on-the-job training.

Respondents in both surveys were asked about multiple episodes of training they had received over time. The NLS elicited information on whether formal training was received since the last interview, and if the response was affirmative, on the source of the 'longest' event in that interval. Thus, only one training event within an interval is reported, but there is information on multiple intervals for each person in the NLS panel.[4] In the NCDS4, respondents were asked how many formal training courses they had attended since secondary school that lasted longer than 14 days or a total of 100 hours. However, details (training source and dates) were only elicited for the first three training courses. Apprentices were also asked about the source of formal training received as part of their apprenticeship program. Finally, respondents provided information on up to four school courses they had taken for higher qualification since secondary school, not including events specifically covered by training and apprenticeship questions. Thus, including apprenticeship training, NCDS4 respondents could report up to four job-related training events and four schooling courses. Few – less than 3 percent – ever exceeded these limits.[5]

For comparability, we structure the training data for both surveys using a common definition of schooling completion – the date an individual completes full-time formal schooling and joins the workforce. An individual completes full-time schooling in a given year if subsequently (at least until the end of the panel), no full-time schooling is reported resulting in an increase in educational attainment. For those reporting a rise in schooling attainment (or qualification), perhaps after an intervening period of work, the date of schooling completion is moved forward to that year. With the date of this school-to-work transition in hand, we then classify training-events as being investments either in formal schooling or in 'post-school' training. Thus, for example, we treat a school-based course taken prior to schooling completion as part of that individual's schooling attainment, but we treat all subsequent courses as post-school training events. This date is also used to define labor-market experience, which begins in the year following schooling completion, as well as the timing of training events.

Overview of Training in the US and Britain

Table 1 shows the cumulative probabilities of getting any training, and training by source, beginning with the period immediately following schooling completion. The first panel refers to the NLS sample, the second and third panels to NCDS4 non-apprentice and ever-apprentice samples, respectively. Reading across rows, we note that the proportion of NLS young men getting some form of training is 12 percent in the first year; with time in the labor-market, the proportion who ever get formal training rises (at a decreasing rate) to about 54 percent by the eighth year. Excluding the 'other' category, company programs, business and technical institutes, and traditional schools appear to be equally important providers of post-school training for youth.

Sample/Sources of Training	Time in the labor market (years)							
	1	2	3	4	5	6	7	8
NLS Young Men								
Any	.12	.19	.31	.38	.42	.52	.52	.54
Company	.02	.05	.08	.10	.12	.15	.15	.17
Bus-Technical	.03	.04	.07	.09	.09	.13	.13	.15
Schools	.02	.04	.07	.10	.11	.16	.16	.17
Other sources	.04	.08	.12	.15	.18	.20	.22	.22
NCDS4 Males: Non-Apprentice								
Any	.27	.35	.40	.43	.46	.47	.47	.47
Company	.07	.10	.12	.12	.14	.15	.15	.15
Off-the-job	.13	.17	.19	.21	.22	.24	.24	.24
Schools	.08	.11	.13	.15	.17	.18	.18	.18
NCDS4 Males: Ever-Apprentice								
Any	.63	.68	.72	.74	.75	.76	.77	.77
Company	.02	.03	.04	.05	.07	.08	.09	.09
Off-the-job	.60	.65	.67	.69	.70	.71	.71	.71
Schools	.02	.03	.04	.05	.06	.08	.09	.10

Table 1. Incidence of training by source: US and UK males.

How do American youth fare in comparison with British youth? Three main differences stand out. First, compared to the NLS, a higher proportion of British youth appear to get some training on entering the labor market. For example, 63 percent of apprentices report training, primarily from off-the-job sources. This should not be surprising since formal study is a requisite for completing an apprenticeship program. However, even among non-apprentices, the proportion training on labor-market entry is twice as high (27 percent) as that in the NLS. Second, and in marked contrast to the NLS, the cumulative probability of training rises relatively slowly with time in the British labor market so that by the eighth year, the training gap between youth in the two countries is reduced considerably. The proportion with training rises from 63 percent to 77 percent for the apprentice group; for non-apprentices, the US-UK training differential is actually reversed! By the eighth year, only 41 percent of British non-apprentices have received training (up from 27 percent in the first year) as compared to 54 percent in the NLS. In Britain, there is apparently less ongoing job-training of the sort found in the US. Finally, in contrast to the NLS, off-the-job training is by far the most common source for British youth. By the eighth year, 24 percent of non-apprentices and 71 percent of apprentices have received off-the-job training. The figures for company-training and school-based training trail behind, at about 15 percent for non-apprentices and 10 percent for the apprentice group.

These cross-national differences in patterns of youth training are striking. The entry-level differences are perhaps not surprising given institutional differences in the educational systems, apprenticeship programs, and public training-schemes. For example, the majority of British students left full-time schooling at the age of 16, often joining apprenticeship programs to acquire job skills. In contrast, although many American young people acquire vocational skills in public and private voc-ed schools prior to labor-market entry, we treat this not as postschool training but as formal schooling. Youth apprenticeship programs in the US are rare (under 1 percent of the labor-force), and training places that are available tend to be concentrated in construction and certain trades, and among older, typically unionized workers (Glower, 1986). The US also had no large public training and job placement program for unemployed youth comparable to Britain's TOPS (Training Opportunities Program), and TOPS may be responsible for some of the off-the-job training reported in the NCDS4.

The cross-national differences in experience-training profiles are less readily explained. Part of the explanation may stem from the timing of the two surveys – the NCDS4 covers a period of fairly depressed economic conditions in the late 1970s and early 1980s, while many NLS respondents entered the labor market during the expansionary period between the late 1960s and early 1970s. Commentators have identified several systemic causes of 'training failure' in Britain, including poor technical preparation of British managers, the short-term perspective of most companies favoring profits over training investments, restrictive practices of craft-based unions that inhibit job training, and company organizational structures ill-suited to the adoption of new technologies (Finegold and Soskice, 1988). However, quantifying these factors, and their relative importance in the two countries, is beyond the scope of this paper. In the following sections, we investigate the determinants and outcomes of training for insights into the factors that might be responsible for these training profiles.

The Determinants of Youth Training

To investigate the determinants of training in the NLS and NCDS4 we estimate probit models separately for each training source using pooled period data. The models for each country include a common set of explanatory variables – level of educational attainment, work experience and job tenure, technological change in the current job, and union or collective bargaining status – as well as control variables for region of residence, aggregate level of economic activity, and missing values. Using these models of the determinants of training, we first examine how training varies with educational attainment and then consider the relationship between training and technological progress. We also study the effect of work experience and union membership on training.

We capture the training effects of schooling by several variables which identify the highest level of educational attainment that an individual has achieved. For the NLS, we define four schooling levels – high school graduates, some college, college graduates, and postgraduates – and compare them to non-high school graduates with less than 12 years of schooling.[6] For the NCDS4 sample, three indicator variables for schooling attainment are used – 'O' levels, 'A' levels, and first degree qualifications – the omitted group being those who leave school at age 16 with the minimum compulsory level of education. Here, our interest is in determining whether schooling and training are complementary or substitute forms of skill investments.

We also investigate the role of technology in influencing the training decisions of employers and workers by considering two sets of hypotheses. First, the perspectives on technical change, and its relationship to training requirements, come from research by Tan (1980). The argument is that many job skills are technology-specific, and are acquired through working with particular production technologies and specialized equipment. As technology advances, technology-specific skill requirements also grow apace. And to the extent that few of these skills are readily available outside the firm, we would expect the demand for in-house company training to increase with the industry rate of technical change. Conversely, the demand for more general kinds of skills provided by outside training institutions – such as vocational schools or business and technical institutes – might be expected to fall, other things equal. Only when technologies become well-understood and widely adopted by other firms do these specific skills become transferable to other employers, in other words, become general ones.

Second, we might also expect differences across educational groups in their training responses to technical change. It has been argued that workers with more education are also more adept at evaluating new information, and therefore respond more readily to technological change (Welch 1970). Bartel and Lichtenberg (1987) provide some evidence for this hypothesis – in US manufacturing, employers use educated workers more intensively when the industry's capital stock is newer (and embodies more recent technologies), especially if research and development spending is also higher. This 'allocative efficiency of schooling' hypothesis suggests that innovative firms in industries experiencing rapid technical change are more likely to use highly educated workers and to provide them with more training relevant to new technologies. Controlling for the level of schooling attainment, this hypothesis predicts a higher likelihood of company training among more educated workers in high-technology industries.

We will test these hypotheses concerning the role of technology in training decisions jointly. For each country, estimates of industry rates of total factor productivity (TFP) growth are used to characterize the technological progressivity of jobs in which individuals are employed. For the US, we rely on TFP estimates developed by Jorgenson, Gollop and Fraumeni (1989) for the period between 1966 and 1979. These measures, derived from constant returns to scale translog production functions, are available for 45 two and three-digit industrial groupings. For Britain, we use O'Mahony and Oulton's (1990) estimates of TFP growth over the 1954-1982 period.[7] Unfortunately, estimates are only available for 130 manufacturing and mining industries; as such, we include a variable to identify those NCDS4 respondents for whom we have missing TFP information. To test the two sets of technology hypotheses jointly, we interact (multiply) these TFP measures with education attainment variables to see (1) whether jobs in industries with high TFP growth involve more company-based training and less outside training as predicted by the technology-specific skills hypothesis, and (2) whether highly educated individuals are more likely to get training as suggested by the allocative-efficiency of schooling hypotheses.

We distinguish between several kinds of work experience. First, we include a quadratic measure of labor market experience (experience and experience squared) to allow for non-linear training effects with time in the labor market. In general, we might expect the probability of training to rise with labor market experience, though at a slower pace over time.[8] For the NCDS4 sample, we also control for pre-entry work experience using variables to measure whether a schooling interruption ('break') occurred, the length of time worked, and if any qualifications were earned during this break. For the NLS, where information on earlier years is less complete, pre-entry work experience is captured simply by a dummy variable for whether there was a break in schooling. The likelihood of post-school training is probably lower if individuals acquire work-relevant skills during this schooling interruption. Finally, we include several (connected) spline variables for job tenure with the current employer. These spline variables constrain training effects to be uniform within a given tenure interval, but allow these effects to vary flexibly across tenure intervals in the first few years on the current job. Employers are most likely to provide training in the first few years on the job, though patterns of training with longer job tenure might differ by training source.

We include a union variable for whether the individual ever belonged to a union, or was covered by a collective bargaining agreement. This definition of 'ever' union member was necessitated by the large number of missing values in the NLS and by the availability of union information only in the first and current or last jobs in the NCDS4. We hypothesize that unions are associated with a lower probability of job training. It is widely believed that in the US and UK unions inhibit employer incentives to provide training because (1) high levels of union-negotiated wages prevent firms from paying lower training wages to finance (workers' share of) training costs, (2) restrictive work practices and job-demarcation rules reduce the potential benefits to employers of providing training, and (3) unions impede the introduction of new technologies that threaten union jobs, but that may require extensive skill upgrading and retraining of workers.

Finally, we include a set of variables to control for a variety of other training determinants. We control for the level of macroeconomic activity in a given year by including the national rate of unemployment. We might expect training incentives to rise when economic conditions are good, and to fall in bad times. For the NCDS4, we included a variable for public-sector employment which is thought to provide more formal training than private-sector employers. Where available, we also included indicator variables for marital status, geographic location, and firm size (NCDS4 only). To test for firm-size differences in training, we define three firm size variables – 25 to 99 workers (termed 'medium size'), 100 to 499 workers ('large firms'), and 500 or more workers ('very large firms') – with the omitted group being firms with less than 25 employees. We expect training likelihood to be higher, the larger the firm, perhaps because they use more skill-intensive technologies, have more capable managers, or attract a more able, stable workforce. Finally, we control for missing values by using indicator variables to control for the effects of partially missing information.

Empirical Results

Table 2 reports the probit results for the NLS, and Tables 3 and 4 the results for NCDS4 non-apprentice and apprentice samples, respectively. Unlike linear models, the coefficients from non-linear models (such as the probit) are not readily interpreted since the estimated effects vary depending on where an individual is located in the underlying training distribution. To facilitate discussion and comparison of results we report the estimated coefficients (partial derivatives) evaluated at the sample mean for each training source.

PARTIAL DERIVATIVES OF PROBIT MODEL

Variables	Any Training	Company Training	Bus-Tech School	School Course	Other Courses
Educational Attainment					
HS graduates	.077 a	.028 a	.032 a	.002	.018 b
Some college	.112 a	.036 a	.033 a	.028 a	.020 a
College graduates	.092 a	.057 a	-.002	.026 a	.009
Post-graduates	.093 a	.032 a	.006	.041 a	.011
Technological change TFP					
TFP * Non-HS grads	.009	-.002	-.003	-.001	.009
TFP * HS grads	-.004	.004	-.002	.000	-.005 b
TFP * Some college	-.013 a	.001	-.002	-.004 b	-.006 b
TFP * College grads	-.003	.006 b	-.008	-.000	-.008 b
TFP * Post-grads	-.016 a	.010 a	-.002	-.008 a	-.013 a
Labor Market Experience					
Work experience	.016 a	.006 a	.000	.003 b	.006 a
Experience squared	-.001 a	-.000 a	-.000	-.000 a	-.000 a
0-1 years tenure	.240 a	.055	.049	.048	.109 a
1-2 years tenure	.008	.008	-.004	-.010	.012 b
2-3 years tenure	.001	.007 b	-.007 b	-.007 b	.005
Over 3 years tenure	-.002	.002	-.003 b	-.004 a	.002
Other Control Variables					
Schooling interruption	.024 b	.009	-.006	-.015 b	.026 a
Started new job	-.100 a	-.015	-.025	-.043 b	-.033 b
Ever union member	.017 a	.006 b	.001	.009 a	-.000
Non-white	-.010	.003	.003	-.003	-.014 a
National unemployment	.006 a	.001	.002 b	.001	.002
2-year interval dummy	.072 a	.010 a	.035 a	.019 a	.009 b

Note· 1. Probit models also included missing value dummy variables.
2. a and b denote statistical significance of associated probit coefficients at the 1 and 5 percent levels, respectively.

Table 2. Determinants of training: NLS young men.

We turn first to the relationship between training and education. In both surveys, the probability of getting most kinds of post-school training rises with schooling attainment. Compared to non-high school graduates, increased educational attainment in the NLS is associated with a higher probability of training, but these peak at different schooling levels for each training source — college graduates in the case of company training, those with some college for training from business-technical schools and miscellaneous sources, and postgraduates for school courses. Similarly, compared to 16-year old school-leavers, NCDS4 males with 'A' level qualifications are between 27 and 29 percent more likely to get training; the corresponding figures for first degree holders range between 41 and 59 percent. Thus, in both countries, education and post-school training appear to be complementary forms of human capital investments.[9] One implication of this 'complementarity' is that individuals with little education face limited training opportunities in the workplace and, if formal training augments productivity, slower wage growth prospects as well.

A pattern of technological change effects on training emerges from Table 2 for the NLS. First, company training is significantly more prevalent in high-TFP industries ('high-tech jobs'), especially for NLS college graduates and postgraduates. For these groups, a 1 percent increase in TFP growth is associated with a 0.6 and 1 percent increase in the probability of company training, respectively. Secondly, and in contrast to training from company sources, high-tech jobs are associated with lower likelihood of training from all sources outside the firm, effects that are increasingly larger and more statistically significant for the highly educated. Compared to the non-high school group, postgraduates have a 0.8 and 1.3 percent lower likelihood of school-based and other training, respectively, as technology rises. Together, these results suggests that in a growing and technologically progressive environment, employers rely more on company training for skill needs, and place less reliance on traditional schools and other outside sources for job-related training.

The effects of technical change in the NCDS4, shown in Tables 3 and 4, are remarkably similar to those reported for the NLS.[10] Probabilities of any training rise with schooling attainment – at least until 'A' level qualifications – as TFP increases. More rapid technical change is also associated with higher probabilities of company training for those with more schooling. From the negative TFP parameter, it is clear that rapid technological change penalizes those with low schooling attainment – they are less likely to get company training than their counterparts in jobs with stable or unchanging technologies. This result is particularly strong for NCDS4 apprentices. Furthermore, high TFP growth reduces the likelihood of training from off-the-job sources for apprentices, and from school sources for non-apprentices. These results, coupled with the NLS findings, provide support for the technology-specific skills model of Tan (1980) and the 'allocative efficiency' hypothesis of Welch (1970).

The training effects of labor market experience are broadly consistent with the training-experience profiles described earlier for the two youth samples. For the NLS, Table 2 indicates that training probability from all sources rises with time in the labor market (though at a diminished rate), while Tables 3 and 4 suggest that most training sources in the NCDS4 decline with work experience. In the NLS, tenure effects vary by training source: training from schools and from business-technical institutes falls off with time in the current job, while company training (and training from other sources) continues to rise slightly with tenure. These NLS tenure effects suggest a pattern of increasing substitution of in-house company training for broad-based general skills supplied by academic and voc-ed institutions as individuals advance into their work careers. In contrast, the NCDS4 results suggest that British employers tend to rely on outside training sources. For both NCDS4 samples, the probability of company training falls continuously with job tenure; training from off-the-job sources and from schools rises, and then begins to decline after the second year on the job. This suggests that other than some entry-level company training, British employers tend to rely on off-the-job training and schools to augment the skills of their workers.

We expected to find a lower probability of training among union members or employees covered by collective bargaining agreements, but did not find any empirical support for this hypothesis. On the contrary, Table 2 shows that union members in the NLS are more likely to get training from company, business-technical institutes, and school sources. Tables 3 and 4 also point to similar union-training effects in Britain. For both NCDS4 samples, unions are associated with a greater likelihood of school-based training. However, union effects are mixed for the other training sources – non-apprentices are more likely to get company training but less off-the-job training, while apprentices are more likely to get training from off-the-job sources but less company training. These results suggest a more complex training role for trade unions than is usually believed. Unions may give rise to more formal training because of union-negotiated agreements, or through their sponsorship of apprenticeship programs. Unions may inhibit less formal kinds of informal on-the-job training, perhaps through job demarcation and work rules – but this issue cannot be addressed here because informal training measures are not available or are of poor quality.

The remaining determinants of training may be summarized briefly as follows. First, in both countries, the probability of training from most sources is usually diminished for those with work experience gained prior to schooling completion, for those with more than 3 previous jobs (NCDS4), or for recent job changers (NLS), possibly because many are bringing skills to the new job from previous employers. Second, when we control for other factors, non-whites are not different from whites in their access to training, with the possible exception of miscellaneous other training which non-whites are less likely to get. Third, NCDS4 respondents in large firms are more likely to get formal training from all sources. While information on employer size is not available in the NLS survey, others have found similar firm-size training effects in the US (Barron, Black and Lowenstein, 1987). Finally, employment in the private sector in Britain is usually associated with a lower likelihood of training, with some exceptions by training source and sample.

Sample/ Explanatory Variables	PARTIAL DERIVATIVES OF PROBIT MODEL			
	Any Training	Company Training	Off-the-job Training	School Training
Educational Attainment				
O levels	.173 a	.026 a	.084 a	.073 a
A levels	.296 a	.041 a	.116 a	.125 a
1st degree	.413 a	.081 a	.161 a	.151 a
Technological Change				
TFP 1954-82	.016	-.011	.009	.030 b
TFP * O levels	.021	.033 b	.006	-.028
TFP * A levels	.171 a	.051 b	.102 a	-.006
TFP * 1st degree	-.009	.095 a	-.032	-.066 a
Labor Market Experience				
Work experience	-.030 a	.011 a	-.027 a	-.014 a
Experience squared	.001	-.001 a	.002 b	.001 b
0-5 months tenure	-.305 a	-.004	-.209 a	-.135 a
6-12 months tenure	.054	-.049 a	.068 a	.071 a
1-2 years tenure	.013	-.026 a	.029 a	.005
2-3 years tenure	.017	-.007	.015 b	.014 b
Over 3 years tenure	-.011 a	-.002	-.013 a	.002
Other Control Variables				
Medium size firm	.052 a	.008	.031 a	.013 a
Large firm	.063 a	.029 a	.030 a	.003
Very large firm	.051 a	.026 a	.011	.013 a
Unionized firm	-.010	.004	-.017 a	.008 b
Private sector	-.092 a	-.053 a	-.044 a	.013 a
Over 3 previous jobs	-.027 b	.001	-.032 a	-.006
Worked before entry	-.064 a	-.011 a	-.029 a	-.016 a
Unemployment rate	-.013 a	-.006 a	-.009 a	.001

Note: 1. Omitted group is sample with minimum compulsory
          education.
      2. a and b denote statistical significance of associated
          probit coefficients at the 1 and 5 percent levels,
          respectively.
      3. Models also included marital status, location, industry
          characteristics, and missing value indicator variables.

Table 3. Determinants of training: NCD4 non-apprentice males.

Labor Market Consequences of Training

Having identified the most important training determinants, we now turn to
the effects of training. We consider two labor market outcomes – the
logarithm of weekly wages, and the likelihood of experiencing a spell of
unemployment. We are interested in whether post-school training enhances
worker productivity (as measured by wage growth), and in identifying the
sources of training that contribute the most to worker productivity. We study

these questions using estimated wage equations which include training effects. We subsequently ask whether trained workers are indeed more valuable to employers, and if so, whether they are less likely to become unemployed. Answers to these questions may yield insights into training incentives in the two countries.

PARTIAL DERIVATIVES OF PROBIT MODEL

Sample/ Explanatory Variables	Any Training	Company Training	Off-the-job Training	School Training
Educational Attainment				
O levels	.200 a	.001	.217 a	.010 a
A levels	.275 a	.013	.249 a	.025 a
1st degree	.590 a	.039 b	.550 a	.003
Technological Change				
TFP 1954-82	-.018	-.017 a	-.044 b	.019 a
TFP * O levels	.013	.059 a	-.027	-.006
TFP * A levels	.088	.096 a	-.054	.014
TFP * 1st degree	.169	.025	-.201	.034
Labor Market Experience				
Work experience	-.073 a	.020 a	-.075 a	.007 b
Experience squared	-.013 a	-.002 a	-.014 a	-.000
0-5 months tenure	-.716 a	.015	-.852 a	-.029
6-12 months tenure	.323 a	-.006	.345 a	.001
1-2 years tenure	.164 a	-.019 a	.183 a	-.009
2-3 years tenure	.268 a	-.003	.316 a	-.004
Over 3 years tenure	-.075 a	-.002	-.075 a	.004 a
Other Control Variables				
Medium size firm	.058 a	.024 a	.060 a	.009 b
Large firm	.087 a	.015 a	.107 a	.015 a
Very large firm	.116 a	.029 a	.118 a	.015 a
Unionized firm	-.003	-.024 a	.074 a	.010 a
Private sector	-.070 a	-.042 a	.038 a	-.003
Over 3 previous jobs	-.071 a	.005	-.125 a	-.013 a
Worked before entry	-.085 a	.002	-.107 a	.009 a
Unemployment rate	.032 a	-.002	.010	.001

Note: 1. Omitted group is sample with minimum compulsory education.
2. a and b denote statistical significance of associated probit coefficients at the 1 and 5 percent levels, respectively.
3. Models also included marital status, location, industry characteristics, and missing value indicator variables.

Table 4. Determinants of training: NDC apprenticed males.

The panel nature of the NLS and NCDS4 datasets allows us to investigate the dynamic pattern of training effects. We will allow job training to affect wages (and unemployment) in several ways. First, whether or not training was received in the current 12-month period: training in the current period may reduce wages through lowered productivity while in training, or may simply reflect the fact that workers 'pay' for training through acceptance of a lower wage. Second, total number of training events taken to date since labor market entry: the occurrence of current and past training events may raise productivity and shift up the wage function (or lower the likelihood of unemployment). We assume that each training occurrence enhances wages (or reduces unemployment) by the same proportion, though each training source may have a different effect. Finally, time elapsed since training, accumulated over all training events: if skill depreciation (or obsolescence) is important, the size of the wage effect of a training event will depend upon how long ago it occurred. We will allow the rate of obsolescence to differ by training source. Together, these training measures form the basis of our analysis of the wage and unemployment outcomes of training.[11]

Wage Effects of Training

The wage analysis is based upon pooled cross-section data. For the NLS, we pool observations from several years – 1967 through 1969, 1973, 1975, and 1980 – where relatively clean data were available on annual wages and number of weeks worked over the past 12-months. This yielded a sample of 9,100 observations. For the NCDS4, we examine weekly wages at one point in time – the current or last job in 1981 – because the NCDS4 only elicited wage information for the first and last jobs. The training measures, however, are constructed from information contained in the entire NCDS4 panel. The final sample comprises 4,537 males who had completed schooling and were observed in wage and salaried employment in 1981. We estimate regression models relating the logarithm of weekly wages (1981 wages in the NCDS4) to the three training measures described above, controlling for a variety of personal and job attributes, location, and labor market conditions.[12]

Results are reported in the first two columns of Table 5 for the NLS and in Table 6 for the NCDS4. Compared to the omitted schooling group, the returns to schooling generally rise with the level of educational attainment. For the NLS, earnings exhibit the familiar quadratic shape, rising with both work experience and job tenure, though at a slower pace at higher experience levels. The NCDS4 results suggest that each year of work experience increases wages by about the same amount as the American sample (5.6 percent as compared to 5.9 percent in the NLS), but that job tenure has no statistically significant effect on weekly wages. Other British training studies have also failed to find any tenure-wage effects (see Baker, 1990; Booth, 1989). Together, these results imply that experience-wage profiles in the US are steeper than in Britain, a difference that stems solely from the larger wage-tenure effects (about 4 percent) in the US. Since these models control for formal training, the residual wage-tenure effects probably reflect (at least in part) investments in informal on-the-job training.[13] If so, the results suggest that there is considerably more informal on-the-job training in the US than in Britain.

Explanatory Variables	Log(Weekly Wages) (1)	(2)	Unemployment Probability
Intercept	4.868 a	4.895 a	-.051 b
Educational Attainment			
High School Graduates	.085 a	.066 b	-.090 a
Some college	.166 a	.142 a	-.127 a
College graduates	.348 a	.320 a	-.215 a
Post-graduate degree	.550 a	.534 a	-.293 a
Technological Change (TFP)			
TFP * Non-HS graduates	.005	.004	-.000
TFP * HS graduates	.006	.006	-.027 a
TFP * Some college	.011	.015	-.003
TFP * College graduates	.056 a	.054 a	-.016
TFP * Post-graduates	.072 a	.073 a	.040 a
Labor Market Experience			
Years of experience	.059 a	.049 a	-.020 a
Experience squared	-.002 a	-.002 a	-.000
Years of job tenure	.039 a	.038 a	-.095 a
Tenure squared	-.002 a	-.002 a	.006 a
Non-whites	-.114 a	-.109 a	.096 a
Ever-union member	.131 a	.129 a	.024 a
Local unemployment rate	.003	.003	.032 a
Training in Current Period			
Company training	.048	.030	
Business-Technical Schools	-.105	.056	
Regular schools	.019	.014	
Other sources	.066	.030	
Number of Training Events			
Company training	.186 a	-.105 b	
Business-Technical Schools	.123 b	-.064	
Regular schools	.067	.005	
Other sources	.099 b	-.003	
Time since Training			
Company training	-.011	.011	
Business-Technical Schools	-.011	.000	
Regular schools	-.007	-.016	
Other sources	-.006	-.003	

Note: 1. a and b denote statistical significance at the 1 and 5 percent levels, respectively.
2. R-squares of wage models are 0.2262 and 0.2374.

Table 5. Labor market effects of training: NLS young men.

The results indicate that the returns to schooling are higher if the individual worked in a high-technology industry. For the NLS sample in Table 5, the estimated interactions between education and TFP are invariably positive, and statistically significant for the two most educated groups. Compared to non-high school graduates, the returns to a college degree rise from 35 to 41 percent (0.35 plus 0.06) when the effects of technical change are included; the corresponding figures are 55 to 62 percent (0.55 plus 0.07) for a postgraduate degree. Broadly similar results are found in NCDS4. In Table 6, the main effect of the TFP variable suggests that NCDS4 males with little formal schooling receive wages that are about 9 percent lower in jobs experiencing rapid technological change. However, the same TFP increase raises the returns to schooling of first degree holders – they earn 10 percent more (-0.09 plus 0.19) than their counterparts employed elsewhere. These findings, which persist even after including training measures, suggest that better educated workers are more adept at responding to technological change, are more productive, and consequently are more highly rewarded.

Before turning to training, the wage effects of several other control variables may be noted. In the NLS, non-whites earn about 10 percent less than other racial groups. In both countries, union members (or jobs with collective bargaining) receive sizable wage premiums – about 12-13 percent in the NLS and 10-14 percent in the NCDS4 – but it is unclear if these reflect economic 'rents' or the effects of unobserved worker attributes. Finally, we find evidence that large firms pay higher wages. Compared to those in small firms with 25 or fewer workers, NCDS4 respondents are paid wages that are 9 percent higher in firms with 100-500 employees, and 15 percent higher in firms with over 500 workers.

In both countries, company-based training appears to have the largest impact on youth wages. In the NLS, company training increases wages by over 18 percent annually, which is considerably larger than the effect of business-technical school training (12 percent), and miscellaneous other sources (10 percent). School-based courses taken after schooling completion have no apparent impact on wages, though we note that educational attainment itself yields large returns. The wage effects of training appear to diminish over time, but they are not measured very precisely. The results for the NCDS4 are similar in terms of the relative productivity of training from each source. In the NCDS4, company training has the largest impact on weekly wages (7 percent), followed by off-the-job training (4 percent). As with the NLS, school-based courses taken after labor market entry have no measurable wage impact. Note that no duration measures were included in the NCDS4 wage models. In other analyses not reported here, we determined that sensible training effects could not be estimated because of the high correlation between training sum and duration variables, which made it necessary to drop the training duration measures.

Explanatory Variables	Logarithm of 1981 Weekly Wages (1)	(2)	Unemployment probability App	Non-App.
Intercept	4.016 a	4.048 a	-.048 b	-.008
Educational Attainment				
O levels	.090 a	.075 a	-.024 a	-.039 a
A levels	.199 a	.183 a	-.053 b	-.038 a
First degree	.342 a	.316 a	-.099	-.068 a
Technological Change TFP				
TFP 1954-1982	-.090 a	-.088 a	-.010	.016
TFP * O levels	.060	.048	.018	-.008
TFP * A levels	.015	-.006	.032	-.003
TFP * first degree	.206 a	.193 a	----	-.053
Labor Market Experience				
Work experience	.056 a	.040 b	.018 a	-.000
Experience squared	.001	.002	.002 b	.003 a
Years of tenure	.005	.010	-.142 a	-.253 a
Tenure squared	-.002	-.002	.014 a	.025 a
Number of previous jobs	.001	.002	-.053 a	-.113 a
Pre-entry certificate	.081 a	.068 a	-.010	-.034 a
Job Characteristics				
Private sector	.008	.024 b	.020 b	.013
Medium size firm	.046 a	.041 a	-.005	-.006
Large firm	.094 a	.092 a	-.004	-.024 b
Very large firm	.152 a	.145 a	-.002	-.036 a
Unionized firm	.103 a	.103 a	.018 a	.058 a
Unemployment rate	--	--	-.012 a	-.004
Currently in Training				
Company	-.058	-.017	-.069 a	
Off-the-job	-.103 a	-.019 b	-.047 a	
At schools	-.034	-.034	-.242 a	
Number of Training Events				
Company	.071 a	-.034 a	.009	
Off-the-job	.041 a	-.031 a	-.026 a	
At schools	.001	-.004	-.008	

Note:
1. Models also included indicator variables for marital status, missing values, and location.
2. a and b denote statistical significance at the levels, respectively.
3. R-squares for wage models are .1509 and .1644.

Table 6. Labor market effects of training: NCDS4 males.

More importantly, the results suggest that the wage effects of formal training in the NLS are roughly twice those in the NCDS4.[14] If these are the price signals facing employers and workers making training decisions, it is clear why neither group in Britain has any incentives to train – the returns to training are probably low compared to other forms of capital investment, including schooling. In the NLS, more ongoing training (both formal and informal) occurs because the returns to training are relatively attractive.[15] There may also be little demand for training in Britain, as evidenced by the existence both of low returns and low levels of training investments in the NCDS4 as compared to the NLS. Demand constraints may arise because of poorly trained British managers, restrictive union work rules, and inflexible corporate structures, but we are unable to evaluate these assertions using our NLS and NCDS4 data.

Training and Unemployment Probability

The remaining columns of Tables 5 and 6 report the results of a probit model to explain whether an individual is either currently unemployed or has been unemployed one month or longer over the past year. This indicator variable is related to the same set of explanatory variables used in the wage analyses. Here, we broaden the NLS sample to include both employed and unemployed young men. The NCDS4 analyses use pooled-period data augmented to include the unemployed, yielding 17,253 and 24,083 observations for the ever-apprenticed and non-apprentice samples, respectively.

Before discussing training, we summarize briefly the effects of other control variables on the probability of unemployment. In both NLS and NCDS4 samples, the likelihood of experiencing a spell of unemployment in a given year is lower for those with higher schooling attainment, and for those with more work experience and longer job tenure. Similarly, unions in both countries are associated with a higher likelihood of unemployment. In addition, the NCDS4 results in Table 6 suggest that employment in large firms is usually associated with greater employment stability, and private sector employment with less stability. For the most part, higher industry rates of technical change in both countries are associated with a lower likelihood of unemployment, though this relationship is only significantly negative for selected schooling groups. For these samples of young men in the US and Britain, we may thus discount concerns that have been raised about technology-induced unemployment.

We turn now to the effect of training on unemployment probabilities. Tables 5 and 6 suggest that training generally reduces the likelihood of youth unemployment in both the NLS and NCDS4. With the exception of company training, these effects are measured rather imprecisely in the NLS. The negative parameter (-.105) suggests that company training significantly lowers the probability of future unemployment, an effect that appears to ameliorate over time, as evidenced by the estimated positive parameter (0.011) of the company training duration variable. The period over which company training has this effect can be calculated by dividing the parameters of the cumulated training and training duration variables (-0.105/.011), namely 10 years. In the NCDS4, the likelihood of unemployment is significantly reduced if the individual got any kind of training over the past year. The total number of training events received to date also inhibits unemployment, but these effects are usually not measured precisely except for apprentices and for non-apprentices in the case of off-the-job training. Unlike the NLS, where company training is most important, there is no clear ranking in the NCDS4 of the different kinds of training in terms of their effects on inhibiting unemployment. For reasons described earlier, no duration effects of training were estimated for the NCDS4.

Conclusion

We have used the NLS and NCDS4 to investigate and compare the incidence, determinants, and labor market effects of youth training in the United States and Britain. In particular we addressed the private sector's provision of training in both countries. Our analyses, though restricted to formal training, nonetheless revealed several similarities and differences in the two countries. Some of these findings, and their policy implications, are discussed below.

In both countries, formal schooling attainment was one of the most important predictors of post-school training and labor market success. Better-educated youth were more likely to get post-school training, especially the more valuable kinds of training provided by employers. Since training has the effect of increasing wages and reducing the likelihood of unemployment, the least educated youth population face relatively bleak economic prospects in the labor market. This conclusion highlights the need for remedial programs targeted at low education groups already in the labor market, and for preventative policies to reduce high school-dropout rates, improve academic achievement, and raise schooling continuation rates for youth still in the educational pipeline.

Technological change reinforces the need for these policies. We found evidence that technical change plays a critical intermediating role in raising educational and skill requirements in jobs. In both countries, rapid technical change increased the likelihood of getting company training, especially for the most educated youth, and generally reduced the likelihood of training from schools and off-the-job sources. The least educated youth received little training from all sources in such high-tech jobs. Current high dropout rates among American youth, and in particular among blacks and other minority groups, raise disturbing questions about how well such groups will fare in the future as the skill requirements in jobs become more demanding. The high rates of school-leaving at age sixteen raise similar policy concerns for Britain.

Contrary to widely-held views, unions in both countries were usually associated with a greater probability of formal training – both from employers and from outside sources. It is often argued that unions, by bidding up wages for their members, reduce employer incentives to provide training through payment of a (low) training wage. Our results suggest a more complex role for unions. The greater likelihood of job training may reflect union-negotiated training and retraining contracts with employers, or union sponsorship of apprenticeship programs. These results pertain only to formal training programs, and unions may have the predicted impact on more informal (but not easily measured) forms of training through restrictive work practices, job demarcation rules, and opposition to the introduction of labor-saving technologies and new forms of work organization.

In both countries, employer-provided training had by far the greatest quantitative impact on increasing youth wages, followed by formal off-the-job training. Course work taken in schools after labor market entry had no measurable wage effects, though schooling attainment itself yields large wage returns. These findings, however, are too preliminary to draw firm policy conclusions about whether public funds are better spent in creating incentives for firm-based training, as compared to existing programs for delivery of training and retraining services, such as under JTPA (Job Training and Partnership Act) that rely on public or private educational and voc-ed institutions. Further research is needed (1) to identify types of training that are more appropriately provided by public or private institutions, or by employers, (2) to evaluate the benefits of training beyond those studied here, and (3) to address measurement issues, including potential biases in our estimates of the returns to training. Biases – arising from unmeasured individual traits, and self-selection into different training programs – may overstate the potential gains from expanding access to company training in the general youth population.

Finally, compared to their counterparts in Britain, American youth appear to get relatively less formal training upon entry into the labor market, but more formal job training with time in the labor market. This training is increasingly company-based, while that in Britain tends to be from schools and off-the-job sources. Some of these differences, especially at the entry level, might be expected given institutional differences in the educational systems, apprenticeship programs, and public training schemes. However, cross-national differences in these experience-training profiles are less readily explained. In particular, why is there so little ongoing training and skill upgrading in Britain? One part of the explanation may lie in relatively high returns to training in the US, which are estimated to be roughly twice as large as those in Britain. With such low returns, incentives for British employers and workers to invest in ongoing job training are also reduced. Depressed economic conditions in the late 1970s may have contributed to low returns and reduced incentives to train in the NCDS4. Other demand-side factors were probably also operative, but they are the subject of future research.

Notes

[1] The World Bank and RAND respectively. Research for this paper was funded by the National Center on Education and Employment at Teachers College, Columbia University, through a grant from the Office of Educational Research, US Department of Education.

[2] Researchers in both countries have only recently begun to exploit self-reported training measures in several national surveys to document the incidence of training. Examples include Lillard and Tan (1986), Lynch (1989), and Mincer (1988) in the US, and Greenhalgh and Stewart (1987), Connaly, Micklewright and Nickell (1989), Booth (1989), and Baker (1990) in Britain. None are explicitly comparative.

[3] This paper is based on a larger comparative study of youth-training in the United States, Britain, and Australia. See Tan, Chapman, Peterson, and Booth (1991).

[4] In the more recent NLS Youth Cohort Surveys, up to three training events may be reported in each interval. Multiple episodes of training in a given interval are not common in this survey, suggesting that under-reporting of job-training in the NLS sample may not be a problem.

[5] We treat these period observations as censored, and drop them from the dataset.

[6] These levels of schooling attainment correspond to less than 12, 12, 13 to 15, 16, and over 16 years of schooling, respectively.

[7] The Jorgenson, Gollop and Fraumeni TFP estimates include quality adjusted indices of capital, labor, and intermediate products. However, while O'Mahony and Oulton control for capital quality, they make no adjustments for labor quality.

[8] The human capital model predicts that most job training will be concentrated early in the work career (Ben-Porath, 1967). Because of a finite worklife, incentives to get (or provide) training late in the career are low since the returns to this investment are received over a shorter period.

[9] We note the caveat that this positive correlation may also reflect the effects of unobserved ability and wealth, both of which are related to greater propensities to get schooling and training.

[10] A different specification of the TFP-schooling interactions is used for the NCDS4. Here, TFP enters by itself (the 'main effect'), and interacts with each educational level except the omitted schooling group. The effect of technology on each level of schooling is simply calculated by adding the main effect to the TFP parameter estimated for each schooling group.

[11] We recognize, but do not address here, potentially important selectivity biases in treating training as being exogenously determined. However, our ongoing research suggests that while selectivity is important, the returns to training reported here are quite close to those estimated by more complex models that account for selectivity and personal heterogeneity.

[12] No training duration measures were included in the models estimated for the NCDS4. In results not reported here, we found training duration and sum of training events to be highly correlated, necessitating the exclusion of one set of variables. This collinearity arises because most training episodes in the NCDS4 are concentrated in the first (or second) year so that the sum of training is often

simply a multiple of the duration variable. In the NLS, this is less an issue since training is more evenly distributed over time.

[13] Some part of this wage-tenure effect may also reflect the quality of the worker-firm match.

[14] The cross-national differences in the wage effects of training are robust with regards to included variables. In results not reported here, training effects for the NCDS4 were estimated excluding firm size (which may be correlated with training and other worker attributes), but these yielded only marginally larger wage effects – the impact of company training rises from 7.1 to 7.5 percent; that of off-the-job training rises from 4.1 to 4.3 percent. Experiments with other variables yielded essentially the same results for the NCDS4.

[15] These wage effects cannot strictly be interpreted as the returns to training without first making several adjustments to incorporate the effects of training duration and intensity, depreciation, and expected job tenure (Mincer, 1989). Data limitations precluded such an exercise in this paper. We note that training courses in the NCDS4 are generally of longer duration than those reported in the NLS, which means that any adjustments for training duration would tend to exacerbate, not reduce, the relative wage returns to training in the two countries. Among NCDS4 males, average duration of training is 4.4 months for company training, 12.6 months for off-the-job training, and 18.5 months for training from schools. The corresponding NLS figures are 4.8 months for company training, 7.9 months for courses from business-technical institutes, 6.4 months for training from regular academic institutions, and 7.1 months for other training courses.

References

Baker, Meredith, 'The Effect of Training on the Earnings of Young Males: An Analysis of the National Child Development Study,' M.A. Thesis, University of Warwick, January 1990.

Barron, John, Dan Black, and Mark Lowenstein, 'Employer Size: The Implications for Search, Training, Capital Investment, Starting Wages, and Wage Growth', Journal of Labor Economics, 5, 1987, pp. 76-89.

Bartel, Anne and Frank Lichtenberg, 'The Comparative Advantage of Educated Workers in Implementing New Technologies', Review of Economics and Statistics, February 1987.

Ben-Porath, Yoram, 'The Production of Human Capital and the Life Cycle of Earnings,' Journal of Political Economy, 1967, pp. 352-62.

Booth, Alison, 'Earning and Learning: What Price Specific Training?', Brunel University, London, Discussion Paper No 8911, November 1989.

Commission on Workforce Quality and Labor Market Efficiency, 'Investing in People', Washington, D.C., 1989.

Connally, S, J. Mickelwright, and S. Nickell, 'The Occupational Success of Young Men Who Left School at Sixteen,' Queen Mary College Discussion Paper No. 190, February 1989.

Finegold, David, and David Soskice, 'The Failure of Training in Britain: Analysis and Prescription,' Oxford Review of Economic Policy, Vol, 4, No. 3, pp 21-53, 1988.

Glower, Robert, 'Apprenticeship Lessons from Abroad', National Center for Research in Vocational Education, Ohio State University, 1986.

Greenhalgh, Christine, and M. Stewart, 'The Effects and Determinants of Training', Oxford Bulletin of Economics and Statistics, 49, pp. 171-89, 1987.

Jorgenson, D.W., Frank Gollop, and B. Fraumeni, 'Productivity and US Economic Growth', Cambridge, Harvard University Press, 1987.

Lillard, Lee and Hong Tan, 'Private Sector Training: Who Gets It and What Are Its Effects,' The RAND Corporation, R-3331-DOL/RC, 1986.

Lynch, Lisa, 'Private Sector Training and Its Impact on the Career Patterns of Young Workers,' unpublished working paper, Massachusetts Institute of Technology, October 1988.

Mincer, Jacob, 'Job Training, Wage Growth, and Labor Turnover', National Bureau of Economic Research, Working Paper No. 2690, August 1988.

Mincer, Jacob, 'Job Training: Costs, Returns, and Wage Profiles', Columbia University Discussion Paper No. 454, December 1989.

Office of Technology Assessment, 'Worker Training: Competing in the New International Economy', US Congress, Washington, D.C., September 1990.

O'Mahony, Mary and Nicholas Oulton, 'Growth of Multi-Factor Productivity in British Industry, 1954-86,' National Institute of Economic and Social Research, Discussion Paper No. 182, July 1990.

Tan, Hong, 'Human Capital and Technological Change: A Study of Wage Differentials in Japanese Manufacturing,' Ph.D. thesis, Yale University, 1980.

Tan, Hong, Bruce Chapman, Christine Peterson, and Allison Booth, 'Youth Training in the United States, Britain, and Australia', R-4022-ED, The RAND Corporation, 1991.

US Department of Labor, 'Work-Based Learning: Training America's Workers', Washington, D.C., 1989.

Welch, Finis, 'Education in Production', Journal of Political Economy, January-February, 1970, pp. 350-366.

USA and UK Government Policy in Youth Training for the New International Economy: Lessons from Abroad

SARAH H. CLEVELAND

In recent years, increasingly competitive international markets and changes in the organization of production have created pressures on the United States and the United Kingdom to reform their education and training systems. Both countries have faced difficulty enacting reforms in youth training because of corporate cultures which traditionally de-emphasized skills, preferring short-term training and quick-fix solutions to meet their skill requirements. Both countries support two-tier education systems which provide neither adequate general nor vocational education to the majority of young people, reinforcing the preference among companies for the low skill path. And both countries are facing a relative decline in living standards on account of the choices they have made.

The two countries' governments have been slow to respond to the challenge of youth training, reflecting a common preference for market-generated solutions. Only grudgingly did they acknowledge a role for central government action. Given the similarities of their international competitive positions, it perhaps should not be surprising that many of the reforms currently being proposed for adoption by the American government have already been introduced in Britain. Because of its sobering bout with high youth unemployment in the early 1980s, Britain identified its youth training problem earlier, and now has a decade of experience in searching for a solution; the United States has only begun to make reforms. Both countries, however, have focused on improving general educational preparation, creating comprehensive vocational training programs that combine work and academic study for the majority of the workforce, and driving these reforms through systems of national educational and vocational standards.

On both sides of the Atlantic, parents, teachers, employers, and government officials, not to mention young people, have become aware that education and training structures are not adequately allocating young people to jobs or providing them with meaningful employment opportunities. Citizens of both countries have become aware that the training in other industrial countries is substantially better for the majority of young people and they accordingly have begun to pressure policy makers for change. The British and American governments therefore also share a common need to observe and learn from other countries' education and training systems.

This paper will examine USA and UK education and training policies in light of training practices elsewhere in Europe. It will also offer recommendations for future reform within the American context. The discussion is largely based on the results of a study of USA and foreign training and employment practices conducted by the Commission on the Skills of the American Workforce [1] between June 1989 and June 1990.

Section I will examine the market equilibrium arguments concerning training in the United States and discuss why there is a need for improved youth training. Section II will contrast the existing occupational preparation of young people in the USA and the UK with the preparation of young people elsewhere in Europe. The third section will discuss the demand side of training and the organization of work in high-skill economies, while the fourth section recommends government policies which might push the USA toward high-skill forms of work. The paper will conclude by relating these recommendations to the recent British reforms, and displaying the need for *systematic* change in both countries' education and training policies.

Why Do We Need Training?

Hong Tan and Christine Peterson's article in this volume on private sector training practices in the USA and Britain argues that while training practices differ among countries, currently there is little reason to believe that the market does not appropriately allocate training to meet employment needs. In the United States, at least, dependence on the market to allocate training resources is a central tenet of the training 'system'. Government has intervened only on behalf of severely disadvantaged or displaced workers, who are perceived to be excluded from the market's proper operation.

Despite the clamor over the need for better skills, the empirical evidence on training practices assembled by the Commission on the Skills of the American Workforce suggests that Tan and Peterson's conclusion is correct. The supply of available skills in the USA roughly matches current skill requirements. As part of its investigation, organized as a strategic, rather than academic study, the Commission questioned hundreds of employers in detail about their current and future employment needs and work practices. [2] Day-long interviews were conducted in a sample of firms selected by both geography and size to be generally representative of their industries.[3] During each of these visits, corporate headquarters staff, production managers, supervisors, human resource managers, union officials, and front line workers were questioned intensively about the organization's business practices and its present and anticipated skill needs.

Most employers surveyed, somewhat surprisingly, did not report a widening skills gap or substantial growth in skills needs. In contrast to predictions that higher order skills are coming increasingly in demand on the shopfloor, 80% of employers reported that their primary concern was that new employees be reliable and have adequate social skills. Very few expected their employees to have substantial occupational or educational skills, and employers who did were concerned about rudimentary math and reading skills – a matter of basic education, not training.

Only 15 percent of employers in all sectors of the USA economy reported difficulty finding employees with adequate skills to fill their job needs. The shortage among this 15 percent was concentrated in two areas, the first being high skill, traditionally female occupations, such as nursing, which do not pay wages high enough to attract qualified individuals into the profession. The second skill 'gap' was in the traditional craft trades, such as plumbing, construction, and skilled manufacture, where apprenticeships have atrophied in recent years due to the long training period and relatively low pay.

Most employers do not expect their requirements to change in the future: only five percent of all employers thought their skill requirements would increase in the next decade.[4] Despite the predictions of the Hudson Institute's *Workforce 2000* and other reports that technological changes and the shift toward a service economy will raise skill requirements, American employers offered little to corroborate this view. Rather, they described an economy where current job categories require very little training, employers and schools provide very little training, and employers do not expect to need anything more. If anything, many employers expect that changing technology and business practices will require even less training of employees.

The findings of the Skills Commission were supported by an intensive community survey conducted by the National Center on Education and the Economy in Rochester, New York.[5] The study posed a similar set of questions to employers and higher education admissions officials, with similar results. Few employers demanded anything above an eighth grade reading and math level from their workers. Neither employers nor college admissions officers maintained any identifiable standards for hiring and admissions. Neither group required prospective students or employees to have skills which would actually prepare them for the positions being filled, whether in work or further education. Both employers and admission officials admitted that if selection were based on skills which were actually relevant to performance, they would not be able to find enough qualified young people to fill the programs.

These findings are consistent with the general configuration of the USA job market in which fewer than one third of all jobs are likely to require a four-year college degree, and another third require only some minimal level of training over a basic education – perhaps a two-year apprenticeship or a secretarial course. A full one third of all jobs in the USA require little or no education and no training.[6] With the exception of the job categories requiring a college degree, which are increasing slightly, this ratio is not likely to change in the near future.

All of this works quite nicely. With few exceptions, American employers are able to fill their skill requirements by providing training or hiring already trained people in the open market. One third of American young people graduate from four-year colleges and are rewarded with relatively high paying jobs. The rest of the workforce is slotted according to the training they have acquired, often into jobs for which they are overqualified. Training demand meets training supply in a convenient match of skills and jobs.

The problem with this scenario is, as David Finegold has argued (see this volume), that the required skills in this equilibrium are low – too low to sustain a middle-class lifestyle for much of the workforce. And as companies buckle under low-wage competition from overseas, the pressure is for skills and wages to go even lower. Modern technology and the use of temporary/part-time workers are two increasingly popular measures adopted by employers to 'de-skill' the American workplace.

Given their interest in accommodating the training needs of companies, government policy makers in the United States and Britain face the prospect of providing the future workforce with a progressively lower level of training and skills. Declining wages, declining productivity, and ultimately declining living standards are the necessary result. The challenge, then, to countries caught in a low-skill vice, is to stimulate both sides of the market – both demand and supply – to increase the quality of jobs as well as skills. The remainder of this chapter will examine how current *government* practices in Britain and the United States obstruct the development of a high-skill economy, how practices in other European countries produce a different result, and what government policies could be adopted in the USA and the UK to help them move onto the high-skill path.

Current Government Practice in the United States and Great Britain

The United States

America is commonly referred to, particularly in contrast to the UK, as the modern success story of universal higher education. Indeed, the prospect of going to college, of equal educational opportunity for all, is a key flagstone of the American dream. Unfortunately, the reality is that a college degree is actually attained in the United States by relatively few. While Americans like to report that half of American young people qualify for college, this figure substantially distorts the truth: of a national group of 100 young people at age 18, only 75 will complete high school with their age group,[7] only about 40 will go on immediately to post-secondary education, and only 22 will complete a four-year degree in a timely fashion.[8]

Of course, a variety of alternatives to four-year college are available. But a surprisingly small number of young people receive degree qualifications through these programs. The result of these combined factors is that approximately 70 percent of American young people – the vast majority of the population – enter the workforce without a college degree or any equivalent. It is a figure which is surprisingly comparable to that in other European countries. What educational opportunities are available for this 70 percent of young people in school? What occupational preparation and opportunities do they have for acquiring skills when they get out? Unfortunately, most of the non-college population in America has minimal opportunities for acquiring valuable skills either in or out of school.

Initial Preparation: The Schools

The myth that America is a society of equal educational opportunity and that all Americans go to college has been institutionalized as reality in America's public schools. Despite the fact that the majority of children never obtain a degree, the American education system directs the lion's share of its energy and resources toward the minority of children (disproportionately white and middle class) who will eventually attend college and fulfill the American dream.

Because college is so deeply rooted in the mindset of parents, teachers, and government officials, the goal for education in United States has become universal higher education. Schools teach for this utopian world.

This everyone-should-go-to-college attitude unfortunately stumbles on some fundamental contradictions. First, universal public education was established in the United States during the industrial era to provide rudimentary education and citizenship training for the burgeoning immigrant population employed in America's factories. The United States has never abandoned this original mold, despite the changing dynamics of international competition.

Second, more than perhaps any other advanced industrial nation, the United States believes that an individual's life chances are determined by native ability and intelligence. This emphasis on ability over effort permeates educational structures and condemns the chances of young people who are not expected to be able to achieve.

Public education in America is designed for the roughly 30 percent of young people who eventually graduate from four-year colleges. These chosen few are channeled into challenging academic courses with standards equalling those anywhere in the world. They receive encouragement and support from teachers, coaches, and administrators who are responsible for helping the students achieve their goal. Colleges publish entrance requirements and guidance counsellors provide students with detailed information about the available options. Grade-point averages, traditional school activities, and scores on standardized achievement tests serve as standards to help students measure their relative progress.

The picture for the other 70 percent of students filling school classrooms looks very different. These students – the more than 20 percent of American students who drop out before finishing high school and the other 50 percent of high school graduates who either do not enter or fail to complete college – receive very little encouragement in school or preparation for working life. These students are identified early as the ordinary workforce based on a variety of factors ranging from the students' interest in class and ease of learning, to their race, socioeconomic status, the way they speak, dress, or wear their hair. Students in this category are relegated to 12 years of mediocre 'general education' or even remedial courses teaching 'life survival skills' – rudimentary programs which provide neither demanding academic content nor useful occupational skills.

Vocational courses are available. Here again, however, the system's logic is inverted. Only 25 percent of vocational courses are taken by the non-college bound. This bias is due, in part, to the fact that vocational courses are considered specialty 'electives' and are therefore taught only at schools able to afford them. Thus, schools with the most disadvantaged children offer 40 percent fewer vocational courses and 50 percent fewer advanced programs than schools with the fewest disadvantaged young people. Even this disparity may not matter, however. Like the general education courses, vocational courses are often either outdated or irrelevant to the skills needed in the contemporary workplace. Only one in eight of all non-college students enters the workforce having actually taken a vocational course related to his or her job.[9]

The problems with vocational preparation in America have been recognized and addressed recently through Congressional legislation and local reform efforts. High schools are responding both by beefing up academic courses and by creating demanding technical programs, often in cooperation with local community colleges. Local school restructuring efforts, apprentice programs based on the European model, and compacts organized by local business leaders to provide jobs for high school graduates are all emerging to fill in the gap. While none of these efforts offers the scale or the systematic approach necessary to tackle the problem head on, all provide promising models for future reforms.

Standards

Part of the problem facing American schools is a lack of standards – standards for all children, not simply the elite, to achieve, standards by which the performance of schools, teachers, and children can be measured and driven. While college-bound students can at least set their sights by SAT performance levels and college admission requirements, no clearly defined goal lies beyond high school to set performance requirements for students not attending college. Thus, teachers and students alike lack any standards for what should be taught and learned.

The one standard that most Americans do obtain, the high school diploma, is facing a crisis of value. For the more than 70 percent of the population who hold the diploma as their primary or even sole credential, it has become a meaningless educational document. According to both the Commission on the Skills of the American Workforce study and the NCEE Rochester survey [10], employers know that a diploma often represents minimal education and few marketable skills. Although many employers require a diploma for employment, 90 percent of them do so because they view the diploma as a measure of obedience and reliability, rather than any level of educational achievement. At bottom, the diploma simply indicates that the holder was reliable enough to show up at school.

Resources

Resources in the public education system are also directed disproportionately to benefit the college bound. Unlike the nationally funded public education systems of Europe and Japan, school financing in the United States is highly decentralized. Over 90 percent of school funds come from state and local tax revenues, with local property taxes alone often contributing 40-50 percent. The amount of funding available to any individual school therefore varies widely both across states and among districts within a given state. Since local property taxes provide such an important source of funding for public education in America, wealthy districts are able to spend significantly more on education for their children. Funding for education in a state such as Ohio, for example, may range from a high of $10,000 per student per year to a low of $2,500 per student, depending on the property wealth of the district.

The cost to poorer districts is doubly high, since schools are funded according to daily attendance and a higher percentage of students in poorer schools drop out. Ironically, such dropouts save the government money in the short term, since few resources are devoted to recovering those who drop out. Although second chance programs such as Job Corps do exist, if divided over the total number of dropouts, the national expenditure per dropout comes to an average of $235 per year as compared with an average in-school per pupil expenditure of more than $4000. In what is probably the saddest irony of the entire education system, dropouts thus bring big windfalls for districts and states trying to tighten overburdened education budgets.

The point of this discussion is not to say that the American system works perfectly for the 30 percent of students who graduate from college. Public education at all levels is approaching a crisis. A study by the

Economic Policy Institute argued that the USA spends less on primary and secondary education than 13 of its major competitors, while American students' academic test scores lag behind other countries.[11] Scholars disagree over the expenditure and educational rankings (Hood, 1990; USA Department of Education, 1990; Perelman, 1990), but certainly it is non-college-bound students who pay the largest price.

Preparation for Work

So what awaits the average American when she or he graduates, or drops out, of high school? Unfortunately, the bias towards academic education in the United States and the 'mass assembly' belief that most workers do not need extensive occupational training also grips the post-high school education and training world. Most students leave high school unprepared for anything but the simplest work, and step into a world which offers little better. The United States has no systematic school-to-work transition program to guide young people to skills and jobs. In its place float a hodge-podge of apprenticeships, community college courses, and under-funded government and state programs which tinker at the margins of the mass labor market.

The apprenticeship system emerged to provide combined school and work-based instruction for occupations which required much broader skills and preparation than those in mass assembly. Apprenticeships however have failed to meet the needs of a changing industrial world. Typically union-led, they remain largely limited to the traditional craft trades, and enroll fewer than 300,000 people – less than 0.3 percent of the adult workforce.[12] Apprenticeships also do not cater to the young in the USA; the average apprentice is 29 years old.

Community Colleges

The American community college system bears primary responsibility for providing training to those students who do not attend a four-year university. Recast from 'junior colleges' to 'community colleges' by the 1947 Truman Commission Report, the institutions were originally intended to provide two years of preparatory work to help less qualified students enter college. Buttressed by federal Pell Grants and Guaranteed Student Loans (GSLs), the colleges now primarily provide vocational preparation for high school leavers. The system is extensive; nationwide 1,000 public institutions enroll 2 million full-time and 3 million part-time students each year (NCES, 1991, Table 123).

The impressive numbers can be deceptive, however. Only about half of community college participants are enrolled in degree programs and fewer than 20 percent of high school graduates who enroll in community college programs receive a degree within four years.[13] Even for those who do enroll and eventually receive a degree, no generalized standards exist and performance is rarely assessed.

Quality among the community colleges varies wildly, and students have no means of determining whether they are being adequately trained or even which schools offer the best preparation. Students sometimes encounter difficulty transferring credits to another institution, and given that 71 percent of community college students do not receive federal financial assistance[14], the probability that any entering student will be able to afford to finish is questionable. Moreover, employers have little way to judge the quality of training represented by a job candidate's diploma. Students cannot even be sure that efforts to complete the course will be rewarded, since many community colleges are not adequately linked to the world of work.

Private Training Organizations or Proprietary Schools

Operating parallel to the publicly funded community college system is a vast network of private business, technical, and clerical proprietary schools offering training of varying quality in a range of popular jobs. In number, private trade schools outnumber colleges and universities. They have been one of the largest beneficiaries of federal financial aid programs, receiving nearly one quarter of the GSLs issued each year.[15]

The problems with quality and lack of standards among the community colleges are even more pronounced in the private system. No performance standards or incentives encourage schools to ensure quality, and the regulatory system in most states is minimal. The only incentive the schools have is to enroll as many students as possible. Once the students' Pell Grants and GSLs have been collected, it is in the schools' interest to have the students drop out.[16] Not surprisingly, dropout rates in the proprietary schools are extremely high and funding abuse is frequent. According to Litow (1989), one school in New York City reportedly enrolled 6,000 people, collected their loans, and then graduated only 7 percent. Nevertheless, as elsewhere in the education system, some of the schools are superb, and the private sector has a rich training potential which, with proper standards and regulatory measures, could prove an invaluable resource.

Federal Programs

In addition to the system of community colleges, state and federal governments support a number of training programs at the municipal, regional, and national level. Federal programs, largely available through the Job Training Partnership Act (JTPA),[17] are severely underfunded and are designed to address only the needs of the nation's most disadvantaged. They do not provide any systematic means for the majority of young people to acquire useful work related skills. State programs, while wider in scope and more diverse, are generally too fragmented to offer anything close to a coherent system.

In addition to providing support for apprenticeships and community colleges, the federal government funds a number of training programs, designed mainly to aid displaced and disadvantaged workers. As noted in the introduction, the American tendency has been to leave training for the mass population to the ad hoc operation of the market. Thus, most of the current government training programs, now subsumed under the JTPA, grew out of President Johnson's war on poverty and were strictly designed to tinker at the margins of this market, providing training to those who were perceived to fall through the cracks.

Even these federal programs have suffered from severe financial constraints during the last decade. The JTPA itself, was adopted in the early 1980s as a cost cutting reform of the Comprehensive Employment Training Act (CETA). Part of JTPA's cost cutting involves a heavy emphasis on performance, measured by the number of graduates receiving jobs. Only programs deemed successful and cost effective are paid. The result is a 'creaming effect': programs selectively enroll candidates who are most likely to be employable, and fewer and fewer in high risk populations are served. In 1987, only five percent of those eligible for JTPA programs were estimated to be able to enroll.[18] JTPA's 1987 budget was only one third of what CETA's had been in 1980 in real terms. Because of the financial pressures, JTPA training tends to be short term and low cost. The average training period is 20 weeks, at a cost of $2287 per terminee, with heavy emphasis on secretarial and clerical courses over costlier, industrial types of training.[19]

The striking exception to the mediocre success of most federal training programs is the Job Corps, a residential training program for problem youth subsumed under JTPA. The program provides remedial and general education, vocational training, counselling and personal skills development to the children of welfare families and school dropouts. Although attrition rates remain high, with nearly a third of those enrolled leaving the program within the first three months, the Job Corps enjoys remarkable success considering the population it serves. Seventy-five percent of Job Corps graduates continue on in employment or further education, at wages which are higher than the participants would previously have earned.[20] Unfortunately, the program serves only 40,000 people per year. Costs are high, [21] and the program accordingly was nearly abandoned by the Reagan administration in the early 1980s.

While Job Corps and other programs do offer some modicum of hope, even proven federal programs are much too poorly funded to reach the majority of the population they are intended to serve. And none of the programs provides any form of training or school to work transition for the mainstream American worker.

State Programs

While federally-funded programs have focused exclusively on the disadvantaged and unemployed, state training programs have taken a broader tack. In the late 1950s, several Southern states included public training as part of state economic development programs to attract new industry. Since that time, such programs have been initiated in a number of states, often being extended to provide training for existing companies as well. States currently spend nearly $1 billion annually on these training programs. While training tends to be narrow and of short duration, it often offers an important supplement to corporate human resource development programs.

State and local governments also support a number of training programs for welfare recipients, minority candidates, and dropouts which supplement federal programs. Fourteen states and a number of cities, for example, operate conservation-corps style programs for disadvantaged youth, based on the model of Job Corps. These programs serve approximately 20,000 people each year.

The primary problem with state programs is that they are often too fragmented for any but the most industrious skills seekers to find a way through the maze. A state like Michigan, for example, supports 70 different training and education programs, administered through nine different government departments. The courses are offered by local providers too numerous to count. Application procedures for each program are separate and qualifications are not transferable from one program to the other. No system of standards or qualifications lends the programs coherence. Quality is difficult to judge and participants often cannot build on the skills they do acquire.

Qualifications and Standards

The lack of any system of standards or recognized qualifications is a consistent problem throughout the USA training system. Rather than maintaining a single rational system of job definitions for training purposes, the federal government alone uses seven different job classification systems, some listing over 12,000 jobs. Hundreds of industry groups and organizations set thousands of additional occupational standards at the national, regional, and local levels.

The result is a crazy quilt of job definitions and training standards which leaves training participants with no means of knowing whether they are enrolling in a quality program. Candidates do not leave with qualifications which are widely recognized by employers or which form part of a coherent program for career advancement. Employers and government are incapable of assessing the quality of the employees they are hiring or of the programs they are funding.

In sum, the youth training 'system' as it currently exists in America provides little or no practical training to young people while they are in school. Nor does it provide a smooth or coherent transition into the world of work. Most training which is available to young workers is short-term and discrete, and provides no tangible connection to the job marketplace or to further educational or occupational advancement. The result is that many young people in the United States waste the first five to ten years out of school floundering between low-skill and part-time jobs. Not until their mid-twenties do most young people land a career track job, and even then they enter the prized job with few more skills than they possessed upon leaving school.[22]

Few structures are in place on either the demand or the supply side to encourage an increase in skills. The USA lacks a national system of occupational preparation for young people which would create a high-skill workforce, and current American incentive structures are either neutral or encourage companies to take the low-skill path. As the following brief overview indicates, the problem of an incoherent qualifications structure has also been prominent in recent British policy debates.

The United Kingdom

Qualifications

As in the USA, Britain has had an education system which distinguishes between ordinary workers and the higher education or university-bound.[23] Young people leaving secondary school in Britain have traditionally had few opportunities to receive quality vocational preparation outside of apprenticeships, which themselves have significantly declined in numbers.

One of the main problems with the British system has been the lack of standards by which training quality and performance may be assessed. Upon completing an apprenticeship, trainees may receive any of a number of forms of recognition, including an oral agreement, an indentured agreement, an apprenticeship certificate, a vocational qualification, or a certificate reflecting both practical and vocational qualifications.[24] Thus in 1986, the Thatcher Government committed itself to establishing a system of National Vocational Qualifications (NVQ's) to develop coherent national standards for all occupations, and the Major Government has continued to pursue this development. These standards have been criticized for perpetuating the problems of training in Britain by over-emphasizing the performance of discrete tasks rather than stressing the creation of flexible work skills, and by setting extremely low standards. At the bottom end of the scale, NVQ Level 1 is the most controversial segment of the NVQ system. The qualification is largely composed of rudimentary tasks, such as making beds and answering a telephone, and is so low that it is not recognized in the European Community. The government defends the qualification on the basis of practicality – that 20 to 33 percent of Britain's adult workers have skills no greater than this and have few chances for improvement. According to the Confederation of British Industry (CBI), for the large number of adult workers with no qualifications, 'the target of an NVQ at Level 2 will seem too much and too far off... An NVQ at Level 1 will offer a more realistic target to stimulate their interest in training and gaining qualifications, and provide a stepping stone to their eventual achievement of qualifications at a higher level.'

The standard is appropriately criticized, however, for simply legitimizing and institutionalizing the essentially unskilled status quo. Britain has no structure for improving the skills of adults once they enter the workforce. In this context, adopting a standard which reflects the current low level of skills simply reinforces the existing low skill economy, rather than creating incentives to train or expanding training opportunities. So, while Britain has begun implementing training standards earlier than the USA, it too is confronted by the significantly higher standards in force in other European and Asian countries.

A View From Abroad

As part of its study of vocational preparation in the USA, the Commission on the Skills of the American Workforce sent research teams to six foreign countries: Germany, Sweden, Denmark, Ireland, Singapore, and Japan. The contrast between the preparation of young people in Britain and America and those elsewhere in Europe could hardly be more striking. Despite the variety of socioeconomic cultures which these countries represent, they all take a highly consistent approach towards occupational training. Each of the systems which the Commission on the Skills of the American Workforce examined shared a number of common features:

- Government, employers, and the general society recognize the importance of training and the economic value of the non-college workforce.
- Governments and societies therefore are committed to providing a high quality general education to all children, not simply those planning to attend college. Each country also maintains a national system of vocational education and training for young people which provides high quality occupational skills to the majority of the nation's work force.
- Training in this system is long-term, often lasting three to four years, and generally combines school and work-based learning.

- Training is given according to national occupational categories and standards designed in cooperation with industry and leads to nationally recognized certifications.
- Programs are designed to encourage progression, allowing young participants to continue on to higher vocational or academic education.
- The initial vocational preparation system is supplemented by an elaborate government training system which provides training for adult unemployed workers.

For the purposes of this paper, European youth training practices will be exemplified by Germany and Sweden. Both of these countries maintain highly successful training systems which have played a key role in pushing the nations toward higher skills. After describing the approach to training, the paper will discuss the recommendations their examples have led the Commission on the Skills of the American Workforce to propose for the United States.

Initial Preparation

Across the board, general education for the mass population tends to be of higher quality for students in Germany, Sweden, Denmark, and Japan than in Britain or the United States. Most of America's competitors provide much more egalitarian schooling, often with higher quality education for all. In Sweden, Denmark, and Japan, tracking is almost unheard of until upper secondary school. Danish children, for example, remain in the same classroom until grade seven. In all of these countries, educational funding is evenly distributed across schools and regions, and some countries, such as Sweden, even provide supplemental funding to schools with high immigrant populations, in remote areas, or with other special needs.[25]

These countries also maintain national performance standards for education which all young people are expected to meet. In Sweden, Denmark, Ireland, and Japan, national examinations are administered to students at the end of compulsory school, around age 16. Performance on these exams is crucial for determining future educational and work opportunities. Employers regularly look at performance on the student's leaving exam as part of the hiring criteria.

While greater emphasis is placed on real academic performance for all students, vocational preparation is also an integral part of every student's education in the Scandinavian countries. Swedish and Danish students receive an early introduction to employment, going on field trips to local firms and visiting their parents at work during middle school. All Swedish students are also required to complete six to ten weeks of work experience in local companies during the last three years of compulsory school.

Germany's more segregated secondary education system places less emphasis on universal vocational preparation.[26] In the Hauptschule and

Realschule, however, students are provided with a wide variety of occupational courses, employment and apprenticeship information, and career counselling. Parents are included in the career preparation.

Upper Secondary Vocational Preparation

After completing compulsory schooling, although most young people continue on to some form of upper secondary program, only a minority of students remain in an exclusively academic course.[27] Two-thirds of young people or more choose among a variety of joint academic and occupational training programs. In Germany, Austria, and Switzerland, most of the job preparation takes place in the company according to an organized apprentice training program. Sweden, like Denmark and France, takes a more traditional school-oriented approach. But regardless of where most of the training occurs, young people are offered clear preparatory paths to careers, with clearly defined standards and nationally-recognized assessment on completion.

Germany: The Dual System

The Germanic countries' apprentice systems have proven unique in their ability to remain flexible and relevant to changing industrial and employment conditions. The German 'dual system', as popularly described, evolved from the craft guild apprentice structures of the Middle Ages. While apprentice systems elsewhere largely have been replaced by other schemes as traditional industries eroded, interest on the part of German companies and youth has remained strong. Both the level of company and union involvement and the regulatory role played by the government have allowed the system to adapt to changing labor market needs.

The German apprentice system is perhaps the most studied of any national youth training system. Nearly two-thirds of German young people spend the years between age 15 or 16 and 18 in an apprenticeship program. Typically, apprentices spend four days training in the firm and one to two days attending a part-time vocational school, where they pursue a curriculum of combined general education and occupation-specific studies.

Training is available in 380 officially recognized occupations and generally lasts two to four years. Training in the company is given according to a detailed training program, drawn up by the national government for each industry in cooperation with employers and organized labor. Within this framework, companies are free to organize training as they wish.

Studies in the school are closely coordinated with the firm's training program, which gradually moves the student from generalized to highly specific training during the course of the apprenticeship. Apprentices are paid a training wage by the company which increases with the young person's abilities and productivity. Wage amounts tend to be quite low, often starting at 20 percent of the skilled worker's starting salary and increasing to about 60 percent in the final year of training.

The apprentice's progress is monitored by local employers' organizations (the local Chamber of Industry and Commerce or Crafts Chamber) which also administer the national finishing exam. Upon successful completion of the program, the apprentice is certified as a nationally recognized skilled worker. Completion also qualifies the apprentice to pursue a higher 'meister' level qualification after several years of work experience.

Sweden

Sweden has taken a rather different tack from the German apprentice model, but seems to offer an equally successful approach to youth training. Upon completing compulsory school at age 16, about 90 percent of Swedish youth continue on to upper secondary school. Currently about 70 percent of these students enter a vocational program in one of 25 occupational areas, ranging from two-year programs in commerce or health care to a four-year technical engineering degree. Although most of the preparation for these programs takes place in school, programs generally include a work component. Work-based learning offers the student a chance to adjust to the work environment and gain experience to ease the later transition into permanent employment. Under reforms currently being adopted in Sweden, all upper secondary vocational programs in Sweden will be increased to at least three years and will include work-based learning. Students in almost all upper secondary programs in the future will spend 10 percent of their first year in a work environment, with the work period increasing to 60 percent by the third year. The level of general education will be expanded allowing students in these programs to continue on to university in most cases, if they so wish.[28]

In adopting these changes, Sweden has acted on a number of concerns about youth training currently being voiced across Europe. Countries such as Germany are concerned that apprentices do not receive enough general education to prepare them for more demanding forms of work. In contrast, countries like Ireland, Denmark, and Sweden, where most youth preparation traditionally has occurred in schools, are attempting to improve students' preparation for working life and strengthen the school to work transition by increasing the amount of work-based learning. The systems across Europe thus seem to be converging on a model of training which combines substantial general education and work experience as providing the smoothest and most flexible transition for young people to future opportunities and working life (OECD, 1985).

Demand Side Pressures on Government Training Policy: The Organization of Work

Thus far, most of the attention in this discussion has been devoted to questions involving the supply side of training: how young people are prepared for work in the USA and Britain versus elsewhere. But as noted in the introduction, a crucial factor in the success of any training system and the creation of a high skill economy is the willingness of employers to demand and utilize high-skilled work.

Not surprisingly, many of the differences identified on the supply side of training in Europe are accompanied by corresponding differences in demand. Graduates of youth qualification programs in Europe's high-skill countries can generally expect to find full-time, career-path jobs at decent wages directly upon entering the job market – a striking contrast from the experience of most American graduating youth. Low-skill jobs are less common; even sales clerks and waiters are treated as professionals. And employers utilize their employees differently, giving them greater responsibility, more challenging tasks, greater opportunities for future skills development, and greater job security. The advanced industrial nations of Europe have not experienced the wage and benefit slashes and the growing dependence on part-time, temporary, and sub-contracted employees witnessed in the USA in the past ten years. Rather, workers in Germany, Sweden, Denmark, and Japan have seen their wages and prospects increase as companies have turned toward the high skill path.

Sweden led the movement toward the reorganization of work with the establishment of the Volvo Kalmar plant in the early 1970s. Team-style production replaced the traditional assembly line, middle management hierarchies were stripped, and decision-making, materials handling, and quality control responsibilities were devolved to the shop floor. Workers supported the changes because they were given more interesting jobs and were more highly valued by the company. The company reaped benefits in shorter cycle times, lower absentee and turnover rates, higher quality, and reduced management and support costs. Since that time, team-style work organizations have been adopted in companies across Scandinavia and in many other countries, including companies like IBM and Federal Express in the United States.

The Swedish model, of course, is not the only form of high-skill work organization. German companies emphasize craft-style production with a focus on individual worker quality. The Japanese lifetime employment 'family' stresses multi-skilling and an egalitarian, cooperative relationship between shop floor workers, technical personnel, and management.[29]

Why do managers in these countries choose high-skill forms of work? For one, it is increasingly the only way that companies in high wage countries can compete without slashing wages. But there are other factors.

Strong pressure from organized labor, highly educated workforces, labor shortages, and above all government policies have created environments in these countries which pressure companies toward the high skill choice.

Since World War II, governments in Germany, Sweden, Denmark, Singapore, and Japan have committed themselves to maintaining high living standards and economic growth for all the society's members. In Sweden, Singapore, and Japan, this commitment has found expression in a policy of full employment – government actively ensures that training and employment are available for all willing and able members of the population. Full employment creates a tight labor market, encouraging employers to compete for employees with rewarding, attractive jobs.

In the countries of Northern Europe, governments have responded to pressure from organized labor by enacting extensive employment protectionist actions such as high minimum wages and restrictions on plant closings, layoffs, and firing. Legally mandated worker councils in German companies give employees a strong voice. Substantial employee benefits, requirements of severance pay, and incentives for companies to retrain rather than dismiss redundant workers all encourage companies to value their employees and to take a long-term economic perspective.

Financial pressures on companies in this direction are also strong. In many major industrial countries, companies are legally required to contribute substantial portions of their payroll to various forms of training, in addition to whatever amount the company ordinarily invests in its own employees. This contribution generally finances apprentice training as well as government training programs for displaced workers and the unemployed.[30] Universally high education standards themselves are probably one of the most crucial forces encouraging companies to demand higher skills. Strong occupational preparation means that employees are both willing and able to take on more responsibility. But it also means that workers are less likely to tolerate menial forms of work. Employers in countries with highly skilled workforces discover that they are unable to either attract or retain workers unless they give workers both the responsibility and the job security which their education merits.

Sweden's experience here is illustrative. Sweden was one of the last European countries to expand its public education system after World War II. In the early 1960s, Sweden increased the length of compulsory education from six to nine years and instituted sweeping public education reforms. Employers strongly opposed the changes, arguing that the sharp increase in education would make the workforce more aggressive and difficult to control. Employers across Sweden now admit that in order to attract the educated young people to employment, they must offer them interesting and responsible jobs. In contrast to the government policies abroad which encourage movement towards a high-skill equilibrium, the incentives in the USA and Britain often operate in the opposite direction. Federal and state labor laws and collective bargaining agreements in the USA which exclude part-time and short-term workers actually encourage employers to de-skill the workplace by hiring low skill, short-term, temporary and part-time workers. Investment incentives and tax codes which emphasize quarterly returns also force companies to take a short term perspective on investments in human and other capital. All the factors – national employment and training policy, labor legislation, corporate tax and investment structures, and even immigration policies – contribute to the overall corporate environment which encourages European companies to make the high-skill choice.

To conclude, although the systems in Germany, Sweden, and elsewhere in Europe take a variety of approaches to youth training, they share in common, and in contradistinction to the USA and Britain, two crucial features: the existence of a comprehensive system of youth vocational preparation with widespread national standards, and demand-side incentives which encourage companies to utilize the skilled workforce the system produces. Young people in each of these countries are able to enter upper secondary school programs which provide them with valuable and recognized vocational qualifications and give them an employment status and opportunities for career advancement unknown to most non-college educated employees in the USA. National standards help to rationalize the systems and allow for the assessment of quality by employees, employers, schools, and governments alike.

Policy Recommendations for the United States Government

Standards are a notable element in the success of foreign training programs, but they are conspicuously absent from the USA system. Standards allow financial incentives for schools and training programs to be based on the actual skills and knowledge acquired, rather than merely on the number of students enrolled or the proportion finding employment. Standards also allow employers to know what to expect from the labor force, and allow them to plan accordingly. Finally, standards motivate students by telling them what they need to learn, and giving them a clear route to their chosen career path.

In making its recommendations, the Commission on the Skills of the American Workforce accordingly focused on standards as the means to raising educational and training qualifications for American youth. The recommendations were as follows:

Recommendation 1: A National Standard of Educational Excellence

A sound foundation in the three R's as well as in the abilities to think, compute, organize, and apply problems are crucial to a young person's subsequent success, whether in a vocational program, in higher education, or simply in life. Given the current state of educational preparation in the

United States, it would be useless to establish a national system of vocational preparatory programs without first addressing the question of basic education. Several countries, notably Ireland and Japan, have created highly skilled workforces primarily by emphasizing general academic skills, while all of the countries maintaining high-skill economies provide quality general education in school before young people choose a vocational program.

In order to raise the quality of general education in the United States and to drive education reform, The Commission recommended a national standard of educational excellence should be established which all students would be expected to achieve, most by age 16. The standard would be benchmarked to the highest equivalent standard in the world.

Student achievement of the standard would be measured in a series of performance examinations taken periodically throughout compulsory school, according to each student's interests and abilities. Examinations would involve problem solving and demonstration of student performance through the completion of a variety of projects. Successful completion of one level would allow the student to advance to the next. The cumulative assessment system would be designed to motivate students and teachers across an extended period and allow multiple opportunities for achievement, rather than simply a high pressure, one-time shot at success.

Demand is crucial to a standard-driven system and achievement of the standard must have real consequences for students and schools. Full completion of the entire series of qualifications would result in the issuance of a Certificate of Initial Mastery (CIM), which would be required for entry into either further academic or vocational programs or into the workforce. Ideally, employers would be prohibited from hiring young people unless they had received the CIM or were actively attending a program which would lead to its completion.[31] Since the legal age of employment is 16 for most occupations, such a requirement would not severely encumber the majority of students. Funding for schools and merit-based compensation for teachers might also be tied to the number of students successfully completing the exams.

Another factor crucial to the success of a high national educational standard is ensuring that all young people will be able to achieve it. It would be easy for an assessment system to set high standards, only to have the vast majority of students fail. This would be the worst possible failure: raising yet another obstacle between disadvantaged young people and mainstream America. On the other hand, to establish the standard at a minimal level which all or even most young people could currently meet would be to fail at the standard's basic purpose of raising the national educational level. Because of the political sensitivity of establishing a standard which many young people will initially fail, many states which have recently attempted to establish a statewide standard of minimal accomplishment, have ended up achieving just that.

Several tacks may be taken to avoid these problems. First, while the standard must be set initially at the desired high level, the accompanying consequences (such as making further educational admission and employment contingent on success) could be delayed from taking effect for five to ten years, until students have had time to be prepared under the new system. Thus, there would be no costs for high initial rates of failure. Secondly, an extensive dropout recovery system should be established to ensure that all students receive the resources and attention necessary to achieve the standard. Such a system could be based on the Swedish Youth Centers. The Youth Centers aggressively recruit young people who do not perform well in the traditional academic setting, offering them employment and recreational opportunities while bringing them back into the educational mainstream through an alternative education setting. Aspects of the Youth Center model have been adopted on a small scale in various USA programs with good results.[32]

Recommendation 2: A System of Occupational Preparation

The failures of the existing education and training system are many. Because of the pro-college bias of American educational institutions, students who do not plan to attend college or who perform better in non-academic forums have few alternatives available which would provide them with instruction more suited to their needs. Young people end up dropping out to get a job which will provide them with ready income and a sense of responsibility, or simply waste their time during the last few years of high school.

Establishing a system of occupational preparation after age 16 would diversify the educational opportunities available for young people while providing a clear path of training and job experience into the world of work. The programs The Commission envision would be three to four years long and would combine general academic subjects with work-based learning. They could be pursued by young people as part of the last two years of high school and beyond, or by adults at any stage in life. Rather than defining a specific curriculum for each job category, the programs would be driven by national occupational categories and standards, designed for each industry by national committees of employers and employees. The standards would build upon criteria which already exist in certain industries and, like the Certificate of Initial Mastery, would be benchmarked to the highest equivalent standards in the world.

Based on the standards promulgated, the specific programs could be designed and offered by any number of private and public providers, including existing high schools, community colleges, private companies and community centers. Both the programs and providers would be certified and accredited by the state before they could enroll participants.

Students would exhibit mastery of an accredited program through successful completion of performance-based exams, established by the national standards committees. Successful candidates would receive a certificate which would qualify them to enter employment as a skilled worker, to attend higher education at a college or university, or to pursue more advanced certification programs. The certificates would be recognized by employers in the industry nationwide.

Employers would have a substantial role in the system. They would be expected to cooperate with local providers, offering work experience and wages for trainees in the programs. Trainees, in turn, could fill the role currently played by part-time and temporary workers while gaining skills for a career job. Employers would then be expected to offer graduates of the programs preferential employment in quality jobs. This would stimulate demand for the programs by creating incentives for young people to join.

Recommendation 3: Creating Demand Incentives

The primary difficulty in the second recommendation, and with raising skill levels in the USA in general, is how to stimulate demand – how to get employers, most of whom currently see no need to alter their existing employment and training practices, to participate in the programs by providing training and by offering graduates higher skill jobs?

As noted earlier, the USA lacks the tight labor market, the strong union movement, and the national commitment to high quality education and full employment which have driven demand in other countries. America's national culture also strongly resists government intervention into corporate affairs. Nevertheless, all countries trying to raise skill levels have confronted problems with employer demand to some degree. Denmark, which supplemented its dated apprentice system with a combined school and work program in the early 1970's, has resorted to employer subsidies at various times and yet still continues to have difficulty encouraging enough employers to participate. Sweden anticipates difficulties as it increases the work component of its training programs, even though the country already has a tremendous corporate demand for skills.

In most cases, the solution has been to subsidize employer participation in training programs. As the British Youth Training Scheme (YTS) and Danish experiences have shown, however, subsidies are an ineffective substitute for the type of true corporate interest which drives training in Germany and Japan.[33] Although subsidies might be necessary to encourage companies to participate, the goal ultimately would be to tie the programs to corporate interests. If trainees are able to perform productive work, it is not unreasonable to expect that employers would be willing to hire them and provide them with pay. This is particularly true if the trainees will be able to complete some of the tasks currently filled by part-time workers.

The more difficult question is how to encourage employers fundamentally to restructure the workplace to offer young people jobs which will utilize their new skills. No student would normally be willing to enter a three- to four-year training program without believing it will provide some tangible reward. The Skills Commission has recommended that a one percent payroll training tax be levied on American employers to raise their legal contribution to roughly equal the lowest level required abroad. The contribution would be reimbursed to companies which offered certain forms of training.[34] Otherwise it could be used to fund public training programs. Quality awards such as the Malcolm Baldridge National Quality Award can also be used to publicize the importance of training and high skill employment. But ultimately, in the American context at least, the responsibility will fall on the voluntary actions of USA companies. Currently a small segment of corporate America – the five percent of USA companies which are subject to direct global competition – thoroughly understands the importance of a well educated workforce and high skill jobs. The burden will fall on these companies to take the lead in organizing training programs and educating the rest of American employers about the advantages of the high-skill path.

Conclusion

In conclusion, the purpose of this paper was to examine the youth education and training problems in the USA and to a lesser extent, the UK, to draw similarities between the obstacles these countries face in increasing skill levels, and how the governments have attempted to respond to these problems. Strong commonalities can be discerned. Both the USA and the UK have developed a two-tier structure for providing basic general education for their youth. Both countries, until recently, have depended almost exclusively on the market to bridge the gap between school and work and to provide adequate job-related training for the majority of their workforces. And, as the American data indicate, the market has substantially fulfilled its mandate. With few exceptions, both countries enjoy a fairly tight match between youth qualifications and the available job requirements.

Unfortunately, in a global trade and economic context which is increasingly dominated by competition from the low-wage developing world, the purely market approach to training adopted by the United States and Britain has proven increasingly incapable of sustaining either a skilled workforce or a livable wage. The result is a double-edged crisis in skill supply and demand.

Yet, here again, governmental policy responses to the looming crisis have been remarkably akin. Both the USA and Britain in the last ten years have increasingly looked toward national standards and examinations and incentive-driven structures to improve the quality, availability, and popularity of youth training. The United Kingdom first piloted the movement toward greater intervention, opting for a national curriculum rather than the weaker national standards currently being discussed in the United States to drive its compulsory education reform. But regardless of the specific character of the reforms adopted, both governments are now beginning to reconcile to the principle that government has an active and obligatory role in sustaining the quality of youth training. Both have recognized a common need to learn from the type of systemic change and comprehensive policies which have been so successful in other advanced industrial states. And both countries, at long last, are turning to more national direction over education and training as the solution to skill problems.

Notes

[1] The study examined public and private training practices in seven countries (Germany, Sweden, Ireland, Denmark, Singapore, Japan and the United States) and included interviews with over 2,000 managers, workers, apprentices, educators, and government officials in over 550 companies and agencies. The work of the Commission was sponsored by the National Center on Education and the Economy based in Rochester, New York.

[2] America's Choice: High Skills or Low Wages!, National Center on Education and the Economy, June 1990.

[3] Seven major economic sectors were covered by the study in both the USA and abroad, including a) banking, financial services and insurance, b) construction, c) government and military, d) health care and education, e) manufacturing, f) oil, gas, mining and agriculture, g) personal services, h) wholesale and retail, and i) transportation, communications, and utilities.

[4] The 5 percent of employers who did expect their skill needs to increase are America's leading manufacturing corporations such as IBM, Motorola, and Ford Motor Company, which are most subject to pressure from foreign competition. These same firms have been the leaders in training and high-skill work organization in the USA during the last decade.

[5] 'High Expectations: What Rochester Graduates Should Know and Be Able to Do.' National Center on Education and the Economy, Sept. 1990 (unpublished).

[6] The approximate ratios are as follows: 30 percent of jobs are highly skilled, 36 percent are semi-skilled, and 34 percent are unskilled. The one third of unskilled jobs primarily require qualifications such as driving ability, a pleasant personality, or physical strength. Data from America's Choice: High Skills or Low Wages!, pp. 26-29, and the USA Bureau of Labor Statistics.

[7] Accurate dropout figures for the United States are difficult to determine. Local dropout rates range from one to 50 percent (or higher in some of the nation's inner cities). Approximately 25 percent of American youth do not graduate with their age group. Some of these may finish school at a later time or may complete a Graduate Equivalency Diploma (GED). According to the William T. Grant Foundation Commission on Work, Family and Citizenship report, The Forgotten Half: Non-College Youth in America, more than 86 percent of young people receive either their high school diploma or their GED by age 29. The distinction between high school diploma holders and dropouts, however, is not relevant for the purposes of this discussion.

[8] These figures are based on high school students in 1980 (Carroll, 1989). Over time the numbers rise as adults obtain additional credentials.

[9] America's Choice: High Skills or Low Wages!, p. 44.

[10] America's Choice: High Skills or Low Wages!, p. 24. See also, 'High Expectations, What Rochester Graduates Should Know and Be Able to Do'.

[11] Sweden, Austria, Switzerland, Norway, Belgium, Denmark, Japan, Canada, West Germany, France, the Netherlands, Britain and Italy all invest a higher portion of their national income on primary and secondary education than the United States, according to the report (Rasell, 1989). In order to reach the 'average' level of spending among the other nations, the United States would have to spend an additional $20 billion on education per year.

[12] Work-Based Learning: Training America's Workers. USA Department of Labor, Employment and Training Administration, November 1989.

[13] According to a study by the National Assessment of Vocational Education (US Department of Education, 1989), of the recent high school graduates entering post-secondary vocational education only 11.2 percent received a bachelor's degree, 5.9 percent an associate's degree, and 1.9 percent a certificate within four years.

[14] US Department of Education, 1992, p. 15.

[15] Stanley Litow, 'Unfair at any Price: Welfare Recipients at New York Proprietary Schools', Interface, Inc., 1989.

[16] Federal regulations now require proprietary schools to establish a refund schedule corresponding to the number of weeks withdrawal from the program.

[17] JTPA is the umbrella for a dozen federal training program, including the Jobs Corps, Jobs for America's Graduates (JAG) and the Summer Youth Employment Program. All of the programs are designed to provide skills development for dislocated or disadvantaged workers. A certain portion of JTPA funding is earmarked for youth.

[18] The JTPA legislation defines the eligible population as those individuals who have an income below the USA Office of Managemnt and Budget poverty line guidelines or who receive Aid for Dependent Children or food stamps.

[19] Program duration and cost data are for program year 1987, and are drawn from 'Job Training Quarterly Survey Special Paper No.10: Review of JTPA Participant Characteristics and Program Outcomes for Program Years 1984 through 1989', Westat for the USA Department of Labor, October 1991.

[20] Commission on Youth Employment Programs, National Research Council. Youth Employment and Training Programs: The YEDPA Years. Washington, D.C.: National Academy Press, 1985, pp. 111.

[21] Participation in Job Corps for an average of seven months cost about $9,200 per student in 1985.

[22] The Forgotten Half: Non-College Youth in America, The William T. Grant Foundation Commission on Work Family and Citizenship, 1988.

[23] For a complete description of the UK education and examination system, and of the evolution of the Youth Training program in Britain, see Raffe and Rumberger in this volume.

[24] Haxby, supra.

[25] In most of the nations of Europe, school funding is allocated equally nationwide, even if locally administered. In Germany, although most funding for schools is collected regionally by the eleven Lander, the federal government supplements state allocations in order to achieve parity in educational financing across the country.

[26] Three different types of secondary school in Germany, the Hauptschule, Realschule, and Gymnasium, separate children into separate career tracks (although there is some room for movement among the schools). The

Hauptschule, traditionally intended to offer practical mass education for working and farming classes, has declined in importance in recent years, but still educates about 40 percent of German youth. It offers the lowest educational qualification recognized in Germany. Above the Hauptschule, the Realschule and Gymnasium offer progressively more academic programs, with the Gymnasium providing explicit preparation for university. The Realschule offers both practical and theoretical studies for students going on to an apprenticeship or to college.

[27] The number of students remaining in academic programs is generally about one third. The exception to this rule is Japan, where the majority of young people remain in a full general academic programs throughout upper secondary school. The lack of emphasis on vocational preparation in Japanese secondary schools is largely due to the fact that under the lifetime employment system, Japanese employers provide most of their employees' vocational preparation. Hiring is based largely on the student's general academic performance.

[28] The number of occupational lines will be reduced to 16 and broadened and the possibilities for specialization will be increased. The existing four-year technical program will become a '2 plus 2' program, with the latter two years spent in an institute of higher education.

[29] High-skill work organization is not universally applied in any of these countries. Germany and Sweden have a history of using inexpensive foreign labor to perform their least desirable jobs. And Japanese multinationals are supported by small suppliers which employ low-skill workers for long hours with little job security. But the trend toward higher skills in all of these countries is strong and clearly visible, and management and employee attitudes toward work offer a striking contrast to those in either the USA or UK.

[30] In Germany, large firm expenditure on apprenticeships may come to 3.5 percent of annual corporate payrolls, above and beyond the 2 to 4 percent of payroll which German companies already regularly contribute toward continuing training for their own employees. In Sweden, Ireland, and Singapore, the legal contribution to public forms of training ranges from 1 to 2.5 percent. Part or all of this contribution can often be recouped by the company for offering certain mandated forms of training. Statistics compiled for America's Choice: High Skills or Low Wages!, pp. 115-118.

[31] One problem confronting both the United States and the UK is the ready availability of employment for young people in the low wage market. Schools find it increasingly difficult to compete with jobs offering $5 per hour for 16 year-olds who are itching to earn money and get on with life. Creating wider opportunities for part-time employment within the education system will improve this situation to some degree. Other countries have dealt with the problem by restricting the ability of employers to hire young people. In Sweden, for example, young people cannot legally work over a certain number of hours per week, or late at night. In Germany, young people between age 15 and 18 who have finished compulsory school must continue to attend a minimum of one to two days of vocational school each week, regardless of whether they are in an apprenticeship, in a job, or unemployed. Employers are legally required to give these young people time off to attend the school.

[32] Notable among these is the dropout recovery program of the Sweetwater Union High School district in San Diego, California. Set up with computerized systems in movable buildings on the school grounds, the program, over a three-year period, has recovered nearly 6,000 pupils and allowed them to finish high school.

[33] Germany and Japan have had little difficulty encouraging companies to train extensively and to organize work around high-skill jobs. In both of these countries, corporate participation is built into the corporate culture as a result of the lifelong employment system of Japan and the medieval craft legacy in Germany. Companies in both of these countries view investment in human resource development as crucial to their overall development strategy, resulting in higher productivity, higher quality, better corporate management, and growth.

[34] This proposal is similar to the levy/grant system which Britain adopted in the 1964 Industrial Training Act, that was later abandoned by the Thatcher Government.

Bibliography

Banerjee, Neela, 'Unfair at Any Price: Welfare Recipients at New York Proprietary Schools', Interface, New York, 1980.

Carroll, Dennis, High School and Beyond: College Persistence and Degree Attainment, USA Department of Education, 1989.

Commission on Youth Employment Programs, National Research Council. Youth Employment and Training Programs: The YEDPA Years. Washington, D.C.: National Academy Press, 1985.

Confederation of British Industry, 'Towards a Skills Revolution', CBI, 1989

Hood, John, 'Education: Is America Spending Too Much?', Cato Institute, 1990.

Litow, Stanley 'Unfair at any Price: Welfare Recipients at New York Proprietary Schools', Interface, Inc., 1989.

National Center for Education Statistics, Digest of Education Statistics 1990, USA Department of Education.

National Center on Education and the Economy, America's Choice: High Skills or Low Wages!, June 1990.

OECD Employment Outlook, Organisation for Economic Co-operation and Development, 1989.

OECD, Employment and Training after Basic Schooling, Paris, OECD, 1985.

Perelman, L., 'The 'Acanemia' Deception: How the Myth that America 'Lags' in Education Spending Threatens to Undermine National Competitiveness', Hudson Institute Briefing Paper No. 120, May 1990.

Rasell, M. Edith, and Mishel, Lawrence, 'Shortchanging Education: How USA Spending on Grades K-12 Lags Behind Other Industrial Nations', Economic Policy Institute, 1990.

US Department of Education, 'Shortchanging Education: A Case Study in Flawed Economics'.

US Department of Education, National Assessment of Vocational Education, Final Report: Postsecondary Vocational Education, Volume IV, 1989.

US Department of Education, Office of Educational Research and Improvement, National Postsecondary Student Aid Study, Students at Less-Than-4-Year Institutions, Contractor report, November 1992, p. 15.

US Department of Labor, Employment and Training Administration, Work-based Learning: training America's workers, November, 1989.

Westat, 'Review of JTPA Participant Characteristics and Program Outcomes for Program Years 1984 through 1989', USA Department of Labor, October 1991.

Education and Training for 16-18 Year Olds in the UK and USA

DAVID RAFFE & RUSSELL W. RUMBERGER

In the UK and the US, as in virtually all industrialized countries, education and training have come under increased scrutiny in recent years. As the international economy has grown, so too has the perception that nations' systems of education and training are critical for their success in the international marketplace. One area of particular concern is the education and training of youth.

In this paper we compare the UK and US education and training systems for 16-18 year olds. There are several reasons for focusing on this age group. Recent policy debates in both countries have identified education and training for 16-18 year olds as in special need of attention. It is the stage which most clearly reflects the different social and economic contexts – in particular the different labour markets – of the two countries. And it is the stage at which institutional contrasts between the two educational systems are sharpest, and most visibly reflect underlying differences in their history and philosophy. Some of these differences are reflected in the different vocabularies used to describe the two systems. The concept of 'vocational education and training' (VET), for example, embodies British (or more precisely English) assumptions which are absent from the American notion of 'voc ed'. As we note below, the contrast between the British phrase 'staying-on' and the American phrase 'dropping-out' conveys a lot about the ways in which participation issues are raised in the two countries. Equally significant are the instances where the same words have different applications or connotations in the two systems, for example 'youth', 'school' and 'college'.

In the first section of this chapter we discuss several important differences concerning the education and training of 16-18 year olds in the two countries. In the second section we identify three central policy issues and compare how these have been presented in recent policy debates in the two countries. Finally, in the concluding section we discuss whether, and how, either system can learn or borrow from the experience of the other.

Contrasts in the Current Provision of Education and Training

Our discussion follows the sequence of student transitions through the system. We consider, in turn, differences between the two countries in the status of 16-year-olds, in the provision of full-time education for 16-18 year olds, in alternatives to full-time education, and in opportunities for youth aged 18 years and over. Before discussing these differences, we should note two important aspects of the systems of education and training in the two countries that bear on our discussion. In both countries there is no single system of education and training for 16-18 year olds. First, the control and provision of education and training involves various levels of government as well as the private sector. Second, there are substantial variations within each country: among local education authorities and among different countries within the UK, particularly between Scotland and the rest of the UK; and, in the US, differences among the 50 state systems of education where the primary authority for public education lies.

The Status of 16 Year Olds

In both countries full-time education is usually compulsory up to age 16, although in some American states the limit is 17 years, and many states do not enforce the compulsory schooling law so that students can leave high school as early as 14 or 15. In both countries most compulsory education is provided in public (state-run) schools, most of which are organized on a comprehensive basis (with the exception, in the UK, of Northern Ireland). In both countries the curriculum up to 16 includes both academic and vocational elements, although academic curricula dominate most students' studies, whether or not the individual is planning to enter post-secondary schooling. The status of 16 year olds, however, differs radically between the two systems. In the UK most 16 year olds have completed a recognized stage of education. They have had the opportunity to gain qualifications that are widely marketable and recognized by employers as well as schools and colleges. In the US, by contrast, 16 year olds are typically only half way through their four-year high-school programmes, which normally last from 14 to 18 years of age and offer no certification or other form of credential to those who leave during that period. The age of 16 is a legitimate transition point in British education; staying on at school is only one of a range of post-16 options all of which have recognized status. By contrast the lack of legitimacy of 16-year-old transitions in the US is connoted by the use of the term 'dropout' to describe those who leave school at this point.

A closely related difference between the two countries is in their labour markets. The British youth labour market is dominated by full-time jobs in a relatively wide range of occupations, many offering relatively high pay. Entering the labour market can be an attractive alternative to continued schooling, not only in the short term but also in the long term, since many training and career opportunities are effectively restricted to those who have left school by 16 or 17. Nearly all young people who leave full-time education at 16 enter the full-time labour market (Raffe and Courtenay, 1988). The US youth labour market, by contrast, is dominated by casual, part-time and low-paid 'secondary' jobs. Neither in the short nor the long term does it offer an attractive alternative to schooling and about a third of young dropouts remain economically inactive outside the labour force (US Bureau of the Census, 1989, Table 636).

These two contrasts – in the educational status of 16 year olds, and in youth labour markets – contribute to what is probably the most important difference between the UK and the US in the provision of education and training at the 16-18 year-old stage. This difference can be described in two alternative ways: one that is less charitable to the UK system; the other is more so. The less charitable interpretation emphasises the UK's low participation in full-time education beyond 16, typically around half the US levels. The more charitable interpretation points to the UK's 'mixed model' of provision and stresses the range of alternatives to full-time education for 16-18 year olds. We discuss these in turn.

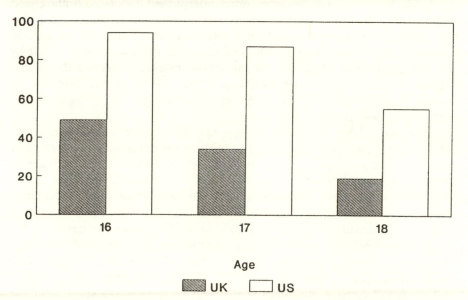

Figure 1. Participation in F-T education (1986). Source: UK Department of Education and Science (1990).

Full-time Education at 16-18

Figure 1 compares full-time participation rates in the two systems. Despite a recent increase in staying-on rates, only about one in two of British 16 year olds continues in full-time education, and slightly more than one in three continues beyond 17. By contrast, more than nine in ten Americans stay on beyond 16, and more than eight in ten stay on beyond 17. The proportion of American students completing high school (typically at age 18) is not known with certainty, but estimates range from 75 to 85 percent (Rumberger, 1987). The comparison between the two countries is even more stark if restricted to secondary school. Whereas almost all US 16 year olds who continue in education remain in high school, only about two-thirds of British stayers (about one-third of all 16 year olds) stay on at secondary school; most of the others enter a college of further education (FE) (UK Department of Employment, 1989). Community colleges, the closest US equivalent to British FE colleges, recruit relatively few students before the age of 18. Scotland is closer than the rest of the UK to the US model; more young people stay on beyond 16, and most do so at school. More Scots leave school at 17, a proportion of whom progress to FE college (Raffe and Courtenay, 1988).

The strongest influence on whether a British 16 year old stays on or leaves full-time education is his or her level of attainment in compulsory schooling (Raffe and Willms, 1989; Gray, Jesson, Pattie and Sime, 1990). The UK's low participation rates are underpinned by a continuing and prevalent perception that staying on, especially at school, is only appropriate or worthwhile for the academically able (Ryrie, 1981). Nor is this perception irrational; it reflects the exclusiveness of the main qualifications pursued by stayers, together with the failure of the labour market to reward those who continue at school but do not substantially increase their qualifications, or who gain only lower-status vocational qualifications (Raffe, 1984; Roberts, Siwek and Parsell, 1989).

Post-compulsory education in the UK is qualifications-driven. Most school stayers take academic courses, either repeating qualifications they attempted at 16 or studying for A levels, the main route to higher education (except in Scotland, described below). A levels are attempted by about 25 percent of the age group, and are typically taken in three subjects over two years (although the AS level, equivalent to half an A level, has recently been introduced to broaden the curriculum). Most 16-year-old entrants to FE college follow one- or two-year courses which lead to a range of vocational qualifications (Gray and Sime, 1990). Some of these are occupationally specific, but the 1980s have seen the development of broader, 'pre-vocational' courses, although these tend to have lower status and the value of the qualifications is more doubtful. A substantial minority of FE college students (more than a quarter) take academic courses, and a smaller minority of school students (about a tenth) take vocational courses (ibid.). Some local authorities have introduced 'tertiary colleges' which offer the range of courses typically available in schools and FE colleges to the 16-plus age group. However, most students pursue courses that are predominantly academic or vocational; there is relatively little mixing.

In Scotland there is somewhat more overlap between academic and vocational curricula (Raffe and Courtenay, 1988). The main academic qualification, the Higher, is typically attempted after a one-year course, and in a broader range of subjects than the A level. A much higher proportion of the age group attempts at least one Higher in Scotland than attempts at least one A level in England. The complex range of vocational qualifications has been replaced in Scotland by a national framework of more than 2000 modules, each of notional 40 hours length, assessed by a single, criterion-referenced and internally assessed National Certificate. Modules may be taken at school or college, and by full- or part-time students or trainees.

The somewhat weaker segregation between academic and vocational tracks in Scotland compared with the rest of the UK brings its school system a little closer to that of the US. There, most students who complete secondary school have taken a combination of vocational and academic courses. Secondary schools in the US are generally comprehensive, offering both academic and vocational programmes. Most states require that a minimum number of academic courses be taken in several areas during the four years of high school. Although the requirements vary from state to state, they would typically include four years of English, two years of mathematics, two years of science and three years of social studies (US Bureau of the Census, 1989, Table 239). In addition, more than half of all high school students take at least some vocational courses, such as typing, industrial arts, and home economics, and about half of these (25 percent of all students) actually specialize in a vocational field, such as automobile mechanics (US Department of Education, 1984).

In the US, students who complete high school receive no certification other than a high school diploma, except those students who complete a recognized vocational programme. There is no national system of comprehensive examinations that all students take comparable to those in the UK; only college-bound students take national exams that cover mandatory verbal and mathematics areas and optional subject specialisms. Some states and local districts require students to complete a comprehensive exam in order to receive a diploma, but the test scores are not normally documented in the student's record. The only record of a student's course of study is a high school transcript, which simply shows the subjects studied and the grades received. In contrast with the UK (where universities are suspicious of internally-assessed credentials) these transcripts are used by colleges and universities for admission decisions, but they are not used by employers for employment decisions.

Alternatives to full-time education at 16 to 18

The more charitable interpretation of the UK system in comparison with the US emphasizes the nature of the UK as a 'mixed model' (OECD, 1985). In contrast to the 'schooling model' of post-compulsory provision exemplified by the US, the UK offers a variety of education and training options for 16-18 year olds who choose to leave school, a majority of whom receive further part-time education or training (Figure 2). There has been a tradition in Britain of apprenticeship and part-time education for young workers, although this has generally been restricted to a narrow range of (mainly 'male' craft) occupations, and the numbers of apprentices fell in the 1970s and early 1980s as recession led to cuts in new recruitment and in investment in training. Since 1983, the government has attempted to improve provision for early leavers through the Youth Training Scheme (YTS), recently re-christened Youth Training (YT).

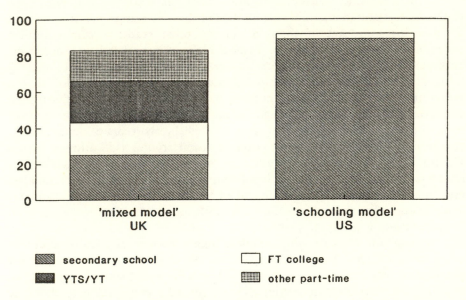

Figure 2. Participation of 16-17 year olds (1988). Source: UK Department of Education and Science (1990); US Bureau of Census (1990).

YT attracts around a quarter of 16 year olds, and a smaller number who enter at 17. Its genealogy is of biblical dimensions but covers a shorter time scale. In 1978 several measures to counter youth unemployment, notably the Job Creation Programme and the Work Experience Programme, begat the Youth Opportunities Programme (YOP); in 1983 the YOP begat the one-year YTS; in 1986 the one-year YTS begat the two-year YTS; in 1990 the two-year YTS begat the YT. The move from the YOP to the YTS was particularly significant, as it marked an abrupt switch in stated objectives from the alleviation of youth unemployment to the promotion of youth training. Unlike the YOP, the YTS was not just a safety net for those who could not find regular employment; it was intended to attract young people in preference to jobs which did not offer equivalent training, and it was even (if implausibly) proclaimed to be of equal value to A levels. However, the institutional change was less abrupt: the YTS inherited the low status of its predecessor, its low position in educational and labour-market hierarchies, and its function as a 'safety-net' for the young unemployed (Raffe, 1988).

All under-18 year olds, not in full-time education or employment, who desired a YTS place were guaranteed one. The delivery of YTS was contracted to managing agents who could be employers (individually or in consortia), private trainers, voluntary organizations or FE colleges. Managing agents in turn could use other employers, colleges or trainers to supply work experience, off-the-job training or other inputs to the training (Lee, Marsden, Rickman and Duncombe, 1990). Schemes had to satisfy certain criteria, including a minimum period of off-the-job training (20 weeks under the two-year scheme). But firms could place their own young employees on YTS, and in effect receive a subsidy for their in-company training. Others used YTS as a 'screening' device or a flexible recruitment pool for future employees (Sako and Dore, 1986; Roberts, Dench and Richardson, 1987).

With the introduction of the YT, the level of government subsidy is being reduced; the scheme is becoming more employer-led; the conditions are being made more flexible (the minimum off-the-job requirement has been dropped); and government control is exercised largely through 'outputs' rather than 'inputs'. Virtually all YT trainees will be expected to work for vocational qualifications to a given level (see section below on national qualifications). Likely consequences of these changes include further polarization within the scheme, with the most sought-after places being those which either offer employed status or are used as channels of recruitment to attractive jobs, and a progressive blurring of the boundaries between the higher-status YT schemes and regular employment.

It is largely the contribution of YT and its predecessor that has allowed the UK government to claim that the UK now occupies an 'intermediate position' in international comparisons of 16-year-old participation (but still a low position in respect of 18 year olds) (UK DES, 1990, p. 6). Whether the implied equivalence between YT and full-time education is merited is debatable. The low skill levels achieved on YTS, and the lack of effective quality control, have been widely criticized (Steedman, 1988; Lee, Marsden, Rickman and Duncombe, 1990). Despite a philosophy emphasizing generic and transferable skills, YTS training appeared to have little value in the external labour market (Raffe, 1988; Roberts and Parsell, 1989; Whitfield and Bourlakis, 1989). However, a final judgement must await the development of YT and especially of the reformed vocational qualifications that will provide the currency for the new training market. The British 'mixed model' is still on trial.

The US, by contrast, approximates to a 'schooling model' of post-compulsory education (OECD, 1985). Young people who leave secondary school before completion have more clearly left the mainstream than have their British peers. However, they still have several options. One is to go back and complete secondary school. Because of recent national concern over the long-term economic and social problems of high school dropouts, many states have developed programmes to serve these groups and provide alternative paths to completing high school (Rumberger, 1990). Students can enrol in adult education classes offered by local school districts or they can attend the local community college and take courses that can be used to secure a high school diploma. Recent studies show that between 20 and 45 percent of high school dropouts eventually earn some sort of secondary school diploma or equivalent certificate (ibid.).

Another option for high school dropouts is to receive further education and training outside of the regular education system. The federal government funds several programmes, most of which provide occupational training rather than formal education. But all these efforts serve a very small fraction of the dropout population. For example, the largest programme, the Job Training Partnership Act (JTPA) Title II-A, serves an average of 200,000 dropouts each year (83,000 below the age of 22) out of an estimated 11 million who are eligible for these services (Rumberger, 1990, Table 5). Moreover, some have questioned how effective such programmes are (Levitan and Gallo, 1988). There is also a host of public and private educational and training programmes for high school dropouts. The lack of any comprehensive federal data makes it difficult to know how many youths are being served by these programmes, but it appears that only a small fraction of all dropouts are assisted.

The other major option for dropouts is regular employment. Approximately 50 percent of all high school dropouts were employed in 1986 (US Bureau of the Census, 1989, Table 636). But employment prospects, both in the short term and the long term, are much worse for dropouts than for high school graduates. For example, in 1987 unemployment rates for high school dropouts 16-24 years old were twice as high as for high school graduates not enrolled at school (ibid.). And dropouts earn, on average, about two-thirds of what a high school graduate earns (Rumberger, 1990).

Largely implicit in the foregoing discussion is the differing extent and nature of flexibility in the two national systems of education and training. In the UK, flexibility is sought largely by offering vocational or work-based alternatives to school. In addition, some students use the first post-compulsory year in full-time education as a catching-up year, either repeating subjects for compulsory-school exams or taking lower-level vocational courses in order to qualify for higher-level ones. In Scotland, the shorter duration (one year) and wider accessibility of the Higher, and the modular structure of vocational qualifications, promote more flexibility than in England. But nowhere in the UK does more than a tiny minority of teenagers return to full-time education having left it, or switch back from vocational to academic tracks (Gray and Sime, 1990). In the US, more individuals return to education to achieve academic qualifications, including young and adult dropouts who can enrol in adult schools and community colleges to complete secondary school and even higher education credentials. It is much more common than in the UK for teenagers to return to full-time education after a break of a year or two (US Department of Education, 1988). It is also much easier to transfer credits between institutions. However there is less flexibility for 16-18 year olds in the sense that all students, no matter what their educational and career aspirations, must complete the same set of academic courses in order to obtain a high school diploma.

Opportunities at 18 and beyond

Only about 20 percent of Britons continue in full-time education beyond 18. A majority of these are in higher education which they enter following two post-compulsory years at school. Most of the remaining 80 percent of the cohort are in the full-time labour market. This group includes 20 percent who are still attending part-time courses, about half of these on day courses, usually on day release from jobs or apprenticeships, and the other half in evening classes only. The proportion in part-time education declines sharply with age. Education and training opportunities for adults, often part-time, are offered by FE colleges, and various private colleges and trainers. About a quarter of UK entrants to higher education are aged 21 or over – the proportion being much higher for polytechnics (34 percent) than for universities (11 percent) (Smithers and Robinson, 1989, p. 9). Apart from government training schemes for the unemployed, most other education or training opportunities for adults are provided or sponsored by firms and are subject to relatively little state subsidy or control.

Upon completion of high school at the age of 18, education and training options for American youth are much greater. About 50 percent of all high school graduates go on to higher education. The higher education system in the US consists of a large number of public and private institutions offering a wide range of academic and vocational programmes, from one- and two-year occupational certificates to doctoral studies. Higher education opportunities remain available throughout a worker's lifetime – almost 40 percent of all enrolments in higher education are over the age of 25 (US Bureau of the Census, 1989, Table 246). In addition, many private-sector firms provide a variety of training courses and programmes to their employees. In fact, most part-time education and training of adults is undertaken by persons already employed – almost 19 million people in 1984, or 18 percent of the employed workforce (US Bureau of the Census, 1989, Table 275).

The other major option at age 18 is full-time employment. About 50 percent of all youth aged 18 to 21 are not enrolled in school, with about 75 percent of this group employed and the remainder either unemployed or not in the labour force. The vast majority of those employed are working full-time (US Bureau of the Census, 1989, Tables 242, 243 and 636).

Overview

Our discussion has pointed to several differences between the two countries: in the British 'mixed model' compared with the US 'schooling model', and the status of alternatives to schooling; in the status of 16 year-old leavers (completers versus dropouts); in youth labour markets; in the formal differentiation of 16-18 year olds; in levels of participation; in the extent of overlap between academic and vocational tracks; in certification; and in the flexibility of educational routes. This should not detract from the enormous variation that exists within each country. We have alluded to national differences within the UK. In some respects Scotland, with its more uniformly comprehensive system, higher participation, more school-based system, less specialized curriculum and more flexible course structure, is closer than England to the US model.

Current Issues

A number of similar issues have arisen recently in both countries regarding ways to improve the provision of education and training for 16-18 year olds. Here we discuss three – raising the participation of 16-18 year olds on education and training programmes, altering the balance of academic and vocational training and reforming the certification that students receive. We describe some features of these debates and explore similarities and differences in the way these issues are characterized and in the responses to them.

Participation

In both countries, current debates about education and training are dominated by the perceived need to raise levels of participation, and consequently levels of attainment, among 16-18 year olds. The diagnosis and explanation of this 'need' are similar in each country. The adoption of new technology is perceived to increase skill needs, and in both countries there have been attempts to promote computer literacy and information technology in the secondary school curriculum. However, it is coming to be realized that such reactions may be based on an inadequate analysis of future employment needs (Wellington, 1989): rather than educating all students in the new technologies themselves, education should try to meet the demands of new methods of production and work organization which new technologies may facilitate (Rumberger and Levin, 1989). The proportion of white-collar jobs, and particularly of professional and managerial jobs, is projected to continue to grow (IER, 1989). More importantly, the reorganization of work is believed to require more flexible and responsive workers with a wider range of skills and with different kinds of skills. 'As manual work declines, the emphasis is on individual responsibility for activities which stress relationships with people and information... Individuals are less likely to be recruited to undertake a specific task and more likely to be hired to help achieve corporate objectives requiring the commitment of abilities, ideas and skills.' (CBI, 1989, p.11). The imperatives of economic change are perceived to be heightened by international competition. Competition from Japan and the Pacific rim is a stimulus for change in both countries, although the UK reforms are directed as much to attracting inward Japanese investment as to winning any outright competition with Japan. Both the UK and the US expect the Single European Market to increase competitive pressures, either within or from the European Community.

However, despite these similarities in economic analysis, there are major differences in the debates about how to increase participation levels. Perhaps most importantly, the context of the debates is very different and this is symbolized by a difference in terminology. In the UK the main concern is to increase 'staying-on'; in the US it is to reduce 'dropping-out'. In the UK the aim is to encourage young people who have already completed a recognized stage of education to begin a new one; in the US the debate is essentially about course completion. In the UK the aim is to convert a minority (who currently remain in full-time education to 18) into a majority; in the US the aim is to reduce an already small minority, whose minority status makes their relative disadvantage even more acute. Arguably, the US problem merely anticipates problems which the UK will face if its current aim of increasing participation is realized. For this aim is only likely to be achieved by targeting the middle-attaining group who are currently on the margins of staying or leaving, and by increasing the educational and economic rewards to middle-attaining stayers relative to low-attaining dropouts. But the US experience suggests that this in turn may aggravate the relative position of those who continue to drop out. It is ironic that some US educational experts seek to introduce greater diversity into 16-plus age group education, and even to develop a system that at first sight has much in common with the UK's mixed model.

A further contextual difference is in the youth labour markets of the two countries. In the UK the labour market provides an alternative to full-time education, and a powerful counter-attraction particularly for middle-attaining 16 year olds. In the US, by contrast, many dropouts do not enter the full-time labour market, and the available jobs offer few rewards in either the short or the long term. By offering casual and part-time employment to enable young people to work their way through school, the US youth labour market is more a complement than an alternative to full-time education (US Department of Education, 1988).

A third difference between debates in the two countries lies in the relative importance attached to participation at 16-18 compared with 18-plus. In the US the main emphasis is on the 16-18 stage; the level of subsequent college participation, at around 50 percent, is generally considered to be already acceptable. The UK debate is more ambivalent. On the one hand there is a widespread feeling, arising especially from international comparisons of attainment in education, that Britain fares worst in respect of the 'bottom half'. On the other hand recruitment difficulties are most likely to be experienced at higher skill levels; and current debates about the 16-18 stage were stimulated in part by fears (since dispelled) that the flow of students to higher education would fall drastically during the current demographic downturn. Staying-on at 16 is the strongest predictor of subsequent demand for higher education, and one of the arguments for improving participation at 16 is that it will increase the flow of students to higher education (Smithers and Robinson, 1989). Ambivalence in the British debate is further reflected in tensions which are mainly latent: should the increased provision for 16-18 year olds be designed primarily to steer them into higher education, or to equip them for entry to the labour force at 18?

Fourth, demographic changes lend a very different flavour to the debate in the two countries. In Britain, the demographic decline has been largely concentrated among the lower social classes who have been most likely to leave at 16 (Smithers and Robinson, 1989). This has led to a crisis in the labour market, particularly in the prosperous South-east, where employers have had to compete for a shrinking supply of young labour. But it has also encouraged a rising trend in participation in full-time education. In the US, by contrast, the ethnic and social groups which have traditionally provided most dropouts have been growing rapidly (Pallas, Natriello and McDill, 1989). For instance, population projections suggest that the number of white 18 to 24 year-olds will decline by 25 percent between 1985 and 2020, while the number of Hispanic youths will increase by 65 percent (US Bureau of the Census, 1986, Table T). In the UK the ethnic minority population is also growing faster than other groups, but this is not perceived to cause general problems for participation levels. This is partly because ethnic minority groups constitute a much smaller proportion of the total population, and partly because they tend, other things being equal, to have lower dropout rates than whites (Gray, Jesson, Pattie and Sime, 1990). Social class differentials are much more important. In the UK, therefore, the policy goal in respect of participation is to reinforce the effects of a favourable demographic trend; in the US it is to alleviate the effects of an unfavourable one. It should be pointed out, however, that both countries face a declining youth population, which will place increased emphasis on the continuing education and retraining of adults (Rumberger and Levin, 1989, NEDO, 1988).

Finally, the two countries tend to produce different answers to the question about which form increased participation should take. Should it be in full-time education or in other (e.g. part-time or work-based) forms of education or training? In the UK, recent proposals have typically been framed in terms of levels of attainment rather than of participation. Targets are proposed for the percentages reaching different qualification levels by 18; the means by which these levels are achieved – whether full-time education, part-time education or work-based training – are left to the individual and/or the 'market'. The existing 'mixed model' is accepted as a given by many contributors to UK debates, with the precise mixture often left to the market to arbitrate. This can add to the confusion of such debates. It is common for commentators to cite low participation in full-time education as evidence of the British problem, but to propose solutions that may leave full-time participation unchanged while raising participation and/or standards in other forms of post-compulsory provision. Conversely, in the US the persistence of the schooling model is generally taken for granted. There are no large movements to break up the monopoly of the comprehensive public high school as the sole provider of education and training for 16-18 year olds. But some states have created or considered creating more options for 16-18 year-old youths. In Minnesota, students can complete the last two years of secondary school at any public or private post-secondary institution within the state. And in California, a recent report issued by an influential group of business leaders called for the completion of secondary education at age 16, at which time students would have several choices: additional academic schooling; vocational schooling; public service; or employment (BW Associates, 1988).

Altering the Mix of Vocational and Academic

The same considerations which have prompted efforts to raise participation are driving debates about the mix between academic and vocational education. Of all current debates in 16-18 year old education this is the hardest to summarize, because the very terms of the debate are contested: it is essentially a debate about the definitions both of vocational education and of general education. The underlying issue is how to prepare future workers for productive participation in a more competitive work environment characterized by the use of new technologies and new forms of workplace organization.

Currently in both the UK and the US there is a mixed system of vocational and academic preparation from which youth can choose. However the boundaries between these sectors are more distinct in the UK, where vocational and academic education tend to be provided for different students, in different institutions, and lead to different qualifications. One consequence is that curricular debates in the UK tend to be framed, and fragmented, by the 'mixed model'; debates are conducted separately in the different sectors with a reluctance to pursue common ground across them (Hodkinson, 1991; IPPR, 1990). In the US, nearly all vocational and academic training takes place within comprehensive high schools where all students have to meet the prescribed academic qualifications for graduation. Vocational training comprises, at most, a part-time programme for those students who elect to take it.

There were two main trends in this area of UK policy during the 1980s: first, a tendency to favour the development of vocational rather than academic education; and second, a gradual re-definition of vocational education to emphasize more generic competencies such as personal and social skills, problem-solving and communication skills which are delivered as much through reforms of pedagogy as through the formal curriculum. Examples of this 'new vocationalism' include the Technical and Vocational Education Initiative (TVEI) in full-time education, new 'pre-vocational' courses such as the Certificate of Pre-Vocational Education (CPVE), and some YTS schemes. These developments have affected compulsory as well as post-compulsory education.

However many of these programmes were initially targeted at lower-attaining students who only remained in education or training because they could not find jobs. As a result, broader-based approaches to vocational education have tended to be stigmatized. Even within vocational education, approaches emphasizing generic competencies tend to be seen as undemanding, trivial in content and suitable only for students who need a more general vocational preparation because they have been unable to find a particular occupation to train for or because the job they have found is too low-level to require more specific training. Despite this, government and business leaders have recently agreed on the need to develop generic competencies, personal and social as well as cognitive, among all 16-18 year olds, in academic as well as vocational programmes (Baker, 1989; CBI, 1989; see also Hodkinson, 1989). A common 'core' curriculum for all 16-18 year olds is now a prospect, even if the development of this core is still taking place separately within academic and vocational sectors.

The US has no national curriculum or minimum standards for graduation from high school. Both of these are set by the 50 state education departments and they vary quite widely. Although several national reform reports have called for national standards for graduation, including four years of English, three years of social studies, three years of science, and three years of mathematics, only about 50 percent of all graduates in 1987 had achieved those levels (US Department of Education, 1989, Table 117).

The striking feature of recent US debates, in comparison with those in the UK, is that the underlying issues and arguments have been very similar, but they have been applied to a different institutional context. Indeed, some of the arguments for vocationalism in the UK are very similar to current arguments for academic education in the US. In the US, the major push has been to increase the academic requirements for high school graduation on the basis that academic skills, especially those referred to as higher-order skills such as reasoning and problem-solving, will be increasingly required in jobs, and that such skills facilitate the future learning of more specific job skills over a worker's lifetime as jobs change and as workers more frequently change jobs. This contrasts with Britain where the 'new vocationalism', rather than academic education, is often expected to meet the need for these skills. The increase in academic requirements in the US has meant that less vocational education is being undertaken at the secondary level and more at the post-secondary level. For example, between 1982 and 1987, students in American high schools increased the average number of courses they completed in academic areas, while they decreased the number of courses they completed in vocational areas (US National Centre for Education Statistics 1989, Table 115). Altogether, about two-thirds of the courses taken by American high school graduates in 1987 were in academic areas compared to about one-sixth in vocational areas (ibid.).

Defenders of secondary vocational education argue that it provides an effective approach for keeping potential high-school dropouts in school and that it can provide viable basic and occupational skills training (Dunham, 1989). These same arguments are used to defend the more institutionalized 'mixed model' of academic and vocational training found in the UK. The argument is that only a suitable mix of vocational and academic training will be able to meet the variable abilities and interests of students and the variable needs of the labour market. Within the academic arena, recent proposals in the US, like the UK, have focused on the need for pedagogical reform and a broadening of the curriculum to cover personal and social skills as well as applied, cognitive skills (National Academy of Sciences, 1984). Some critics have argued that schools should broaden not only the types of academic skills they teach, but also the manner in which they are taught and the way they are assessed, in order to make these skills more relevant and functional to their actual use in the workplace (Resnick, 1987). The vocational education community has come to realize that the only way to save a place for vocational education in the secondary schools is to make the skills training more generic. For instance, the recently enacted US Vocational Education Act calls for more academic training in vocational curricula and mandates that states assess the impact of vocational training in four areas: basic skills; industrial competency; decision-making; and problem-solving (*Education Week*, 1 August, 1990).

These differences are difficult to summarize. The UK seems to have made more progress in implementing the kinds of pedagogical reforms and broader concepts of skill that are the subject of current debate in the US. Conversely minimum requirements for graduation in the US have – albeit with wide state variations – enforced a kind of core curriculum, a concept towards which the UK is slowly moving. In both countries there is wide agreement on the general need to defer occupationally specific training. However the clearest conclusion from our comparison is that the conventional labels of 'academic' and 'vocational' are inadequate to describe current debates on the curriculum, which have as much to do with qualitative differences within these categories as with the balance between them.

Certification

The British education and training system is substantially qualifications-driven and most proposals to reform it have implications for certification. Recent government policies have focused on vocational qualifications, which are awarded by a large and poorly coordinated collection of examining/validating bodies. In 1986 the government established a National Council for Vocational Qualifications (NCVQ) to provide greater coordination. The NCVQ does not itself award certifications, but it accredits qualifications that satisfy certain criteria as National Vocational Qualifications (NVQs). NVQs must normally be based on industry-defined standards; 'lead bodies' have been nominated for each sector of industry to define standards for each occupation and thus to help identify appropriate NVQs. The NCVQ's remit does not extend to Scotland. Indeed there is something distinctively English about the NCVQ approach. The warring fiefdoms of the numerous examining/validating bodies are left unchallenged, while rationalization and simplification are pursued by introducing yet further layers of institutions, procedures and acronyms. In Scotland, a more radical reform of vocational qualifications was carried out earlier in the 1980s, when nearly all non-advanced vocational qualifications were replaced by a single National Certificate, which included more than 2000 modules designed to a standard framework. However, throughout the UK the main academic qualifications (the A level and the Higher) remain largely unreformed. The NCVQ has been criticized for obstructing further integration of academic and vocational qualifications by imposing criteria that stress workplace competence and assessment and by recognizing excessively narrow qualifications as NVQs (Spours, 1989). The Scottish National Certificate is more 'education-led' and less vulnerable to this accusation (Raffe, 1991).

As described earlier, there is no national system of certification for secondary school graduates in the US except for a high school diploma, which only signifies whether a person has successfully completed the requirements of graduation. Thus, employers have information neither concerning what subjects students have studied nor how well they performed in those subjects. Moreover, some employers complain that the standards for high school graduation are so lax that some graduates are functionally illiterate (US Departments of Labor, Education, and Commerce, 1988), and that their inability to discriminate among job-applicants discourages their recruiting high school graduates for more responsible jobs. Conversely, the absence of certification means that high school students who do not plan to enter college have little incentive to achieve more than the minimum required for a high school diploma (Bishop, 1989). As a result, several proposals have been introduced to provide a comprehensive system of certification for high school graduates. Already several states have begun working on state systems that would document the competencies of graduates, not only in traditional academic areas, but also in vocational fields and such areas as attendance and leadership. During the fall of 1989, the National Business Association called for the development of a national system of certification that would also provide employers with detailed information on high school graduates in a broad array of areas (*Education Week*, 15 November, 1989). At present, there is no national system of certification for post-secondary vocational programmes since both the provision and the certification of post-secondary programmes are left to the states.

The terms of the debate concerning certification thus differ between the two countries. The US debate is about developing public certification. The UK already has public certification, which plays an important role in structuring the education and training system; reform of certification is therefore a means to reform wider aspects of the system. Arguments about participation and the curriculum, discussed above, have typically been expressed in terms of proposals to reform academic and/or vocational qualifications, or to integrate the two.

Despite this, there are several similarities between UK and US debates about certification. In both countries the reform (or introduction) of national certification is perceived to promote a number of common objectives: to raise standards of attainment; to improve student motivation; to increase the relevance of education (or training) to employment; and to promote uniformity, or at least coherence, within the education and training system. Underlying these common objectives, effective certification is perceived in both countries as a way to promote market mechanisms. Qualifications comprise the currency for education and training markets. In the UK, NVQs seek to provide reliable information on 'outputs', so that decisions on educational 'inputs' can be left to individual choice and/or the market. NVQs can also be seen as part of a strategy to revive occupational labour markets, which can only function effectively when there is agreement on occupational definitions and standards (see Marsden, 1986). In the US, it is argued that certification would encourage employers, not only to recruit high school graduates with more confidence (and therefore to more responsible jobs), but also to discriminate in favour of more 'relevant' programmes (Bishop, 1989). In both countries certification can strengthen the labour market for the relevant age group. Ironically this is an argument for introducing public certification at 18 in the US, in order to strengthen the 18-plus age group labour market, and for abolishing it at 16 in the UK, where the 16-plus age group labour market is already too strong. One problem of the strategy of qualifications-as-currency is that it rests heavily on the validity and (equally important) the credibility of assessment. If this is lacking, as is perhaps the case in respect of personal and interpersonal skills, the currency is debased and the market cannot operate effectively.

Learning not Borrowing

Despite the enormous differences between the two systems, our account has revealed several common themes. Other areas of current debate – notably the introduction of market mechanisms into education, discussed elsewhere in this volume – also reveal underlying similarities. But we have also demonstrated important differences, not only in the institutions of education and training but also in their social, labour-market and governmental contexts. This raises the question of appropriability: are attempts to learn or borrow from each other's experience invalidated by these institutional and contextual differences? Or can useful learning take place, despite these differences? There are, we think, at least four forms which such learning or borrowing could profitably take.

Increasing self-awareness.   First, making comparisons can, at the very least, identify alternatives to the present system that may not be apparent otherwise. For instance, our analysis confirms the utility of a broad distinction between 'mixed' and 'schooling' models of post-compulsory education. In the UK, the 'mixed model' tends to be taken for granted. Most policy debates are not only premised on the 'mixed model' but also fragmented by it, with parallel but separate debates and reforms within the different sectors (Hodkinson, 1991). One effect of UK comparisons with school-based systems such as the US may be to place the persistence, modification or abolition of the 'mixed model' on the explicit policy agenda (IPPR, 1990; Raffe, 1992). Conversely the US system, and US differences, have often been premised on the role of schools as principal providers up to 18, and on a common core in the high school programme; alternative sources or types of provision have at best a marginal and interstitial role.

Negative borrowing. A second, though similar, type of learning can take place when increased self-awareness helps a country recognize features of its own system that are dysfunctional, or which obstruct other policy aims. The UK system can learn from the absence of public certification at the age of 16 in the US, and from its lack of a strong labour market for 16-18 year olds. Both of these features of the British system obstruct efforts to raise participation in full-time education.

Warnings. A third type of learning can take place through more direct comparisons between specific features or policies in the two systems. While education systems may not evolve according to a uniform linear model, it is possible for each system to observe in the other features that it expects or hopes to develop in the future. This can provide warnings as well as encouragement. For example, the high rates of participation in the US may encourage attempts to raise participation in the UK; but the US experience also suggests that some diversity of provision will still be required. Even in a predominantly school-based system, it may be unrealistic to expect a single institution such as school (or college) to cater to everybody (Rumberger, 1987). Conversely the UK experience may offer a warning to those Americans pursuing reforms of pedagogy and a broadening of the curriculum in favour of personal and social skills. The introduction of such reforms must be handled carefully if the new pedagogy and curriculum are not to be stigmatized as appropriate only for the less able or the less employable.

Functional equivalences. A fourth type of learning can take place when comparisons are made between functionally equivalent stages or sectors of educational systems rather than, for example, between similar age groups. A possible starting point is Squires' (1989) distinction between general, foundation and specific stages of education. Our comparison suggests that while 16-18 year old education and training may span a range of these stages within each country (especially within the more differentiated UK system), on balance it tends to represent a more 'advanced' stage in the UK than in the US system. This in turn reflects earlier leaving patterns in the UK, where students of a given age are, on average, closer to finishing their initial education and training. It is possible that the UK system at 16-plus has as much in common with the US system at 18-plus as with the US system at 16-plus. Certainly the participation rates, institutional diversity and increased differentiation of US education beyond 18 resemble those of UK education beyond 16. US community colleges perform a similar function to FE colleges in the UK, despite the different average ages of their students (although both cater for a very wide age range). Americans interested in public certification at 18, and in its potential for motivating students and encouraging a labour market for high school graduates, would probably learn more from studying UK certification at 16 years than at 18 years. Lessons from YTS and other training schemes for 16-18 year-olds in the UK are probably more applicable to young adults than to under-18s in America. However while American borrowing from the UK may be based on stage rather than age, the converse (that is, UK borrowing from the US on this basis) may not always apply. Rather than accept its different relation of stage to age as a 'given', might not the UK wish to defer some of the stages of education so that they more clearly match the US pattern?

Conclusion

While each of these types of learning can take place through international comparisons between education and training systems, there are two important limitations that may inhibit such learning. This is especially true in the third and fourth types listed above, where direct comparisons and borrowing take place. The first limitation is that any comparisons must recognize and respect institutional and contextual differences in the two systems of education and training. Successful borrowing always involves a degree of analytical abstraction in the identification of the feature that is borrowed. The greater the institutional and contextual differences, the greater the level of abstraction required. For this reason, it may be more useful to talk about 'learning' than about 'borrowing'. One cannot simply import specific foreign institutions or policies. It is debatable whether this lesson has been heeded in recent examples of policy borrowing. For example, when Private Industry Councils (PICs) crossed the Atlantic to become Training and Enterprise Councils (TECs or LECs) (Bailey, this volume, Part 3), was there any serious consideration of the differences between the 'mixed' and 'schooling' models, and in particular of the different roles of public training programmes and their different relationships with the education system? Whatever their potential benefits, TECs threaten to aggravate the problems of coordination and coherence in education and training for 16-18 year olds. This threat would not have been apparent from observing US PICs, which have had relatively little to do with this age group.

The second potential limitation is inherent in the political process. Would policy-makers make appropriate use of comparative evidence, even if such evidence took these contextual differences into account? Some commentators perceive policy-making as a largely political process that makes limited use of existing data and empirical evidence (Bulmer, Banting, Blume, Carley and Weiss, 1986). Others observe that policy borrowing – at least in the UK – has tended to be unreflective, ad hoc and ideologically filtered, and has tended to inhibit the coherence and stability badly needed in the system (Keep, 1991). However we believe that various forms of learning and borrowing can be useful, provided that policy-makers are prepared to learn before they borrow.

Acknowledgements

The support of the UK Economic and Social Research Council, of which the Centre for Educational Sociology is a Designated Research Centre [grant no. XCOO 280004] is gratefully acknowledged.

References

Baker, K. (1989) 'Further education: A new strategy', Speech at the annual conference of the Association of Colleges of Further and Higher Education, 15 February, London, DES.

Bishop, J.H. (1989) 'Why the apathy in American high schools?' Educational Researcher, 18, pp.6-10.

Bulmer, M., Banting, K.G., Blume, S.S., Carley, M. and Weiss, C.H. (1986) Social Science and Social Policy, London, Allen & Unwin.

BW Associates (1988) Restructuring California Education, Recommendations to the California Business Roundtable, Berkeley, CA, Berman Weiler Associates.

Confederation of British Industry (1989) Towards a Skills Revolution: A Youth Charter, London, CBI.

Dunham, D.B. (1989) 'Vocational education in the secondary school: the case for continuation', Economics of Education Review, 8, 1, pp.89-74.

Education Week, 15 November 1989, p.1. Education Week, 1 August 1990, p.2.

Gray, J., Jesson, D., Pattie, C. and Sime, N. (1990) Education and Training Opportunities in the Inner City, Research and Development No. 51, Youth Cohort Series No. 7, Sheffield, Training Agency.

Gray, J. and Sime, N. (1990) Patterns of Participation in Full-Time Post-Compulsory Education, Research and Development No. 61, Sheffield, Training Agency.

Hodkinson, P. (1989) 'Crossing the academic/vocational divide: Personal effectiveness and autonomy as an integrating theme in post-16 education', British Journal of Educational Studies, 37, 4, pp.369-383.

Hodkinson, P. (1991, forthcoming) 'Liberal education and the new vocationalism: A progressive partnership', Oxford Review of Education.

Institute for Employment Research (1989) Review of the Economy and Employment: Occupational Assessment, IER, University of Warwick.

Institute for Public Policy Research (1990) A British 'Baccalaureat'? Ending the Division between Education and Training, London, IPPR.

Keep, E. (1991) 'The grass looked greener: Some thoughts on the influence of comparative vocational training research on the UK policy debate', in Ryan, P. (ed) International Comparisons of Vocational Education and Training for Intermediate Skills, Basingstoke, Falmer.

Lee, D., Marsden, D., Rickman, P. and Duncombe, J. (1990) Scheming for Youth: A Study of YTS in the Enterprise Culture, Milton Keynes, Open University.

Levitan, S.A. and Gallo, F (1988) A Second Chance: Training for Jobs, Kalamazoo, MI, W E Upjohn Institute for Employment Research.

Marsden, D. (1986) The End of Economic Man? Custom and Competition in Labour Markets, Brighton, Wheatsheaf.

National Academy of Sciences (1984) High Schools and the Changing Workforce, Report of the Panel on Secondary School Education for the Changing Workplace, Washington DC, National Academy Press.

National Economic Development Office (1988) Young People and the Labour Market: A Challenge for the 1990s, London, Training Commission and NEDO.

Organisation for Economic Cooperation and Development (1985) Education and Training after Basic Schooling, Paris, OECD.

Pallas, A.M., Natriello, G. and McDill, E.L. (1989) 'The changing nature of the disadvantaged population: Current dimensions and future trends', Educational Researcher, 18, pp.16-22.

Raffe, D. (1984) 'School attainment and the labour market' in Raffe, D. (ed.) Fourteen to Eighteen, Aberdeen, Aberdeen University Press.

Raffe, D. (1988) 'Going with the grain: Youth training in transition', in Brown, S. and Wake, R. (eds) Education in Transition, Edinburgh, Scottish Council for Research in Education.

Raffe, D. (1991) 'Scotland v England: The place of "home internationals" in comparative research', in Ryan, P. (ed) International Comparisons of Vocational Education and Training for Intermediate Skills, Basingstoke, Falmer.

Raffe, D. (1992) 'Beyond the "mixed model": Social research and the case for reform of 16-18s education in Britain', in Crouch, C. and Heath, A. (eds) Social Research and Social Reform, Oxford, Oxford University Press.

Raffe, D. and Courtenay, G. (1988) '16-18 on both sides of the border', in Raffe, D. (ed) Education and the Youth Labour Market, Basingstoke, Falmer.

Raffe, D. and Willms, J.D. (1989) 'Schooling the discouraged worker: Local-labour-market effects on educational participation', Sociology, 23, 4, pp.559-581.

Resnick, L. (1987) 'Learning in school and out', Educational Researcher, 16, 9, pp.13-20.

Roberts, K., Dench, S. and Richardson, D. (1987) The Changing Structure of Youth Labour Markets, Research Paper No. 59, London, Department of Employment.

Roberts, K. and Parsell, G. (1989) 'The stratification of youth training', ESRC 16-19 Initiative Occasional Paper 11, London, City University, Social Statistics Research Unit.

Roberts, K. Siwek, M. and Parsell, G. (1989) 'What are Britain's 16-19 year olds learning?', ESRC Initiative Occasional Paper 10, London, City University, Social Statistics Research Unit.

Rumberger, R.W. (1987) 'High School dropouts: A review of issues and evidence', Review of Educational Research, 57, 2, pp.101-121.

Rumberger, R.W. (1990) 'Second chance for high school dropouts: Dropout recovery programs in the United States', in Inbar, D. (ed.), Second chance in education: An interdisciplinary and international perspective, Philadelphia, Falmer Press.

Rumberger, R.W. and Levin, H. (1989) 'Schooling for the modern workplace', in Commission on Workforce Quality and Labour Market Efficiency, Investing in People: A Strategy for Addressing America's Workforce Crisis, Background Papers, Vol.1, Washington DC, US Department of Labor.

Ryrie, A.C. (1981) Routes and Results: A Study of the Later Years of Schooling, Sevenoaks, Hodder and Stoughton.

Sako, M. and Dore, R. (1986) 'How the Youth Training Scheme helps employers', Employment Gazette, 95, 6, pp.195-204.

Smithers, A. and Robinson, P. (1989) Increasing Participation in Higher Education, London, BP Educational Service.

Spours, K. (1989) 'Promoting progression: Prospects for a post-16 modular framework', Post 16 Education Centre, University of London Institute of Education (mimeo).

Squires, G. (1989) Pathways to learning, Paris, OECD.

Steedman, H. (1988) 'Vocational training in France and Britain: Mechanical and electrical craftsmen', Discussion Paper No. 130, London, National Institute of Economic and Social Research.

UK Department of Education and Science (1990) International Statistical Comparisons of the Education and Training of 16 to 18 Year Olds, Statistical Bulletin 1/90, London, DES.

UK Department of Employment (1989) 'Education and labour market status of young people in Great Britain', Employment Gazette, 97, May, pp.262-263.

US Bureau of the Census (1986) Projections of the Hispanic Population: 1987 to 2080, Current Population Reports, Series P-25, No. 995. Washington DC, US Government Printing Office.

US Bureau of the Census (1989) Statistical Abstract of the United States, 1989, 109th edition, Washington DC, US Government Printing Office.

US Bureau of the Census (1990) School Enrolment: Social and Economic Characteristics of Students: October 1987 and 1988, Current Population Reports, Series P-20, No. 443. Washington DC, US Government Printing Office.

US Department of Education (1984) The Condition of Education, 1984 edition, Washington DC, US Government Printing Office.

US Department of Education (1988) Education and Training of 16-19 Year Olds after Compulsory Schooling in the United States, Paris, OECD.

US Departments of Labor, Education & Commerce (1988) Building A Quality Work Force, Washington DC, US Government Printing Office.

US National Centre for Educational Statistics (1989) Digest of Education Statistics 1989, 25th edition, Washington DC, US Government Printing Office.

Wellington, J. J. (1989) Education for Employment: The Place of Information Technology, Windsor, NFER-Nelson.

Whitfield, K. and Bourlakis, C. (1989) 'An empirical analysis of YTS, employment and earnings', Discussion Paper No. 42, Institute for Employment Research, University of Warwick.

Part 3

Part 3

The Mission of TECs and Private Sector Involvement in Training: Lessons from Private Industry Councils

THOMAS BAILEY

In the United States and Great Britain, substantial educational reform is underway, shaped by the perceptions that the education systems are failing to prepare the workforce for the challenges of a modern, fast changing, global economy. That some policy makers in Great Britain should have looked across the Atlantic for answers to their educational problems is perhaps surprising, given the current low repute, justified or not, of American schooling. Nevertheless, during the spring of 1990, based to a large extent on a model imported from the United States, the Training and Enterprise Councils (TECs) were launched with a broad mission to promote radical reform in the training of the British workforce.

The inspiration for the TECs came more or less directly from the Private Industry Councils (PICs) that have existed in the US since 1978. The PICs currently oversee the local administration of programs under the Job Training Partnership Act (JTPA)– the most important federal program in the United States charged with training and job search assistance for the poor.

The TEC strategy was first advocated in 1988 by the Employment Secretary, Norman Fowler, after a visit to some PICs in the United States. The debt that the TECs owe to the PICs is further revealed by the prominent role that Americans, like Catherine Stratton, have played in advising the British government on the design and implementation of the TECs. She was retained because of her experience working with the Boston PIC. Additionally, the discussion around the planning and implementation of the TECs is replete with references to experience of the PICs.[1]

This chapter has two objectives. The first is to analyze whether the PICs as they have developed in the United States are an appropriate model for the objectives that the TECs are designed to meet. The short answer to this question is that while there are many similarities between the objectives of the PICs and the TECs, there are some fundamental differences. In particular, the PICs are charged with a mission that is much narrower than the mission advocated for the TECs. The first section of the chapter describes the evolution of JTPA, analyzing its original structure and intent, as well as more recent modifications. The section then compares PICs with TECs, and finds that their differences call into question the extent to which PICs should be seen as a model for TECs.

The second objective is to draw some lessons for the TECs from existing research on the PIC experience. In particular, the chapter focuses on the disappointing contribution of business executives in improving JTPA performance, and on the way performance standards shape PIC activity. Here, the brief conclusion is that PIC experience suggests private sector involvement is unlikely to have the impact that the TEC planners expect. Indeed, there is little evidence that the PICs have had a positive influence. During the early stages of the JTPA, there was great enthusiasm for a direct and extensive private sector involvement. Although the participation and support of prominent business people is still sought and valued, current discussions of JTPA reform suggest a diminished reliance on private sector involvement as a central engine of change.

This is not to say that the TEC strategy will be unable to improve the training of the British labor force – such a conclusion is beyond the scope of this chapter. Rather the purpose of the chapter is to help clarify what can or cannot be learned from the US experience with the PICs. Can something be learned from a program with a different scope and purpose? Will involvement of the private sector have the kind of effects the UK hopes? Does US experience suggest key features that present TEC design overlooks?

The Job Training Partnership Act

The Job Training Partnership Act (JTPA) was passed in 1982 with a spending authorization of $3.6 billion. The JTPA replaced the Comprehensive, Employment, and Training Act (CETA) of 1973. The JTPA was a product of the intense antagonism towards the public sector of the early Reagan years. During the late 1970s, federal employment and training initiatives funded by the CETA appeared to exemplify the failure of public sector activities isolated from the discipline of the market. For example, much of the CETA money was spent on providing clients with public sector employment (PSE). These jobs were often considered useless 'make work.' Although subsequent research has indicated that PSE raised earnings as much as other types of training, [2] a widespread impression existed that few clients left their public sector placements for un-subsidized jobs. Studies and evaluations found serious weaknesses in the management and monitoring structure of the CETA.[3] And so, justified or not, a general aura of waste, inefficiency, and even scandal developed around all of the CETA programs.

When JTPA replaced the CETA, it represented a sharp cut in federal training expenditures – by 1984, real federal expenditures on employment and training were almost 80 percent less than they had been during the late 1970s.[4] In addition to cuts in funding, the administration and Congress made four crucial changes during the introduction of JTPA. Each change offers lessons to the designers of TECs. The first change marked a shift in control from the US Department of Labor to the states; two other changes involved shifting training initiatives to a more market-oriented model; and the fourth involved efforts to increase the local-level co-ordination among related employment and training initiatives.

Decentralization. Under CETA, the US Department of Labor (DOL) retained significant control over federally funded employment and training efforts. The DOL contracted with hundreds of 'prime sponsors' – non-profit or local government agencies that were charged with administering the programs at the local level, usually through a network of subcontractors. Administrative control was exercised by regional DOL offices which highly scrutinized the operation of the prime sponsors and their sub-contractors. The states had only a minor role in CETA. With JTPA, however, the states assumed responsibility for oversight of local activities of the Service Delivery Areas (SDAs), the JTPA successors to CETA's prime sponsors, and for the allocation of funds and accountability.

Private Industry Councils. The Act explicitly gave people in private business some control over the design and management of the programs through the PICs. The PICs had been established as part of a small initiative to involve the private sector in the 1978 amendments to CETA, but their role was vastly expanded by the JTPA. According to the Act, the SDA policy is under the joint control of the PICs and local elected officials. The PICs are chaired by and have majority memberships of private businessmen who must be owners, chief executive officers, or officers with substantial policy positions in private firms. The locally elected officials are usually mayors, county executives, or a consortia of these officials in SDAs that encompass more than one political jurisdiction. The PIC and the elected officials jointly act as a board of directors for the local JTPA activities. They set policy as well as choose and oversee the individuals or organizations that carry out the policy.

Creating an Outcome-Oriented Program. The second market-oriented change involved a shift to an output driven accountability system. The JTPA replaced the administrative system in which the Department of Labor was directly involved in monitoring and regulating the programs at the local level, with a system that relies on providing incentives and sanctions to the SDAs when they achieve or fail to achieve prescribed standards of performance. SDA activities are judged against seven performance standards that measure the percent of the participants who are placed in jobs or other specified alternatives, the wages earned by the graduates, and the cost per participant.[5] The Act also established a structure of financial rewards for achieving the standards as well as sanctions for falling short. Thus, in effect, the JTPA set a price for a particular level of performance; then it gave the service delivery areas flexibility in how to achieve the goals. The report by the Senate Committee on Labor and Human Resources about the JTPA explicitly states the purpose of the standards:

> The legislation must insist on performance. The current CETA system does not have any effective means of measuring program results or penalizing non-performance. The new legislation will provide standards for judging the programs for what they accomplish – by whether those trained are hired and earn more as a result of training. It will end federal involvement with the process of how people are trained. It will provide for measurement of the outcomes and remove the Federal government from involvement in the details of program operations.[6]

The parallel to a market-oriented system emerges clearly in the relationship between the SDAs and the individual contracting firms or organizations that provide the services. The legislation encouraged the use of 'performance-based contracts.' Under CETA, subcontracts were based on detailed specifications of the costs of staffing and services used to provide training. Performance-based contracts simply set a price to be paid for providing a given service, such as placing a client on a job.

Local-Level Coordination. The JTPA emphasized the need to coordinate the various employment and training services available for the poor or unemployed. Funds were authorized by the Act to be used, under the direction of the PICs, to encourage institutional linkages and communication between JTPA contractors, welfare agencies, the employment service (federally funded job finding assistance linked to unemployment insurance), and other relevant institutions.

The PICs and the TECs Compared

Descriptions of the Training and Enterprise Councils reveal strong similarities between the approach that they represent on the one hand and the PICs and the JTPA on the other. The Training Agency prospectus states that "at least two thirds of the TEC board should be private sector employers who are chairmen, chief executives or top operational managers at the local level of major companies." The prospectus outlines five principles that will shape their character:[7]

(1) A locally based system
(2) An employer-led partnership
(3) A focused approach
(4) An accent on performance

(5) An enterprise organization

The first four principles correspond to the four changes that the JTPA brought about in the federal employment and training initiative. (The focused approach concept is based on the need to co-ordinate the various educational services and programs to create a coherent whole). The fifth principle, 'an enterprise organization' is described in the TEC Prospectus as follows:

> a new kind of organization will be needed, capable of driving radical reform. It must be locally based with the power and credibility to set goals, manage delivery and assess the impact of its investment. It must be an organization, born of the enterprise culture, with a bold vision that stretches beyond existing programmes, institutions, and traditional methods of delivery.[8]

The vision of the JTPA authors need only be stretched slightly to correspond to this view. Certainly they hoped that the PICs would inject a bottom-line business orientation into employment and training and would add credibility and power. Moreover, they expected that the private sector representatives would also support attempts to break out of traditional approaches and support new ideas and initiatives.

But while these principles seem to be shared by both TECs and PICs, there are some fundamental differences in the motivations for establishing them and their current stated missions. First, the Training Agency Prospectus makes it clear that the TEC strategy emerges from the current preoccupation with international competitiveness and economic growth:

> This Prospectus is about people and jobs in a changing world. It is about enterprise and competitiveness in an increasingly competitive world market-place. It is about opportunity and access to opportunity. But above all, it is about a new institutional framework, founded on the principle that people are our most valuable resource and the key to business success and economic growth.[9]

Second, taking into account the size of the population of the two countries, the national budget for the TECs is several times the JTPA budget. But more important, although most of the initial funding for the TECs will come from the Youth Training (YT) and Employment Training (ET) programs for school leavers and the long-term unemployed, all of the TEC advocates call for the eventual development of a much broader role. The Prospectus states, "The fundamental aim of every TEC will be to foster economic growth and contribute to the regeneration of the community it serves. Its special focus will be on strengthening the skill base and assisting local enterprise to expand and compete effectively".[10] The favorable report by the Confederation of British Industries (CBI) on the TECs argues that in order for the TECs to reach their full potential, they must have 'a wider remit, including being responsible for "overseeing" the local delivery of all relevant vocational education and training'.[11] Academics and policy analysts also call for broad strategic roles for the TECs that involve planning and co-ordinating general education, vocational education, training, employment, and economic development policies.[12]

In contrast, the PICs did not emerge primarily from a concern about international competition. And they have never been looked to, in any practical sense, for leadership in the development and co-ordination of broad education and economic development policy.

Modern United States employment and training programs date from the passage of the federal Manpower Development and Training Act of 1962 (MDTA). The MDTA was a re-training program designed to provide modern vocational training to workers whose skills had been made obsolete by technological advancement. As the specter of automation-induced unemployment faded in the mid-1960s, the American middle class became aware of widespread poverty in the Appalachian Mountains and elsewhere. The focus of the employment and training system shifted to training and job search assistance for the poor. Numerous programs were established under the auspices of several federal agencies.

When CETA was passed in 1973, it was designed to consolidate most of these programs under the Department of Labor. Most of CETA's funds went to local government to create PSE jobs. Indeed by 1978, $5.8 billion out of a total allocation of $9.5 billion (61 percent) was devoted to direct job creation. In that year, only 16 percent of CETA enrolees were engaged in classroom-based job-related skills programs.[13] As pointed out earlier, by the late 1970s, political support for CETA had weakened as the impression spread that PSE participants rarely found un-subsidized jobs in the public sector.

It was in this environment that the proposals for greater private sector involvement arose. The PICs were established by Title VII of the 1978 amendments to CETA, and were allocated $500 million out of a total CETA authorization of over $8 billion. The Act stated that 'It is the purpose of this title to demonstrate the effectiveness of a variety of approaches to increase the involvement of the business community...in employment and training activities...and to increase private sector employment opportunities for unemployed or underemployed persons who are economically disadvantaged.'[14] The private sector effort was established in juxtaposition to the perceived problem that few PSE participants found non-government jobs. The authors believed that this could be remedied by involving private sector employers. As the legislative history of the amendments states, 'Who knows better than the employers what employers want?'

Thus, the PICs were first established as an explicit part of a strategy to find employment for the poor and long term unemployed. At that time, there was little discussion of the problems of international competitiveness and the link between education and the loss of US economic hegemony was simply not an issue.[15]

Despite some change in rhetorical emphasis, the much expanded role of the PICs after the 1982 passage of the JTPA remains focused on training for the poor and disadvantaged. Early in the history of the JTPA, PIC members argued that the JTPA should be oriented towards serving the needs of local business, rather than be defined as a social program serving the needs of the poor. But JTPA eligibility is restricted to individuals with incomes below a prescribed standard; even if the PICs have a wholehearted commitment to serving the needs of local business, they only have this clientele to offer. In tight labor markets in some industries, the JTPA eligible population might indeed be the foundation of the labour supply, but for most employers, the needs that can be met by services provided by the PICs are no more than marginal to the operation of their firms. There has been little serious attempt to involve PICs in broader planning for vocational education offered at community colleges and secondary schools, and no effort to give PICs a major role in shaping the whole education system to be more appropriate and responsive to the contemporary economy.

In short, the PICs were set up in 1978 and expanded in 1982 because policy makers thought that employers were in the best position to determine what skills and services disadvantaged individuals needed to become established in the labor force, not because employers were believed to be in the best position to design aspects of the overall educational system. Indeed, in the United States, the current educational reform movement that emerged after the PICs were set up, has seen PICs as marginal players at most, although partnerships with business people have played a role in the drive to reform schools.

Education Reform and PICs

There are two broad reasons why the PICs have not been central to the current educational reform movement. First, there is and has been a sharp philosophical, cultural, and institutional distinction between employment and training policy and broader educational policy. Employment and training policy is focused on preparing the disadvantaged and unemployed for work and is controlled at the federal level by the Department of Labor. Broader educational policy concerned with schooling for all at the federal level is the responsibility of the Department of Education. Employment and training policy is discussed, planned, implemented, and evaluated by economists and general policy analysts while educational policy is the concern of the huge educational policy and research community. Although there are individuals who bridge these two worlds, the chasm between them is immense.

There have been some official efforts to co-ordinate JTPA and education policy. Interagency co-ordination is, at least in theory, an important element of the JTPA strategy. Early evidence suggested that this was not particularly successful [16] — agencies cooperated more on paper than in reality — but in any case, this coordination primarily involved the

Employment Service (a Department of Labor responsibility) or welfare agencies. When there was co-ordination between the JTPA and schools or colleges, this involved working together specifically on services to JTPA clients. With one or two exceptions, the PICs did not get involved with general school reform. The federal Vocational Education Act does call for monitoring of the co-ordination between the JTPA and vocational education, and recent concern about the link between education and competitiveness has started to bring these two worlds together at an official level. In 1989, the Departments of Labor and Education mounted a joint Commission on Workforce Quality and Labor Market Efficiency and there is interaction between the Departments on issues such as workplace literacy, but these developments are still tentative.

The second reason why the PICs have had only minor roles in educational reform is that while power and funding of employment and training policy is centered in Washington (which delegates some responsibilities to the states), the state capitals have overwhelming control over primary, secondary, and post-secondary education – the Department of Education is essentially a research and advisory agency.

One of the innovations of the JTPA was the devolution of some power over training to the states. In principle, the states could choose to give broad educational responsibilities to the PICs or to the state-level public/private partnerships established by the JTPA (the State Job Training Co-ordinating Councils), but why should they? The JTPA represents a tiny fraction of national educational funding. For example, the national JTPA expenditures are less than $4 billion, while the annual expenditures of New York City Board of Education exceed $6 billion. JTPA expenditures in New York City only total about $100 million while the City spends more than $1 billion on public post-secondary education and tens of thousands of students of all ages who attend private educational institutions that are regulated by the state. Even if the comparison is limited to expenditure on individuals 16 and over, the JTPA still represents only a minuscule percentage. National post-secondary expenditure totalled about $110 billion in 1988, and much of the secondary school expenditure go to serving students at least 16 years old. And the cost of employer provided education is believed to exceed $100 billion.

Governors simply have no incentive to give any more power or influence to the PICs than that required by the Federal government as a condition for receiving the JTPA funds. This does not mean that state governors are not interested in educational reform. Indeed several have built national reputations based on their advocacy of reform. But they are hardly going to turn the initiative, and the credit, for educational reform over to a federal program in exchange for control over a few tens of millions of dollars – in any case, they get the money even if they continue to define the PICs' roles in the narrowest of terms.

What might this imply for the TECs? It is possible that the traditional cultural and institutional differences that separate employment and training from education in the United States are less salient in Great Britain. Moreover, the federal structure that gives so little power over education to Washington may be less of a barrier to the integration of employment and training and education in Great Britain. Thus, there may be more potential to develop a broader role for the TECs. But this also means that policy makers in England who want to see the TECs take on a broad strategic role in planning the trajectory of the country's education should not look to the PICs for lessons. The PICs have had responsibility for a narrowly defined program aimed at a specific part of the population. Moreover, that program represents a minuscule part of the total educational expenditures in the country.

Another possibility is that while the rhetoric of the TECs suggests a much broader strategic role than the one played by the PICs, in reality the two approaches are much closer. About 90 percent of the TECs' funds initially will simply come from the Youth Training Scheme (now YT) and Employment Training (ET), programs aimed primarily at school leavers and the long-term unemployed. Presently, falling expenditure on YT and ET make it even more difficult to believe that a strategy based primarily on these funding streams can be the basis of fundamental educational reform or a revitalization of the economy through training. Moreover, press reports in early 1990 already indicated that some employers who had been initially enthusiastic about the TECs had become disillusioned precisely because the TECs seemed to be concerned primarily with YT and ET when they had been billed as organizations that would develop grand training strategies as weapons in the international competitive wars.[17] In the end, the greater the relevance of PIC experience to the TECs, the further the TECs will be from the more ambitious roles on which much of their political support is based.

Private Sector Involvement

The planners of the TECs put a great deal of emphasis on the participation of private-sector employers on the TEC boards. This section explores the impact of this type of private-sector involvement on the PICs. Much of the information relied on for this discussion was collected during field visits to 25 SDAs in 15 states during the first three years of the operation of the JTPA.[18] Why did policy makers in America and Britain believe that private sector involvement would improve the operation of employment and training policy? Three important arguments are usually advanced. First, prominent businessmen bring prestige, power, and influence to the programs. This increases their credibility and political support. Second, business people are believed to be in the best position to know the types of skills needed for employment in the private sector. Third, policy makers believe that employers will bring more efficient private sector, bottom-line oriented administrative procedures to the operation of these programs. Each argument will be examined below.

Private Sector Clout and Prestige. In discussing the selection of TEC directors, Catherine Stratton argued that they must be 'the real power brokers in their communities. They must be the acknowledged leaders whose presence will give the TEC instant prestige and influence...[They must] have the muscle to act as real change agents: to influence public institutions or their fellow employers.'[19] The importance of high-profile, private-sector involvement in strengthening the credibility of the JTPA was a common theme in interviews with employers and public sector employees involved with the JTPA. This was believed to be particularly important during the early years of the Act when it had to confront CETA's tarnished reputation. The JTPA Advisory Committee convened by the Secretary of Labor in 1988 and 1989 to suggest changes in the legislation concluded that the PICs have 'increased the awareness of major public issues among key private sector actors.'[20] Thus although there is no systematic research that establishes the importance of this factor, there is a consensus that the PICs have strengthened the credibility and awareness of the problems and accomplishments of the JTPA in the private sector and the public at large.

The PICs as a Source of Labor Market Information. The notion that it is only employers who know what skills are needed in the workplace runs through the discussions of both the PICs and the TECs. This idea lay behind the establishment of the PICs in 1978 and survived into the discussion of the JTPA. The report of the Senate Committee on Labor and Human Resources advocated the involvement of the business community (through the PICs) in the administration of the JTPA because

> it is the private sector which will employ the graduates of the training programs, and it is only those who will employ the graduates who can really define the kinds of training programs that are needed.[21]

Likewise, the TEC Prospectus, in explaining the need for an employer-led partnership states: 'Employers are best placed to identify key skill needs and to ensure that the level and quality of training and business services meets those needs'.[22]

It seems plausible enough that employers are in the best position to know the skills needed in the workplace. But the contention that CEOs and high-level, private-sector officers serving on organizations such as the PICs or TECs are in the best position to plan a broad training strategy cannot stand up to close scrutiny. First, employers can only be expected to have any precise understanding of the needs of their own firms. Second, field researchers who study the skill needs of workplaces often find that high executives, at least in large firms, have only vague ideas about the types of skills that their lower-level employees need. Third, there is also something odd about relying on employers to spearhead a national training policy aimed at strengthening international competitiveness. Certainly the policies and strategies of employers must bear substantial blame for the problems of competitiveness to begin with. Indeed, the first role of the TECs outlined by the Training Agency is to 'promote more effective training by employers and individuals in their areas, using public programmes and private funds'.[23] This seems to suggest that employers may not be conducting the most effective training. Some employers may know the skills required in their industries, but only the government is in a position to gather data useful for broad policy. In the United States, there is no private sector source of broad occupational and skill information even remotely adequate for this purpose.

In this respect, the experience of the PICs is instructive. Early enthusiasm on the part of PIC members for generating their own labor market information quickly faded. A review of the first nine months of the operation of the PICs under the JTPA found:

> During the initial phase of the JTPA considerable interest was evinced by the PICs in developing labor market information for use by the SDAs in developing training programs. Twenty of the 25 field survey PICs reported establishing internal committees to create strategies for improving labor market information. By the end of the first program year, PIC activity in this area had decreased. Despite the initial interest, most PICs ultimately turned to traditional sources for obtaining such data: the Employment Service, other government agencies, and local universities. Eight of the 25 PICs had undertaken employer surveys to determine trends in local hiring needs. Most of the SDAs reported that these surveys were disappointing either because the response was insufficient or because they revealed little additional information beyond what was already available. Overall, the impact of PICs on developing labor market information was limited, SDAs rarely reported that training strategies were significantly altered as a result of PIC input.[24]

The 1989 report of the National JTPA Advisory Committee seems to abandon completely the notion that the PICs will be a primary source of labor market information. The discussion in that report of the need for improved labor market information (LMI) does not even mention the PICs. The report states that:

> Those who rely on LMI generally believe that knowing how to make better use of existing information should take priority over obtaining more data; the first means of improving communication with users of LMI can be accomplished by increasing its meaning through more and improved analysis. In addition, increased training is needed for both producers and users.

> Under JTPA's decentralized approach, efforts to share new technology and developments across states have not been fully successful. An organized and consistent federal effort is needed to assure that new and innovative developments are shared effectively with those who use them.[25]

Moreover, the emphasis on using the educational system to diffuse information about technology and skills to employers, rather than having employers tell educational systems what to do, has taken on an increasingly important role in American efforts to strengthen the industrial base in the face of growing international competition.[26]

PIC Influence on the Operations and Efficiency of the JTPA. Private sector representatives involved with the JTPA during the 1980s very much saw their role as bringing business methods and practices to the local operation of the JTPA. They adopted an approach closely associated with the system of performance standards promulgated by the Act. The performance approach continues to generate tremendous controversy. It is beyond the scope of this chapter to discuss the complexities of the issue, but simplistically, critics argue that the performance standards do not measure the actual goals of the JTPA and that they encourage "creaming" – recruiting those eligible participants least in need of services in order to bolster placement and wage rates. Thus performance standards simply encourage contractors to be more selective rather than to sharpen up the effectiveness of their operations. To some extent, the authors of the JTPA tried to counteract this problem by restricting the contractors' discretion in choosing participants, for example by requiring that each SDA spend 40 percent of its training funds on youth.[27]

Private sector PIC members placed a great deal of emphasis on these standards, arguing that they were the key to a bottom-line, business-like approach to program operation. According to the Act, the PICs were to be involved with general policy development and strategic planning. The Act listed several objectives: reducing unemployment and welfare dependency; increasing wage levels; increasing the employability of young workers; providing services to those most in need; serving the needs of local businesses; and co-ordinating the activities of public sector agencies. The PICs had a mandate to set policy and to establish an appropriate balance of emphasis among these goals. Nevertheless, meeting the prescribed targets was, for the most part, considered an indication of successful operation whether or not there was any indication of progress on the broader stated goals of the Act.

The field interviews consistently revealed differences between the orientation of public and private sector representatives towards the performance standards and the JTPA structure. The majority of the private sector PIC members had accepted and approved of the constraints imposed by the performance standards. In contrast, government officials and public sector employees were more likely to express frustration at the law's implicit incentives to avoid those clients with more serious problems and barriers to employment. Thus, increased private sector involvement could be indicated by a movement towards more highly qualified participants, and towards training such as direct placement programs and on-the-job training (which program operators believe to have high placement rates).

As a whole, federal job training programs under the JTPA are cheaper and shorter than previous programs. During the 1980s, operators became more selective and increased their emphasis on placement.[28] But these developments could be the result either of the performance standards or of the increased private sector involvement.

In order to differentiate between these two factors, I compared the performance, program and client characteristics in SDAs that had a strong and active private sector involvement to the same factors in SDAs that had weak PICs.[29] The 25 SDAs of the study sample were placed into three categories according to the relative influence of the two leadership partners – the PICs and the local elected officials. Eleven of the 25 service delivery areas (45 percent) were classified as government-led SDAs. In ten of the SDAs, the local elected officials remained on the sidelines, while the PICs set policy and had primary influence over the employment and training staff. These were referred to as PIC-led SDAs. In four sites, no dominant partner emerged, and these were classified as shared-leadership SDAs.[30]

The analysis considered four factors. First, if the greater influence of the private sector results in more efficient operations, or if government-led SDAs are less selective in their recruitment and enrolment, then PIC-led SDAs would have better performance records than SDAs with inactive PICs. Second, if PIC-led SDAs are more selective, then these SDAs would enroll greater numbers of presumably easier-to-place high school graduates. Third, a greater emphasis on client selection and on meeting the labor needs of local businesses might result in PIC-led SDAs underemphasizing services to young clients. If this is the case, then PIC-led SDAs would be more likely to fall short of their youth expenditure requirements. Fourth, programs oriented towards high placement rates will put a greater emphasis on on-the-job training since it is widely believed to result in a stronger placement record. The analysis revealed neither statistically nor substantively significant differences between PIC-led and government-led SDAs with the single exception of expenditures on on-the-job training. And in that case, contrary to the expectations, it is the government-led SDAs that spend more on this type of training. In sum, these data suggest that a strong and active PIC did not result in greater program efficiency (at least according to available measures) or in more selective recruitment.

Although private sector representatives often saw their primary role as assuring the achievement of standards themselves, the research suggested that the emphasis was already guaranteed by the effects of the performance standards. Public sector personnel involved with the JTPA expressed frustration at the bottom-line approach, but apparently fell in line in order to hit their targets. But while duplicating the effects of the performance standards, the PICs did not take leadership in confronting the broader strategic issues involving the JTPA – particularly the problem that the original performance standards were only tenuously associated with the stated goals of the Act.

Current Reform in the JTPA

The above analysis was based on a study from 1985. While data are not available to update the analysis, subsequent developments and discussions suggest that the outcome orientation has continued to grow and attract attention while the role of the business representatives has waned. In 1988, the Secretary of Labor appointed an advisory committee of employment and training experts, including public, private, and non-profit sector representatives. Their report was published in March 1989 and gives an indication of future policy directions.

The advisory committee came up with seven broad recommendations:

(1) Target the program more directly on those disadvantaged persons with serious skills deficiencies.

(2) Individualize and substantially intensify the quality of services provided.

(3) Realign the services currently authorized for youth into a new, consolidated year-round program title for at-risk youth with increased funding.

(4) Redesign outcome measures to reflect more accurately the program's goals of increasing the long-term economic self-sufficiency of participants.

(5) Substantially relax program constraints to increase the responsiveness of the system overall and to improve its capacity for effectively serving participants with serious barriers to employment.

(6) Increase the productivity of the JTPA system by undertaking a major training and research effort to improve program quality and build the capacity of the staff who administer and deliver the program at the state and local level.

(7) Create expanded public/private partnership arrangements to achieve linkages between JTPA and other human resources programs in order to serve a larger proportion of the eligible population more effectively with a broader range of services.[31]

Several interesting points can be made concerning these recommendations. Most importantly, the committee advocated a continued emphasis on serving the disadvantaged. The first and fourth recommendations are explicit attempts to sharpen the performance-based system but at the same time limit the discretion that service providers have in selecting clients with the fewest problems from the eligible population (creaming). The second and sixth recommendations suggest that the committee was not satisfied with the quality of services provided under the JTPA and that it thought the federal government should have an increased role in strengthening the skills and capacity of the training delivery system. The fifth recommendation (relax program constraints) was primarily aimed at eliminating some administrative regulations, such as the constraints on work experience and stipends, that were included in the JTPA as a reaction against presumably wasteful features of the CETA. Thus, in general, the proposed reforms can be interpreted as an attempt to improve the outcome standards and service while guaranteeing the continued focus on the disadvantaged. The emphasis on performance standards continues to be controversial. Though most critics of the performance system will not be satisfied by the report, it seems fair to say that this reform agenda is an attempt to create a more effective market-oriented system that delivers meaningful services to clients with serious problems.

At the same time, the strident emphasis on direct and detailed private sector participation that characterized early discussions of the JTPA is gone. In this light, it is interesting to examine the comments accompanying the committee's seventh recommendation to expand public-private partnerships. The report states:

> Building upon existing institutions, such as the Private Industry Councils and the State Job Training Co-ordinating Councils, partnership institutions at the national, state, and local levels should foster greater *interagency collaboration* in the planning and delivery of services to the disadvantaged, dislocated workers, and other groups in need of assistance to qualify for employment. To facilitate this linkage process, *federal agencies serving similar client groups should adopt common outcome measures.*[32]

Although it is the PICs that are mentioned, the partnerships discussed by the report's authors are between public agencies rather than between private business people and the public sector.

Performance and the TECs

Thus, for the JTPA, the market-oriented or bottom-line approach has indeed carried the day, but this has been focused on the performance standards and eligibility criteria rather than business participation. Although the plans for the TECs call for 'an accent on performance,' so far the discussions and writings about the TECs have placed a much greater emphasis on private sector involvement than on considering performance standards or how to measure them. For example, a May 1989 paper on the TECs by Bennett, McCoshan and Sellgren (1989) has only a short discussion of performance measures, simply emphasizing the extent to which performance standards limit local autonomy. And the July 1989 collection of conference papers edited by the same three authors includes only the most rudimentary discussion of performance standards.[33] A November 1989 conference at the University of Warwick did have a session devoted to evaluation and performance assessment, [34] but veterans of the performance standards wars in the United States would find the discussion in Britain to be at an early stage.

Perhaps then, the performance standards controversy represents the greatest lesson from abroad for TECs. Certainly there is much to be learned from the PICs, but it should be remembered that the JTPA has a much more restricted mission than the mission proposed for the TECs. The JTPA performance standards all involve measures of post-program employment or educational participation of participants. Performance evaluation is simplified for the JTPA because the program serves only a small fraction of the eligible population, and even in this case, evaluation has presented great difficulties. But in contrast to the PICs' emphasis on the disadvantaged, the TECs are charged with bringing about radical change in areas of the broader education system. It may be possible to devise performance standards to measure achievement of these broad goals, but this has not even been attempted by the planners of the JTPA. Thus performance standards lessons from the PICs can only be relevant to the TECs if the TECs choose to climb down from their ambitious goals.

Conclusion

If British policy makers are serious about using the TECs to bring about a radical restructuring of the country's educational system, then they should be skeptical of lessons from across the Atlantic. British goals are wider and deeper than the ones embedded in JTPA. There is indeed a tremendous amount of educational reform activity in the United States, with as yet unknown effects, but the vast preponderance of this activity is not driven or coordinated by local-level partnerships led by business people. That is not to say that such partnerships may not be the key to solving Britain's presumed educational problems. But however one judges the success or failure of the PICs with respect to JTPA, they are minor players in the broader educational reform movement. At most, the PICs have significant local-level control over a relatively small education and employment program aimed at the poor.

Even within the much narrower JTPA mission, the PIC experience suggests that the participation of private employers in program planning and oversight is only one among many elements that defines a successful program.

The original authors of the JTPA believed that by setting performance goals, moving authority out of Washington and involving business representatives who were believed to know what the market needed, they could create a more efficient program free from the heavy bureaucratic hand of the public sector. In 1990, the JTPA was moving towards an even greater emphasis on performance standards, including attempts to respond to the many critics of the approach. But the JTPA experience suggests that for performance standards to be effective, they must be designed and implemented based on extensive information and analysis that usually require an abundance of regulations, record keeping, paperwork and detailed evaluation – just the bureaucratic processes that a market approach and outcome-oriented monitoring are meant to obviate. But while the performance-standard strategy appears to be moving ahead, the emphasis on private sector involvement has stalled. Representatives of business are still sought out for support of various kinds, but private sector involvement appears to be losing its place as the central pillar on which federal employment and training policy rests.

The analysis of PICs and TECs also raises some larger questions about policy borrowing in general. The different missions of PICs and TECs mean that opportunities to learn from the other's experience will be limited. Furthermore, research in America suggests that the actual mechanism British policy makers borrowed – the private sector boards charged with making decisions about the allocation government training funds – is not the source of recent improvements in program efficiency. British policy makers will have to examine the other contributors to training efficiency in the United States to avoid putting too much faith in a single mechanism. This case study suggests that countries should beware of drawing inappropriate lessons from programs run for different reasons. In the rush to adopt another nation's program, they may overlook other aspects of a system that can, in reality, be critical determinants of program results.

Notes

[1] See for example Robert Bennett, Andrew McCoshan, and John Sellgren, "TECs and VET: The Practical Requirements: Organization, Geography and International Comparison with the USA and Germany," Research Paper, Department of Geography, London School of Economics, May 1989; Catherine Stratton, "The TECs and PICs: The Key Issues Which Lie Ahead," in "Training and Enterprise Councils (TECs) and Vocational Education and Training (VET): Conference Papers on Practical Requirements," Bennett, McCoshan, and Sellgren, (eds.) Research Papers, London School of Economics, Department of Geography, July 1989, pp. 21-30; and Education-Business Partnerships: Lessons from America, Training Agency and BiC, 1989.

[2] Burt S. Barnow, "The Impact of CETA Programs on Earnings," Journal of Human Resources, 22 (Spring 1987): 157-193.

[3] Paul Osterman, "The Politics and Economics of CETA Programs," Journal of the American Institute of Planners 47 (October 1981): 434-446; and Carl Van Horne, "Implementing CETA: the Federal Role," Policy Analysis 4 (Spring, 1978): pp. 159-183.

[4] CETA outlays in 1978 were $9.5 billion (Employment and Training Report of the President, 1979, p. 32). The 1984 JTPA allocation was $3.6 billion or $2.1 billion in 1978 dollars (Walker 1984, p. 1).

[5] These standards were changed in 1990.

[6] United States Senate Committee on Labor and Human Resources, (S. Rpt. 97-469), Washington, D.C.: United States Government Printing Office, 1982.

[7] The Training Agency, Training and Enterprise Councils: a Prospectus for the 1990s. London: Training Agency, 1989, pp. 4, 11.

[8] Ibid, p. 4.

[9] Ibid, p. 3.

[10] Ibid, p. 1.

[11] Confederation of British Industries, "Training and Enterprise Councils–The Way Forward," Interim report to the Vocational Education and the Training Task Force, 1989.

[12] See (Bennett, McCoshan, and Sellgren, April 1989); and (Stratton, 1989) for example.

[13] Employment and Training Report of the President 1979, p. 32.

[14] Public Law 95-524, Section 701, October 27, 1978.

[15] For a more detailed discussion of the origins, history, and effects of Title VII of the 1978 amendments to CETA, see Thomas J. Smith, Private Sector Initiative Program: Documentation and Assessment of CETA Title VII Implementation, Final Report. Philadelphia, PA: Public/Private Ventures, April 1982.

[16] Gary Walker, Thomas Bailey, Katherine Solow, and Harvey Shapiro (1986), "An Independent Sector Assessment of the Job Training Partnership Act. Final Report: Program Year 1985" (Washington, D.C.: The National Commission for Employment Policy, 1986).

[17] "The Training Trap," The Economist, April 21, 1990, pp. 63-64.

[18] For a detailed description of the selection and characteristics of the sample SDAs and other methodological issues, see Gary Walker, "An Independent Sector Assessment of the Job Training Partnership Act: Phase I" (Washington, D.C.: The National Commission for Employment Policy, March 1984). Additional results from the project are reported in Gary Walker, Hilary Feldstein and Katherine Solow, "An Independent Sector Assessment of the Job Training Partnership Act: Phase II" (Washington, D.C.: The National Commission for Employment Policy, January 1985); and Walker and others 1986.

[19] Stratton, 1989, p. 22.

[20] Job Training Partnership Act (JTPA) Advisory Committee, Working Capital: JTPA Investments for the 1990s. Washington, DC.: The United States Department of Labor, March 1989, p. 7.

[21] Senate 97th Congress, 2d Session–Report #97-469, p. 1-2.

[22] The Training Agency, p.4.

[23] "The Training and Enterprise Councils," Skills Bulletin, Issue No.9, Summer 1989. p. 28.

[24] Walker, Feldstein, and Solow, 1985, pp. 101-102.

[25] The JTPA Advisory Committee.

[26] Philip Shapira, Modernizing Manufacturing: New Policies to Build Industrial Extension Services. Washington, D.C.: Economic Policy Institute, 1990.

[27] For an extensive development of this argument see Thomas Bailey, "Market Forces and Private Sector Processes in Government Policy: The Job Training

Partnership Act," Journal of Policy Analysis and Management 7, No. 2 (1988), pp. 300-315.

[28] Bailey, 1988.

[29] Bailey, 1988.

[30] This classification system was based on extensive interviews with PIC members; elected officials; welfare, job service, board of education and employment and training staff members; and training contractors in all of the SDAs. In most cases, a consensus existed about the relative roles of the partners. In cases where there was disagreement, the classification was based on an examination of the discussion and attendance at PIC meetings, the extent to which the PICs or the local government initiated activities or policies, and whether those initiatives were implemented. When ambiguity remained, the SDA was put in the shared-leadership category.

[31] JTPA Advisory Committee, 1989, pp. 10-11.

[32] JTPA Advisory Committee, 1989, p. 11.

[33] Robert Bennett, Andrew McCoshan, and John Sellgren, "Training and Enterprise Councils (TECs) and Vocational Education and Training (VET): Conference Papers on Practical Requirements," Research Paper, London School of Economics, Department of Geography, July 1989.

[34] National Workshop on TECs," VET Forum Newsletter, University of Warwick. Issue Number 2, 1990, p. 5.

Bibliography

Bailey, Thomas "Market Forces and Private Sector Processes in Government Policy: The Job Training Partnership Act," Journal of Policy Analysis and Management 7, No. 2, 1988.

Barnow, Burt S., "The Impact of CETA Programs on Earnings," Journal of Human Resources, 22 (Spring, 1987).

Bennett, Robert, Andrew McCoshan, and John Sellgren, "Training and Enterprise Councils (TECs) and Vocational Education and Training (VET): Conference Papers on Practical Requirements," Research Paper, London School of Economics, Department of Geography, July 1989.

Bennett, Robert, Andrew McCoshan, and John Sellgren, "TECs and VET: The Practical Requirements: Organization, Geography and International Comparison with the USA and Germany," Department of Geography, London School of Economics, May 1989;

Confederation of British Industries, "Training and Enterprise Councils – The Way Forward," Interim report to the Vocational Education and the Training Task Force, 1989.

Economist, "The Training Trap", April 21, 1990.

Employment and Training Report of the President, 1979

Finegold, David and David Soskice, "The Failure of Training in Britain: Analysis and Prescription," Oxford Review of Economic Policy Vol. 4, No. 3, 1988.

Job Training Partnership Act Advisory Committee, Working Capital: JTPA Investments for the 1990s. Washington, DC.: The United States Department of Labor, March 1989.

Osterman, Paul, "The Politics and Economics of CETA Programs," Journal of the American Institute of Planners 47 (October 1981).

Shapira, Philip, Modernizing Manufacturing: New Policies to Build Industrial Extension Services. Washington, D.C.: Economic Policy Institute, 1990.

Smith, Thomas J., Private Sector Initiative Program: Documentation and Assessment of CETA Title VII Implementation, Final Report. Philadelphia, PA: Public/Private Ventures, April 1982.

Stratton, Catherine "The TECs and PICs: The Key Issues Which Lie Ahead," in "Training and Enterprise Councils (TECs) and Vocational Education and Training (VET): Conference Papers on Practical Requirements," Bennett, McCoshan and Sellgren, (eds.). London School of Economics, Department of Geography, July 1989.

The Training Agency, Training and Enterprise Councils: a Prospectus for the 1990s. London: Training Agency, 1989.

The Training Agency and BiC, Education-Business Partnerships: Lessons from America, 1989.

"The Training and Enterprise Councils," Skills Bulletin, Issue No.9, Summer 1989.

United States Senate Committee on Labor and Human Resources, (S. Rpt. 97-469), Washington, D.C.: United States Government Printing Office, 1982.

United States Senate 97th Congress, 2d Session – Report #97-469.

Van Horne, Carl, "Implementing CETA: the Federal Role," Policy Analysis 4 (Spring, 1978).

Walker, Gary "An Independent Sector Assessment of the Job Training Partnership Act: Phase I" Washington, D.C.: The National Commission for Employment Policy, March 1984.

Walker, Gary, Hilary Feldstein and Katherine Solow, "An Independent Sector Assessment of the Job Training Partnership Act: Phase II" , Washington, D.C.: The National Commission for Employment Policy, January 1985.

Walker, Gary, Thomas Bailey, Katherine Solow, and Harvey Shapiro, "An Independent Sector Assessment of the Job Training Partnership Act. Final Report: Program Year 1985", Washington, D.Cs.: The National Commission for Employment Policy, 1986.

Employers as an Instrument of School Reform? Education–Business 'Compacts' in Britain and America

WILLIAM RICHARDSON

During the 1980s there developed an increasing interest in America and Britain in fostering the relationship between education and industry, with a particular thrust on stimulating greater business involvement at the schools level.

This chapter selects the compact device, one of the most influential models of school-business collaboration, and examines its origins in the specific US urban setting of Boston, Mass. before moving to a consideration of its widespread replication in America and Britain up to the summer of 1990. The record of the first eight years of the Boston Compact (1982-90) is examined and set within its local context of fluctuating economic, labour market and education reform conditions. Moving to a wider assessment of the influence of the compact after 1986, three distinct phases or episodes of policy borrowing are discussed: the replication of the compact idea in the US; the adoption of the Boston model by a pioneering British group in East London; and the national promotion of compact replication by the government in England, Scotland and Wales.

Arising from this analysis of policy borrowing, a number of wider themes are identified which point to achievements and limitations in the operation of compacts in the 75 American and British cities where they have been established. In particular, an assessment is made of the would-be role of employers as an instrument of school reform – a strong feature of the compact in Boston; the relationship of labour market conditions to compact 'success'; and the issue of policy focus in compact operation.

The Boston Compact

Background and Early Momentum, 1982-5

The specific social and economic conditions out of which the compact policy model first arose in the US forms an important context when considering its subsequent replication in other American cities and overseas.

The Boston Compact was conceived against a background of increasingly severe urban problems in America.[1] National trends included a 5.5% rise in urban high school drop-out rates between 1972 and 1982; employment rates for 16-19 year old ethnic minority males fell from 53% to 26% between 1955 and 1981 whilst remaining at 50% for non-minority males; in 1985 46% of white female 16-19 year olds were employed compared to 21% from minority groups.

In Boston itself school enrolment had fallen by one third during 1972-82 as middle class parents moved to the suburbs or took their children out of the publicly funded schools in favour of the parochial schools system. A set of circumstances was combining which required Robert Spillane, the Superintendent of the Local School District, urgently to seek a new powerful constituency that would challenge the claimed ineffectiveness of the city's School Committee and speak up for the schools directly.

Simultaneously, business leaders were faced with an economic boom, and a labour shortage. According to the President of the Federal Reserve Bank of Boston, "people were coming into the labour force from the schools [who] were often functionally illiterate. The schools system was not doing its job". This combination of events and Spillane's business-like approach in introducing new accountabilities and management disciplines into the city's school system won the confidence of Boston's business leaders. In reflecting on the conditions which led to the creation of the compact Catherine Stratton, the Boston Private Industry Council (PIC) Executive Director recalled that "part of it was [Spillane's] presence; part of it was his credibility. And part of it was probably the sense of desperation that existed: 'If this person doesn't make it, what's going to happen to our schools?'".

The Boston Compact was, therefore, born out of conditions of extreme concern for the future of inner-city schooling. Spillane was able to build upon a faltering range of school-business partnerships – many forced on a reluctant schools system by a 1974 court order enforcing desegregation – and use his own authority to commit the city's schools to unambiguous goals for their students (Farrar and Cipollone, 1988[a] pp. 92-7). The result was that on 22 September 1982 fifteen city businesses agreed to offer 400 school leavers permanent jobs the following June, to increase that number to 1,000 students within two years providing they met entry-level requirements, to stimulate the work of the PIC in employment training and school to work programmes, to increase the availability of summer jobs, and to recruit 300 companies by 1984 to join the priority hiring commitment of the compact. The Schools Department, meanwhile, made a public commitment to reduce truancy and 'drop-out rates' (those high school students failing to 'graduate' at age 18) by 5% annually and to increase by 5% annually the number of students who took a job or went on to college after school. In addition, it agreed to introduce minimum standards in maths and reading for all students by 1986 (Rossano, 1987; Farrar and Cipollone, 1988[a], p. 90)

It was this basic formula of mutual target-setting – an exchange of jobs or training places by the business community for tangible achievement targets set for low-attaining students by the education sector – which was followed by the 12 American cities and 62 British cities that set about establishing Boston-style compacts in the late 1980s.

The Compact as a Policy Tool

From the outset in Boston the compact idea appealed to a wide variety of political and economic interest groups. Paradoxically, whilst the compact appeared to offer unusually specific commitments by both sectors to numerical targets for student performance and employer involvement, in the early stages, at least, these were of secondary importance to the political flexibility of the compact in the eyes of its operators. As Farrar and Cipollone's interviews in Boston demonstrated:

> People see in it and make of it the things they want to ...At one level it is a politically astute and cleverly crafted agreement that people have used to accomplish a broad range of objectives. But at another level, the Compact is a programme that has expanded beyond its initial push to find jobs for Boston youth to a strategy for introducing broad-based improvements in the city's high schools. Part of its success results from the many different and sometimes competing purposes that it serves. This makes it useful for everyone... (ibid. p. 91)

Farrar and Cipollone conducted their first study of Boston's Compact in 1985 and were, at that time, sanguine as to its prospects for continued growth and success. By then 500 businesses were participating and 876 school-leavers had been placed in jobs that summer (ibid. p. 92). By 1986 the figures had risen to 600 companies and 967 permanent jobs (Rossano, 1987 p. 9). Meanwhile, the potential of the compact idea began to be stressed increasingly in newspaper articles and in the pages of practitioner journals within education and business, a majority of which concentrated primarily upon the managerial aspects of running a compact (eg: NAB, 1987, Rickhaus, 1989).

Subsequently a second, more ambitious claim began to be made on behalf of the compact idea – that, through the technique of goal-setting and review, it represented a mechanism which could form the basis of a permanent education-business partnership. At the time of the Boston signing The Boston Globe commented on the long-term significance and commitment of the Compact partners; by 1989, the National Alliance of Business had picked up the same point, commending the national spread of compacts as 'partnerships with long-term measurable goals for school improvement in exchange for business' pledge of employment opportunities' (Farrar & Cipollone, 1988[a]; NAB, 1989[c] p. 1).

Growing Difficulties, 1985-90

Ominously for those who, from 1986 began to put so much faith in the compact model, the continuing experience in Boston became beset with difficulties. Problems began in the summer of 1985 with the departure of Superintendent Spillane, the subsequent absorption of the Compact into the Schools Department's bureaucracy and the departure of other founders of the project to new jobs, including responsibility for compact replication in other cities. Consequently, the energy on the education side of the Compact began to dissolve; in British terminology, its phase as a targeted 'initiative' was coming to a close. Simultaneously a tension in the original claims made for the Compact began to be exposed as its 'ideological' commitment to school-based, bottom-up planning was revealed to have been largely dependent upon Spillane's leadership.

A second set of problems encountered in Boston surrounded employers' motivations. Educationalists began to observe that periods of labour shortage were a fertile environment for employer enthusiasm toward education. Such enthusiasm, however, could come to seem hollow if reinforced by techniques such as shallow marketing and public relations campaigns. Boston's youth programme manager, for example, was struck by the level 'of theater attached [to the Compact]; the amount is astonishing' (Farrar and Cippolone, 1988 [a] pp. 118, 106, 117).

The result of these tensions was that as the Compact itself became marooned in the city's Schools Department, the intensifying public relations surrounding corporate donations to education further dissipated the original partnership ideal. During 1985-88 Boston companies' contributions totalled over $25m (compared to an annual city education budget of $327m). Yet donations were made in a climate where, 'after years of racial discord and political controversy, urban education had become a safe and popular corporate cause [providing a] platform for corporate leadership and visibility'. This favourable atmosphere for employer largesse was coupled with a funding mechanism which allowed companies to manage their own programmes and by-pass the Schools Department, further isolating the Compact's officers (Farrar and Cippolone, 1988 [b] pp. 9-10,23).

Education leaders began to feel dwarfed by this display of corporate muscle. At the same time the new superintendent replaced Spillane's insistence upon school-based improvement planning with a more traditional, centralised improvement plan which was anathema to the Compact officers. As the partnership unravelled, concerns and hostilities surfaced. Business leaders wondered if they had 'over-invested' in the school system's success at a time when the confidence in the leadership provided by the superintendent was eroding: 'we may have more turmoil in the schools', said one company representative, 'and we're going to look embarrassed with a number of business communities saying "we thought Boston solved all these problems", because we haven't'. Critics in the school system meanwhile argued that increased school-leaver employment was due more to demographic shifts and severe labour shortages than any positive influence of the Compact. One widely reported educationalist was led to describe the Compact as 'the biggest fraud ever perpetrated on the city's schools' (Farrar and Cippolone, 1988 [b] p. 11; P.E., 1989).

This distancing of relations between business and education in Boston led to a crisis in late 1988 when employers refused to re-sign the annual pledge, disenchanted with 'the public schools' lack of progress' on basic educational standards (Jack, 1989[a]). Anxious to avoid a political debacle the Schools Department accepted new goals for a relaunched Compact in the spring of 1989 which shifted the Compact's emphasis away from student targets toward more general, yet still numerically measurable goals for the education system. These were directed at institutional reform through the increased accountability of each school for a range of policies. The new goals retained the priority of tackling drop out rates and test scores but went on to introduce new measures for parental involvement, student follow-up procedures and accountable, school-based management systems 'to improve the quality of education' provided by each school (NAB, 1989[c], pp. 25-26; Jack 1989[b]).

Through such a mechanism the Boston business community had re-asserted a decentralised school improvement plan upon the city's Schools Department, returning the Compact more closely to the operating plans pursued by Spillane during 1982-85. This time, however, the demands for school-based reform were to be imposed from without by non-educationalists and were to broaden the objectives of business funding beyond that of students' incentives to include the introduction of managerial structures required to raise school performance.

Compact Replication

The US National Alliance of Business

In June 1986, the US National Alliance of Business (NAB) had initiated a 'major national demonstration project' to assist with the development of compacts in seven other US cities (NAB, 1989[a] p. 1). Launched with principal support funding from the US Department of Health and Human

Services, 70 cities were initially screened by NAB officials. Subsequently, ten 'semifinalist cities' were asked to convene competing 'leadership meetings', and seven cities were chosen to develop compacts. These 'demonstration sites' were joined by five additional compacts when the project was expanded in 1988.

Despite this confident language, the NAB project was suffering from having been launched at the peak of Boston's consensual progress in 1986. Meanwhile, increased employer demands of schooling in Boston seemed in tune with the bullish tones of the NAB compact replication project which began to publish detailed descriptions of its progress in 1989. 'The Boston Business community', the NAB asserted, 'was widely recognised for having met and surpassed its goals .. however the schools in Boston have not been as successful' with the result that the only course of action left to the corporate sector was to place 'a renewed emphasis on fundamental school change and accountability' (NAB 1989 [b] p. iv).

Despite bullish support of demands by Boston business leaders for fundamental school reform, difficulties in the compact replication process were becoming apparent. On the one hand, realisation grew amongst staff that the systemic education problems facing inner city schools 'were beyond the scope of a jobs programme'. Simultaneously it became clear that in other cities a relatively booming economy rendered the job-based incentive for students redundant. As a result, by mid 1989 only three of the twelve 'demonstration cities' had established quantified, long-term measurable goals of the Boston type, despite this being a requirement of acceptance onto the project. Other cities, as NAB acknowledged, were still 'outlining planning structures and coalescing necessary leadership'. At this point in its development the American project appeared to be at something of a crossroads with the NAB insisting upon measurable goals and the provision of 'base line data' from all cities whilst acknowledging that Boston-style goals were not readily applicable across the country (NAB 1989 [b], pp. 5, 65).

UK Pioneers in East London

Three months after the launch of the NAB replication project in June 1986, Boston played host to a visiting English delegation of business and education leaders from London (Martineau, 1989 p. 38). The London team was concerned by large pockets of unemployment close to the City of London and the new Docklands development and had crossed the Atlantic to 'see whether the Compact could not be brought to Britain' (Martineau, 1988, p. 12). In the context of policy replication, the timing of this visit at the peak of Boston's success was highly significant, in the light both of the difficulties subsequently encountered in Boston and the very rapid speed with which the compact idea was to be spread on both sides of the Atlantic.

The English visitors had already formed the London Business Education Partnership as a direct result of ideas gleaned from a visit to New

York in 1984. Using this existing partnership as a basis, the group was able to secure commitment to the establishment of a compact from six London schools, one college, a core of businesses and from the Inner London Education Authority (ILEA) within six months of their Boston visit.

The East London Compact was launched in September 1987 targeting 50 employers who between them would offer 300 permanent jobs to school leavers. The idea of common employer and school goals was directly borrowed from Boston with very similar aims being subscribed to by both sectors. Employers were to offer permanent jobs with training; pupils were to achieve attendance and punctuality targets as well as 'graded results in a recognised exam in English and Maths' (Martineau, ibid.).

In its initial stage, the East London Compact sought to establish itself, to avoid Boston's problems and to adapt an American social partnership model to British political conditions. An official HMI inspection of the Compact was conducted in the spring of 1988, was published the following November and provided the Compact with a fair wind in its initial stages. In the first year of operation (1987-88) the Compact organisers had claimed a school attendance rate rise of 8% and a dramatic increase in staying-on rates 'from about 40% to about 65-70%'. The result was that only ten of the 212 compact jobs offered were taken up (Martineau 1989, p. 40; Barker, 1989). Twelve employers were surveyed about this issue and appeared not unduly concerned – all those questioned recruited sixteen year old school leavers prior to joining the Compact but expressed willingness to take on Compact students at the age of eighteen (ILEA, 1989 [c], pp. 20, 24)

Compared to Boston's concentration on school reform, it is noticeable how the 50 employers involved at this stage of the East London Compact were content to participate with educational partners on a consensual agenda of activities set within the process-oriented 'schools-industry movement' in Britain: work experience; teacher secondment; visits to schools by employers; industrial school governors; student records of achievement; and curriculum projects such as mini-enterprise. By 1989, this situation was being echoed in some NAB compact cities such as Albuquerque where a strikingly British-style agenda included general objectives for the partnership such as building consensus and providing more comprehensiveness in the linkages between education and business (NAB 1989 [b] p. 8).

The situation in both East London and Albuquerque was in stark contrast with the position reached in Boston by 1990. There 1,000 participating employers with eight years experience of the Compact were tightly organised through the PIC and felt enabled to impose terms of educational reform on schools within the city. In East London employers have been content to emulate national policies and in so doing to encourage specialist middle and junior managers to take charge of education liaison activities (ILEA 1989 [c], p. 25). This contrast to the stance of employers in Boston is in part explained by the considerably more developed national government policy environment in education-business relations in Britain compared to America. In this context much of the literature from East London has emphasised how the compact can act as a coherent 'umbrella' for ameliorating the many policy demands made upon British companies to become involved in education.

The experience in East London of a very low take-up of compact jobs by students is also set in a specific national context of government and individual company policies. Negative student attitudes among goal-achievers in London to those Compact jobs which were part of the government's Youth Training Scheme appears to have been one factor contributing to low take-up. A second cause was the practice of some employers in making the job 'guarantee' conditional upon company-specific selection and aptitude tests (ILEA, 1989[b] pp. 25-26).[2]

It is also probable that East London employers were to some extent disarmed by the detailed evaluation of the Compact undertaken by the Research and Statistics Branch of ILEA. This included a detailed discussion of the statistical difficulties inherent in evaluating individual schools' performance against strict 'improvement' goals for student punctuality and attendance and led the ILEA researchers to two conclusions: that the 5% improvement target for schools 'should be phased out' and that the 'school compact goals should not lead to a comparison of one school's performance with another' as this failed to take account of social variables outside the control of the compact and of the individual school (ILEA 1989 [a], pp. 39-40). The logic behind the first statement was not clearly presented. The second argument directly challenged other government policies which sought to encourage statistical comparisons between schools as an aid to parental choice. For government ministers the stance of the evaluation report could be seen as political interference, as typical of the ILEA (which was the only local authority in the English education system of sufficient size to support its own research operation) and as beyond the remit of an education authority to adjudicate. This clash of interests was solved from the government's point of view by the abolition of ILEA in March 1990.

UK Government Replication of Compacts

The HMI report (DES, 1989) on the East London Compact appeared far quicker than was normal for the DES. The inspection was carried out in only the second school term of the Compact's operation, and designed 'to contribute to the successful development of the project' (ibid. p. 2). Such an unreserved endorsement of a policy initiative is unusual from HMI and may indicate that the DES sought rapid and positive identification with a project that a rival department of government – with rival policy aims – was proposing to support with a large injection of funding.

For, as the DES inspectors were going about their work, in March 1988 Secretary of State for Employment Norman Fowler launched a £12m national compact initiative. Enthused by his own study visit to Boston,

Fowler announced that the Department of Employment would take the lead in providing for twelve new compacts, offering each £100,000 funding per year for four years in addition to £50,000 preliminary development funding. The initiative was to be part of the government's inter-departmental 'Action for Cities' initiative and the compacts were to start operation in 1989.

If the DES was keen to be part of the compacts movement, there was clear annoyance among the London Compact organisers at the turn of events. 'These compacts will be set up before we have evaluated the first' was the testy reaction of the chief executive of the London Enterprise Agency (Wright, 1988 p. 17); the London organisers began to re-describe their project as a 'pilot' for the whole of Britain. Richard Martineau commented that the government's scheme had been launched 'for better or worse' and expressed concerns about 'the government's centralising tendencies' (Martineau, 1988 p. 12; 1989 pp. 39, 40–41).

This was politely coded language hinting at a general sense of outrage amongst those involved with compacts at the government's handling of the national launch of its scheme. Not only had the original study visit of the London group pre-dated Fowler's own by over two years but the East London Compact's pioneering role was completely omitted from the government's press launch and from the Employment Department literature which accompanied it. This snub was apparently the result of Education Secretary Kenneth Baker's announcement in the House of Commons five weeks earlier that the ILEA was to be abolished due to its purported inefficiency and poor record in maintaining education standards. Media coverage of the national compacts launch concluded that any reference to ILEA's central role in the East London Compact would have been a political embarrassment, particularly as supporting government rhetoric justifying ILEA's abolition included general charges of its betraying left-wing bias and being anti-business.

In portraying the arrival of compacts in Britain as Mr Fowler's inspired vision, it was left unsaid that ten other British cities had already begun developing compact plans, using East London as their model (Wright, 1988 p. 12; Nash 1988 p. 1). Where Martineau had been restrained, *The Times Educational Supplement*'s view was forthright:

> There is something unbelievably childish in this desire to slight ILEA: certainly it does nothing to foster a belief that ministers understand or care about the kind of close co-operation between education authorities and industry which is needed if the 'compact' idea is to spread (*TES* 1988 p. 2).

Elsewhere in the press, the government's limited view of a comprehensive concept of 'partnership' was noted. 'There was no mention of the role of local authorities', *The Guardian* observed, adding, somewhat pointedly, that 'an imaginative government would have been looking at ways in which to encourage these partnerships, which have been particularly successful in the U.S.' (*Guardian*, 1988).

Despite the skirmishing it was clear that the Conservative Government had alighted on compacts as an ideal vehicle for satisfying a number of specifically British education policy prerogatives: employers could exert greater direct influence over school policies at the expense of local education authorities; a spontaneous coming together of business leaders and education managers in a number of British cities could be appropriated and officially 'launched' at very little cost and claimed as the government's own innovation; ministers' respect for selected examples of free market dynamism in President Reagan's America could be demonstrated through imitation; the establishment of numerical performance targets for inner-city schools could reinforce both their accountability to business and to government as well as providing a further yardstick for informed parental choice between schools.

Perhaps the most attractive feature of compacts to a government increasingly concerned to stress accountability and measures of performance in education was that the structure, goals and function of compacts appeared simple to understand, applicable to any urban environment, could be established quickly and could be monitored and evaluated in a straightforward way. There was also a belief that this kind of partnership between education and business was more sophisticated than those which had preceded it. Training Agency promotional literature claimed that 'by establishing clear, measurable goals' compacts took partnerships 'a stage further, focusing effort on improving the quality of the future workforce and giving young people a more effective entry into employment or further education'. Subsequent preliminary evaluations of British compacts have hinted, however, that much of the substance of such claims is based upon the most rudimentary understanding of the incentives which influence student choice and employer involvement (T.A., 1988; Fuller, 1990, p. 15).

Patterns of National Compact Replication in America and Britain

In its publicity, the NAB used virtually identical wording to that of the Training Agency in Britain to explain its rationale, commending compacts as partnerships 'with long-term, measurable goals [helping to] reinforce the importance and benefits for at-risk youth of completing a successful transition to work or higher education (NAB, 1989[a], p.1). Absent from the American replication project, however, was the British Training Agency's ambivalence about whether compacts were primarily concerned with increased inner-city job opportunities or should be seen as supplementing the wider urban education effort (Jackson, 1989). In America, where issues of urban social decay and its impact upon schooling were widely perceived to have reached a much more serious point, the business community had become confident in insisting that compacts were designed to effect 'systemic change in education through business involvement with public education'. American compact cities, unlike their British counterparts, were required both to use 'a business intermediary such as the Private Industry Council' to co-ordinate the jobs effort and to demonstrate 'the school Superintendent's commitment to working with city leaders to improve education'.[3] This Boston-inspired design was reinforced through a national steering committee for the NAB project with strong Boston representation including a former Boston compact director, two Boston PIC directors and the former superintendent (NAB, 1989[a], pp. 1, 3, 15; NAB 1989[b], p. 5).

In Britain, compact development had, until the launch of TECs in 1990 (see Bailey, this volume), no equivalent to the PIC structure around which to coalesce employer involvement in education. One consequence was that, despite rumours about the problems being experienced in Boston, student targets, linked to job or training opportunities, remained the basis of the British compact model and the instrument which demonstrated employer commitment to inner-city education.

A further, fundamental difference in the British context was the interplay of Conservative education policies. The compact programme was considerably enlarged during 1988-90 – funding was eventually made available for the operation of 60 compacts – during a period when local education authorities (LEAs) began to come under increasing political pressure.[4] In a Training Agency publication, Matthew Nicholas, the head of the government's new Compact Support Unit, alluded to various 'concerns' expressed by LEAs about compact development. The planned abolition of ILEA had not helped ease such worries. Neither had government ministers attempted to smooth relations with Nicholas Ridley observing that the principle behind all inner city policy was 'a shift in the function of local authorities' from providers to regulators of services (T.A., 1989[a]; Burns, 1988). In addition to anxiety about their long-term prospects for survival, several LEAs were worried about the potential of compacts to narrow student opportunity.

By the end of 1989 a more general concern was being expressed that, despite early East London experience, existing compacts had the potential to hamper increased staying on rates. This prompted the London Business Education Partnership to unveil a prototype 'higher education compact' with polytechnics and universities reserving places on specified courses for students attaining compact goals. The plan resembled the Boston Higher Education Partnership launched for similar reasons in 1983 and served to underline the London organisers' continued pioneering role, despite a lack of recognition by government departments. Moreover, the British education press, reporting on the new plan, alluded to tensions between policy departments:

> So far the Department of Employment, which funds compacts under
> the Government's urban programme as a way of getting school leavers
> into jobs, has not been involved. But the Department of Education and

Science, far more concerned with staying on rates, is following the development closely (Jack, 1989 [b]; Jackson, 1989).

Undaunted, the local, non-governmental pioneers of compacts in England continued to stress an independent line. The London Education Business Partnership provided an 'umbrella' for the three new London compacts in 1989 and, in one of its last publications, ILEA produced a practical handbook for other cities running compacts – a full year before the Training Agency was in a position to do so (Martineau, 1989 p. 40; ILEA 1989 [d]).

Training Agency figures released in April 1990 summarised the growth and spread of the national compact initiative in Britain: 3,800 employers and training organisations were 'actively involved' as were 255 schools 'with more than 36,000 young people offered a job with training in return for the achievement of agreed personal objectives'. Training Agency funding rules required that British compacts set measurable, numerical performance goals for pupils. In America the national Compact Project was in a more diffuse state having abandoned the attempt to replicate conditions in Boston. The National Alliance of Business reported, rather lamely, that 'the 12 Compact Projects are at 12 different points in compact development' with only a minority of cities choosing to adopt long-term, measurable goals. (T.A., 1990 p. 11; NAB, 1989 [b] p. 65).

Policy Issues Underlying Compacts

The Problem of Policy Focus

For the policy analyst much of the interest of compacts lies in the various and competing claims made on their behalf – by politicians as well as by the various constituent groups involved in the initiative.

A central problem facing those who promote compacts is that, in both America and Britain, confusion remains as to their main objective: are they an education reform policy, an employment policy or a social policy? If it is claimed that they are all three then their capacity to effect lasting change in any one policy area is likely to be considerably diluted, for reasons discussed below.[5]

The organisation, logic and operation of the Boston Compact during 1982-90 demonstrates a marked shift among the three aims. What started out as an experiment in employment policy with some implications for school reform became unequivocally an experiment in school-reform policy. The measures of success drawn up in Boston were, to begin with, those determined by employment policy considerations. These focused on improving labour market supply of young people to employers through the operation of incentives – money for the public sector and employment prospects for young people based upon minimum performance standards.[6] Later, when labour market conditions eased and when the school reform focus became blurred, the Boston employers promptly exerted greater public pressure over the issue of school performance.

Three themes are important to note. First, in the education policy context, it is evident that, after eight years of very great influence, the Boston Compact in 1990 remained highly experimental with no sustained research information on its impact upon young people. In addition, in a situation such as that of Boston where, after 1986, employers sought to dominate the school reform agenda by insisting upon measures of efficiency, education 'partners' in the compact became disenchanted. This disenchantment arose within on education management culture which returned to a model of equality of provision through bureaucratic, centralised management.

Second, in the employment policy context, it seems probable that the Boston Compact and business-education 'partnerships' styled upon it require, for their impetus, either a tight youth labour market where employer demand outstrips student supply, or a determination by the business sector to insist upon an agenda of school reform based upon a management-by-objectives framework. In the absence of either pressure there is, as yet, no evidence in the Boston case that either side of the partnership can be sustained. Furthermore, in both America and Britain during the 1980s business intervention in schools has been encouraged by governments keen to invoke employer-led solutions to education and training policy based upon an appeal both to the efficiency of the labour market and the role of employers in providing incentives for young people to attain educational qualifications. The problem that this combined situation poses for compacts is that the determinants of improved student attainment brought about by the compact idea per se are difficult to identify. An additional complication, particularly in Britain, has been a pressure on employers not to recruit 16 year-olds in the face of national targets for improving staying on-rates.[7]

Third, the social policy context within which formal business-education 'partnerships' need to be assessed tends to suggest that they receive additional momentum when established in conditions such as those of the inner-city. Here minority and ethnic community issues combine with wider social problems of youth alienation and drug abuse to disrupt efficient labour supply and contribute to familiar problems of urban decay. It is significant that in America, where such problems are considerably more severe than in Britain, NAB's funding for the Compacts Project was secured from the federal Department of Health and Human Services. In Britain, where formal 'partnerships' in rural and provincial communities have been relatively underdeveloped, it is the example of the inner-city 'compact' model that has been influential.[8] If directly replicated in rural areas, however, the distinguishing characteristics of compacts – employer concern about the economic stability of the community and interdependent city networks - is more difficult for compact managers to exploit.

183

Such a three-way split between education reform, employment, and social policy objectives is a clear feature of compacts and of many business-education 'partnerships'. This diffuse focus reduces the risk of outright failure and may help to ensure their continued use as a policy mechanism for the foreseeable future. But it also weakens compacts' capacity to effect significant change. Each interest group, for example, can explain lack of success through the inadequacy of other participants. This problem was well illustrated in Boston where the compact organisers complained of being continually obstructed by 'the curriculum and instruction people' in the Schools Department whereas the employers concluded that the schools themselves had hindered the Compact's success (Farrar and Cipollone, 1988 [b], p. 16; Boston PIC, 1988 p. 2).

More importantly, diffuse policy objectives allow considerable scope for disagreement as to what constitutes compact 'success'. This problem is particularly well disguised by the tendency of those concerned with compact replication to stress the managerial "do's and don't's" of getting established to the detriment of developing a sophisticated research method for assessing the compact's impact upon its basic client group of young people. If the compact's ambition is limited to such a managerial outlook, the main criteria for 'success' is limited to the survival of the partnership itself.

Furthermore, the problems which compacts face in assessing their impact upon young people caused by competing policy objectives and the primary goal of their own institutional survival have been compounded by their status as components of a highly fashionable 'initiative'. Both American and British educationalists complain of their subjection to a battery of externally-imposed policy initiatives, arguing that such intervention is an inadequate political response to the fundamental problems of public education provision. Compact advocates counter that the programme brings selective incentives to a notoriously unmanageable and inefficient part of the public sector.

The terms of the debate considerably underestimate the complexity and difficulty of the task facing both countries. Where is the evidence that the incentive argument has a significant impact upon the educational experience of young people? Conversely, what compelling counter-strategies can critics of incentive-based policy intervention offer as a realistic revitalising mechanism for the loss of confidence in the management theory and practice of inner-city schooling?

Private Sector Intervention in School Reform

Because British, community-based, education-business ventures are strongly grounded on consensus and because local labour markets are less clearly dominated by powerful employer lobbies than those in America, it is difficult to envisage even the most confident Training and Enterprise Council (TEC) in Britain declaring, as did the Boston PIC in 1989, that whilst employment objectives for the compact had been achieved, 'real school improvement remained an unfulfilled promise' (Boston PIC, 1988, pp. 1-2). Apart from British employers' traditional reticence directly to confront local educational provision in this way, continuity in national education and training policy in Britain is notoriously elusive. If a TEC was to strike such a confrontational pose many educationalists would content themselves with the prospect of the TEC-centred policy imperative being removed upon a change of government.

American business people are apparently more aware of and alarmed about the economic implications of the mix of demographic change, ethnic minority trends and inner-city social statistics than are their British counterparts (T.A., 1989[b], p. 3). There is no evidence, however, that the American corporate community has any more imaginative, coherent or consistent view concerning the content of educational reform than the impoverished understanding of their opposite numbers in Britain (Keep, 1988; CBI, 1988 pp. 17, 22). Indeed, in the British context, a national employers' study of the relationship between schools and companies was happy to recommend the greater involvement of business in the existing diverse and often competing 'menu' of activities on offer. The same CBI study also struck a note which would be highly implausible in America: 'since 1979 this Government has met most if not all the demands which business might reasonably have made with respect to the education system'. Not only had the government played its part but it was concluded that 'the education service has never been more willing to receive an input from industry than it is today' (CBI, 1988 pp. 25, 13).

It is in such a benign policy environment that varieties of the Boston Compact have been propagated in Britain. Without the government's intervention it is unlikely that measurable student goals would have been insisted upon; more likely, employers and educationalists in local communities would have formulated the more generalised agreements resorted to in most of the NAB's American compacts. For Boston's business leaders, these compacts are already a compromise and a backwards step. The Boston PIC Director was quite clear in 1989 that his local business community was not 'backing off'. He insisted instead that the employers would proceed 'full speed ahead. They're becoming more aggressive, stepping forward, getting involved in fundamental school reform' (NAB, 1989[d] p. 1)

Thus the Boston Compact continues to offer a provocative lead to its imitators. Having abandoned its belief that job-guarantee incentives can stem the drop-out rate without parallel school reform it was, by 1990, seeking the imposition of specific forms of school management and accountability based upon private sector theory and practice through which schools would be required to manage themselves.

National reforms of a similar nature, labelled Local Management of Schools (LMS), have been implemented in Britain but these are concerned with financial accountability. Academic standards in Britain are to be raised through the National Curriculum. Yet Boston business leaders reject this approach arguing for LMS as a tool for academic accountability because 'asking for academic improvement from the system as a whole doesn't work' (ibid p. 2).

Nevertheless, it would appear in the interests of neither the compacts nor their funders to see a strong, outspoken business lobby divert the compact agenda to the more intractable problem of the extent to which school reform should be conducted upon private sector lines. This territory is complex and politically volatile. Broadly speaking, the 74 American and British compacts which have modelled themselves on Boston have erred on the side of pragmatism and mutual tolerance in setting their goals. Only in Boston, the progenitor compact, is the message still uncompromisingly harsh. 'Are the schools good enough?' asks the Boston PIC chairman. 'Without hesitation, we are compelled to answer "no"' (ibid. p. 1).

Compacts and Policy Borrowing

In the late 1980s, British government policy makers identified a lack of vision in the management theory and practice of inner-city schooling. As an antidote they prescribed salvation through the study and replication of American practice. In 1989 the Training Agency even went so far as to commission a glossy leaflet entitled *Education Business Partnerships: Lessons from America*. This document speaks enthusiastically of an American 'tide of emotion and enterprise that has led to a staggering range of partnership schemes'. It then goes on to confirm the diffuse policy goals served by this process – social policy, employment policy and 'the major target' of school reform policy. So compelling was the American vision thought to be that most of the report 'consists solely of practical advice and tips' for those entrusted with managerial responsibility for generating such conditions in Britain. At the same time as *Lessons from America* appeared, the sense of fervour was reinforced by the British pressure group Business in the Community which reported on a study tour by British business and education leaders who found American practice to be 'dazzling' and the experience of visiting America to have 'lifted the level of thinking among activists' in British business-education partnerships (T.A., 1989[b] pp. 2-5; BIC, 1989 p. 1)

What have been the lessons of this example of policy borrowing? First, such outbursts of enthusiasm tend to breed caution and suspicion amongst uninitiated non-'activists' outside the charmed circle of government advisers. Offence in British education circles was caused, for example, when, at the launch of the compacts initiative, the Department of Employment announced the appointment of Catherine Stratton as 'special adviser' to Norman Fowler. Her background with the Boston PIC did not commend her to the British education press which felt that the government should have turned 'to those who had first-hand experience of adapting the Boston model to English conditions in East London'. To this claimed insensitivity was added the accusation that politicians were merely 'putting in a small amount of money to buy the right to make the rules for future school/industry compacts' (TES, 1988).

Significantly, however, criticism was not levelled against the concept of policy borrowing from America for *The Times Educational Supplement* labelled the Boston Compact as a 'brilliant local initiative'. Rather, it was fuelled by suspicion of the appropriation of compacts as an official, national 'initiative' which would otherwise have taken root in Britain spontaneously. As it was, the TES concluded that the local authorities would have to 'pocket their pride and humour the childish arrogance of ministers who cannot bear to think anyone might have a good idea but themselves' (ibid). Yet such language was itself somewhat immature and missed the point for without the 'small amount of public money' there was no guarantee of compacts setting numerical, measurable goals – a wider objective of government policies for local government accountability. Furthermore, it is notable that those American business-education partnership specialists who observed British developments, enthused over the national awareness, financial stimulus and rapid spread of compact ideas arising from central government intervention of a kind not possible in the USA.

Because the compact idea has been transplanted ostensibly intact from the American situation to Britain, authoritative comparison of the education policy context of each country may be made with more than usual confidence. It is apparent that a greater infrastructure for policy delivery exists in Britain than in America, with most British companies involved in compacts aware of a broadly-based, consensual agenda for 'education-industry' activity not specifically related to labour market or social policy measures. From its beginnings, the East London Compact sought to co-ordinate this agenda of 'soft' policies in a way that would have appeared unappetising to the Boston PIC (TES, 1988; Martineau, 1989, P.M., 1989, p. 63). Such a climate in Britain owes much to the exploratory nature of the Technical and Vocational Education Initiative (TVEI) and Industry Year in 1986 which sought to engage schools, local authorities and companies in dialogue rather than in contractual goal-setting. The ground was further prepared in Britain in 1988 when the government set itself the goals providing work experience for all pupils by the age of 16 and an annual target of seconding 10% of teachers to work in business for two weeks. These performance measures resulted in government-appointed education-industry advisers lobbying business in each local authority area – a further example of an awareness programme that could not conceivably be run nationally from Washington DC (DTI, 1988).

For some in Britain such activity, though relatively thorough, has been too leisurely and compacts have been exhorted to emulate what the Training Agency described as the American virtue of getting 'as much happening as fast as possible' (BIC, 1989 p. 1; T.A., 1989[b] p. 3). There is a consensus, however, amongst those from Britain who have observed American compacts and 'partnerships' at first hand that they are less sophisticated than equivalent British practice in terms of curriculum development and critical evaluation (Hofkins, 1990). This view has been summarised in *Lessons from America*:

> At first sight the British team did not find evidence of what we understand as rigorous evaluation – yet a closer look revealed [that] nearly all [U.S.] schemes set great store by it but that the universal intent was to pull out the positive lessons rather than the negative. This had the effect of stoking enthusiasm...(T.A. 1989[b] p. 3).

If developed in an unfettered way in Britain such uncritical enthusiasm will further disquiet the sensibilities of many British educationalists, academics and education journalists. This, in turn, could cause considerable problems for the national compact initiative should inner-city schools begin to encounter the problems experienced in Boston where student improvement goals were discovered to be unattainable.

More likely than a Boston-style debacle is that British compact schools will achieve most of their government-endorsed student goals which typically aim at individual attendance rates of 85% and punctuality rates of 90%, the 'completion' of designated courses and, in a minority of compacts, 'performance commensurate with ability' in English and Mathematics. By sanctioning such a mix of improvement measures – the last, very reminiscent of officially discredited ILEA thinking – the government can point to compacts as addressing employers' labour market needs and as remaining true to the Boston principle of insisting on long-term, measurable goals for 'school improvement'.

As a policy device, compacts in both countries have made a significant impact and have shown that the basic compact idea is easy to grasp, flexible in operation and, accordingly, is a good vehicle for replication. Despite this, a number of important weaknesses endanger the claims for compacts' longer-term significance in confronting the problems of inner-city schooling: the dilution of compact objectives across too wide a policy canvass; the reliance of compacts on a tight labour market to secure from employers job guarantees for students; and lack of clarity about the basic school improvement objectives of compacts – compounded, in Britain, by excessive emphasis on the managerial techniques of running a successful compact and, in America, by a lack of critical evaluation.

Notes

[1] The story of the Boston compact has been told many times (eg: Caradonio & Spring, 1983; Willie, 1984; NAB, 1987; Rickhuss, 1989). Most accounts are descriptive and designed to encourage other cities to emulate the model. Only two of the many of articles spawned can claim to provide a significant analysis of

the policy process of the compact and the impact it has made. Both are by Eleanor Farrar and Anthony Cipollone (1988[a]; 1988[b]).

Uncritical 'research' literature about the business-education relationship is a general problem. This movement has generated a mass of accompanying literature, most of which is non-analytic but descriptive and expository in nature. In 1980 there was virtually no such literature on the rationale for active school-business collaboration other than academic articles discussing the state of vocational education in general. By December 1989, however, the Educational Research Information Center (ERIC) database of abstracts in Washington DC listed 3,036 articles published since 1982 under its category of 'schools-business relationship'. A mere thirty seven abstracts (1.2%), however, attempted evaluation or critical analysis of the mass of activity linking schools and business.

[2] Richard Martineau, the chief executive of the London Business Education Partnership, reported that such an increase fitted in with 'the needs of many employers who would rather take on young people at 18 with better qualifications'. An HMI inspection report was more cautious as to the cause of increased staying-on rates, observing that 'many pupils seemed uncertain about what the employers would be offering and about their motives' (Martineau, 1988; DES, 1989 p. 9).

[3] This arrangement was adopted in Britain in 1991 when it was announced that compacts would normally work through the TEC structure.

[4] The government's original announcement in March 1988 of 12 compacts costing £12m had been rapidly extended to allow for three more inner cities to become involved. Five months later the Department of Employment announced that support would double from fifteen to thirty compacts with the result that the minister could point to 'a very real prospect of establishing Compacts in inner city areas throughout the country' (DE, 1988). This goal was subsequently brought closer to realisation by a further doubling of the target to sixty compacts being in operation by 1991.

[5] The British government's enthusiastic adoption of compacts represents the clearest example of the operational flexibility and political capital available to all compact participants first highlighted in interviews by Farrar and Cipollone with the originators of the Boston Compact (Farrar and Cipollone 1988 [a], p. 91).

[6] It is clear that those who were involved at the outset of the Boston Compact identified the initiative as a programme designed primarily to establish a smooth school to work transition for students where this had broken down. There appear to have been two main causes of the rupture. On the one hand, the Schools Department and individual schools had seemingly become disorientated by external changes in the youth labour market and social demography in inner Boston. Middle class families moved out at a time when the youth recruitment needs of downtown employers increased. Simultaneously, it seems that the management and organisation of the schools system came under increasing criticism from the outside.

As a result, business leaders and the new schools Superintendent joined forces in an attempt to exact specific changes in school organisation and goals. Among the specific outcomes which they sought to achieve through the compact were: greater stress on school leadership; extra resources for schools; increased staff development; enhanced student motivation; raised expectations amongst teachers, student and administrators; and accountability of schools to publicly-set goals. To reinforce the point the compact office in Boston made a proud boast. 'We had an ideological approach that we weren't going to deviate from'; this was to require institutional change from the bottom upwards (Farrar and Cipollone, 1988[a], pp. 100-06).

The early support of educationalists for the compact rested on the claim not merely that drop-out rates would fall but that 'the quality of education' in schools would be improved, specifically through the attainment by students of the most rudimentary reading and mathematical skills. It is at this point that tensions may be detected. In Boston in 1985 the Compact was generating considerable publicity as a school reform policy, yet it was acknowledged privately, within the compact office, that devolving school plans to teachers would not in itself generate the resources required to improve teaching. Vital instruments for overall school improvements such as in-service training, curriculum development and intensive coaching for slow learners were core educational activities which could not expect to be the subject of business funding.

Such admissions confirmed that, after all, the Boston compact was, in practice, a school to work programme which reached its high point in terms of consensual progress in 1986. That autumn the PIC director reported that, 'with the class of 1986, I think we've reached a point where we can say that every Boston high school graduate can either go on to college or can get a job. That is probably the outstanding achievement of the Compact, and maybe the Compact itself will never be able to achieve more' (Farrar and Cipollone, 1988 [b] p. 5).

[7] Government support for compacts in Britain – from the UK Department of Employment – as well as specific statements by NAB suggest that, fundamentally, they are funded as school to work programmes (NAB 1989 [b] p. 5).

[8] The British Government announced in 1991 the further replication of the 'compact approach' to non-urban areas (DES/DE; 1991).

References

Barker P. (1989) 'A compact with Disillusion', The Independent, 15 June, 1989

B.I.C. (1989) 'Learning from America' in Partnership Points, Number 1, January/February 1989 (misdated 1988), Business in the Community, London

Boston PIC (1988) 'Proposed New Goals presented at the Boston Private Industry Council Annual Meeting, 3 October, 1988', unpublished committee paper

Burns A. (1988) 'Thatcher launches high profile line on inner city policies', in The Independent, 7 March, 1988

Caradornio J. & Spring W. (1983) 'The Boston Compact' in Journal of Vocational Education (U.S.A.), Vol. 58, No. 3, April, 1983

C.B.I. (1988) Building a Stronger Partnership Between Business and Secondary Education, Report of the CBI Business Education Task force, Confederation of British Industry, London

D.E. (1988[a]) 'Compacts', internal Manpower Services Commission memorandum, April 1988

D.E. (1988[b]) 'Norman Fowler announces funding for 30 Inner City compacts, Department of Employment Press Release, 17 August, 1988

DES (1989) Report by HM Inspectors on the London Education Business Partnership, The London Compact: East London Phase, HMSO

DES/D.E. (1991) Education and Training for the 21st Century, HMSO

D.T.I. (1988) DTI – The Department for Enterprise, HMSO

Farrar E. & Cippolone A. (1988[a]) 'After the Signing: The Boston Compact 1982 to 1985' in Levine M. & Trachtman R. (eds.) American Business and the Public School, Teachers' College Press, New York

Farrar E. & Cippolone A. (1988[b]) 'The Business Community and School Reform: The Boston Compact at Five Years', unpublished paper, March 1989, available from the Private Industry Council, Boston, Mass.

Fuller A. (1990) 'Compacts: the emerging issues', in Education and Training, Vol. 32, No.4, pp. 13-16.

Guardian (1988) Leading article on the 'Action for Cities' launch, The Guardian, 8 March, 1988

Hofkins D. (1990) 'Shared concern on inner-city failure' in Times Higher Educational Supplement, 9 March 1990

ILEA (1989[a]) East London Compact Evaluation report No. 1: Goal Achievement and Student Destinations, Inner London Education Authority, May 1989

ILEA (1989[b]) East London Compact Evaluation report No. 2: The Compact Jobs, Inner London Education Authority, May 1989

ILEA (1989[c]) East London Compact Evaluation report No. 3: Employers' Perceptions and Experiences, Inner London Education Authority, May 1989

ILEA (1989[d]) The London Compact Handbook, Inner London Education Authority

Jack A. (1989[a]) 'A Troubled Compact' in Boston Globe (Mass.) 3 July, 1989

Jack A. (1989[b]) 'Business Education Compacts: Trans-Atlantic Lessons' unpublished draft paper

Jackson M. (1989) 'London Compact to promise H E places', in The Times Educational Supplement, 8 December.

Keep, E.J. (1988) 'What do Employers Want from Education? A Question more Easily asked than Answered', unpublished paper, University of Warwick

Martineau R. (1988) 'How we got going with Compact' in CBI News, 27 May – 9 June, 1988, Confederation of British Industry, London

Martineau R. (1989) 'First term report on the London Compact' in Personnel Management, April, 1989

N.A.B. (1987) The Fourth R: Workforce Readiness, National Alliance of Business, Washington DC

N.A.B. (1989[a]) 'The Compact', promotional brochure, National Alliance of Business, Washington DC, Spring 1989

N.A.B. (1989[b]) The Compact Project: School Business Partnerships for Improving Education, National Alliance of Business, Washington DC

N.A.B. (1989[c]) America's Business Leaders Speak Out on Business Education Partnerships, National Alliance of Business, Washington DC

N.A.B. (1989[d]) 'The Boston Compact: Stalemate or Rebirth?' in Work America, Vol. 6, No. 4, March 1989, National Alliance of Business, Washington DC

Nash I. (1988) 'Cities take radical steps to boost leavers' job prospects', The Times Educational Supplement, 26 February.

Nash I. (1989) 'Boston trailblazers loose their way' in Times Educational Supplement, 19 June, 1989

P.M. (1989) 'East London Compact Scores Limited Goals' in Personnel Management, July 1989

P.E. (1989) Education Compacts: Local Economic and Development Information Service (LEDIS) Overview No. B.85', June 1989, The Planning Exchange, Glasgow

Rickhaus T. (1989) 'Business Education Partnerships for Progress: The American Experience' in Training and Development, U.K. July, 1989

Rossano K. (1987) 'The Boston Experience', unidentified source

T.A. (1988) 'Compacts: Strengthening the Partnership between Employers and Education', Training Agency publicity leaflet, published November, 1988

T.A. (1989[a]) 'Compacts off to a Flying Start', in-house publicity leaflet, Training Agency, Sheffield, 1989

T.A. (1989[b]) Education Industry Partnerships: Lessons from America, Training Agency, Sheffield

T.A. (1990) Training Agency Research Annual Report 1990, Training Agency, Sheffield

T.E.S. (1988) 'Will the MSC Wreck the Compact?', leader article, Times Educational Supplement, 11 March, 1988

Willie C. (1984) 'The Boston Compact: A Model for Inter Agency Collaboration and School Improvement', in Equity and Choice (U.S.A.), Vol. 1 No. 1, Fall 1984

Wright B. (1988) 'The Compact Route from London to Boston' in Transition, May 1988

Top-up Student Loans:
American Models of Student Aid
and British Public Policy

LAUREL McFARLAND[1]

On November 9, 1988, the British Government issued a White Paper outlining a new system for financing students' living costs. A year and a half later the student loan proposal was law, and for the first time in the post-war period, loans became part of the British system of student aid. This sharp departure from a forty year commitment to the provision of free higher education has provoked sharp debate and criticism. Opponents have singled out the forthrightly American approach as indicative of the Government's betrayal of the British post-war consensus on higher education.

The loan program reflects an unmistakable American influence. To understand the relationship between American loan programs and the British loan design, this chapter will undertake a systematic examination of the appropriability [2] of American student loan programs for British policy-makers. It will explore why American models were used in the British student loan program, and which models were applied. At a deeper level, it will also analyze the borrowing process, to identify the critical factors and agents in various stages of the policy transfer. The structure of this analysis will be straightforward: it will begin with a brief description of the Conservative Government White Paper on top-up loans, including a discussion of why British policy-makers chose to adopt an American-style program. It will then analyze the two American student aid plans that were influential in the British loan system's design. The next step is to examine the changes made in the program from the White Paper to its final enactment, examining some of the economic and political reasons for the changes. It will then consider the specific problems of transferring educational programs between the two countries, examining seven political and economic conditions in Britain that may limit the appropriability of the American designs. The chapter will close with an analysis of the borrowing process and a discussion of the wider implications of imposing American aid models on the British system, including the likely effect on other stated government goals such as expanded access to higher education.

Top-up Loans and the British Policy-Making Process

The first step in analyzing the appropriability of America's student aid models to Britain is to identify the nature of the current British policy-making process, in order to show why American models were incorporated into the top-up loan program.[3] A concise, if somewhat cynical interpretation of present government social policy attributes two overriding goals to Conservative policy: reduction of the Public Sector Borrowing Requirement (PSBR) and a commitment to dismantle the welfare state. In the political and fiscal environment of Mrs Thatcher's third term, both goals were placed at the very top of the Tory agenda, and the proposed changes in educational policy should be viewed in this light. In deference to public opinion concerning education, public pronouncements have downplayed these primary motivations in favor of more palatable appeals for expanded access to higher education, and decreased "dependence" on government. Thus, the Conservative Government has a two layer motivation for adopting an American student loan framework: its "private" agenda of reducing PSBR and the welfare state, and the publicly stated objectives of increased equity and access.

The Conservative Party's consolidation of power in the years following the 1983 landslide re-election was dramatic. In the late 1980s, the Conservative Party under Margaret Thatcher not only was the dominant voice in policy formation, but it also succeeded in altering the fundamental agenda of British public policy. The Government's early struggles were with economic matters: restraining inflation, weakening trade unions, returning public enterprises to the private sector, and above all, reducing government borrowing. Controlling government and restricting its interference in economic activity succeeded to a point at which, particularly between the 1987 election and Mrs. Thatcher's 1990 resignation, the Government tried to find its way towards a post-welfare state in which market forces also replace central government planning and control in spheres of social policy. Despite successes with their economic agenda, ministers had no precedent, and little experience in how to achieve this goal. Furthermore, the policy process was emasculated by the lack of opposition in Parliament: prior beliefs dominated Tory ministers' policy initiatives, and the closed and secretive nature of British government restricted input from outside. Given this situation, it is not surprising that ministers turned to American social policy for guidance. In its rush for reform and its pursuit of the ideological high ground, the Thatcher government convinced itself that the American system of student aid offered lower cost per aided student, less PSBR pressure, and hypothetically, access for all. American aid programs, while not the only influence on British student aid reform, were used frequently as ammunition in the Conservatives' battle to alter the finance of higher education. Secretary of Education Kenneth Baker made three trips to the United States in the late 1980s to discuss American student aid programs, and made repeated references in speeches and in print to the benefits of the American system of loans (Walker, 1989). Baker sought to change the existing British system for financing students, which provided free tuition and a maintenance grant for living expenses. By the late 1980s, inflation had seriously eroded the adequacy of the grants, and by not indexing them, the Conservative Government had begun to challenge the assumption that students and their families should contribute only a small share of the total cost of higher education. The argument over who should make up the widening gap provided the impetus for the Government's consideration of a top-up loans program.

The Influence of American Student Loan Models in Britain

In formulating the top-up loans proposal, the British borrowed from two student loan designs, the US Government's Guaranteed Student Loan ("GSL" program), and income contingent loan models, popularized in the U.S. by 1988 presidential candidate Dukakis's Student Tuition and Repayment System (STARS).[4] The GSL program was first developed in 1965 after the passage of the Higher Education Act. It was conceived as one part of a tripod of federally-funded student aid for higher education: work-study, "Pell" grants to low-income students, and federally-guaranteed student loans. The government paid the interest while the student was attending college, subsidized the rate of interest during repayment, and provided a guarantee to the private bank that issued the loan. Eligibility guidelines and interest rate subsidies have been changed several times since 1965 in order to contain costs and prevent abuses, but nonetheless, GSLs have increased from a total of $1.015 billion in 1970 to $6.2 billion in 1980, and most recently to about $12.4 billion (1991 College Board estimate). The number of borrowers has quadrupled from 1.017 million in 1970 to 3.98 million in 1990.

The STARS proposal put forward by Democratic presidential candidate Dukakis in 1988 was the most recent American incarnation of the income-contingent loan concept which has been introduced in Australia and other countries. The income contingency idea is conceptually simple, but complex in implementation and enforcement. It is also distinctly American, dating back to Milton Friedman's writings in the 1950s and to the Zacharias education proposals of the 1960s, but the proposals have never become law. With Dukakis's defeat, the plan was shelved once again, but it certainly influenced British policy-makers, particularly Baker. The Dukakis proposal envisioned banks loaning any college student the amount he or she needed, receiving principal and the market interest rate from the federal government which, in turn, would exact payment from borrowers in the form of a lifetime payroll tax. Estimates of the cost to the student ranged from one-eighth to one-quarter of one percent surcharge on tax per $1000 borrowed, depending on the rate of interest charged and incomes within the pool of borrowers (Blyska and Hodge, 1988).

The influence of these two models on the final version of the British top-up loans scheme is quite clear: there was a pronounced shift towards a mortgage-style GSL loan between the White Paper and the Student Loans Act, though the loan amounts and the loan:grant ratio plans stayed about the same. The White Paper proposed phasing in a loan program by gradually replacing parental contributions and government grants for living expenses with a privately funded, government-guaranteed loan. At this point the administrative mechanisms resembled the GSL, even down to the 9 month grace period before repayment began, but the repayment terms would have placed a fair number of students in an income contingent repayment category. And, like the GSL, interest on the British student loan would have been subsidized after graduation, and completely covered by the government while the student was still at university. In the enacted version, the interest rate subsidy has essentially become an interest rate waiver, with the outstanding loan amount increased only by the inflation rate. Both the White Paper and the Act suggested a £420 loan be made available in the first year of operation (1990-91), and £1150 for three years of study. By 2007, however, the "top-up" loan would become the principal method of funding students' living costs, and in 1989 prices would provide about £5000 over three years.

The White Paper, however, reflected the influence of income-contingent loan designs more than the Act: monthly repayments would be tailored to an individual's economic circumstances. Deferments or even write-offs were to be possible for low-earning individuals, and in general the White Paper's proposal was income contingent: installments would be calculated as a percentage of taxable income, somewhere in the vicinity of 4%. British policy-makers at first chose to address the occupational diversion risks of the American loan examples, while ignoring other problems. The Government's White Paper addressed this issue explicitly, stating, "A choice to pursue a vocation where earnings are low should not be inhibited by an obligation to complete repayment of the loan" (UK Govt., 1988)." The government projected that about 15% of graduates each year would not make any repayments because of low incomes. There was a GSL-type mortgage option in the White Paper, though, so that high-earning individuals could convert their income contingent loan to a conventionally amortized, short-term loan. Thus, in the White Paper the Government designed a top-up loans program based upon the GSL, but with provisions for income-contingent repayment plans for many borrowers.

The subsequent Student Loan Act departed significantly from the White Paper. The widely publicized collapse of the bank consortium formed to administer the loans led to the most obvious alteration: the creation of a government-owned student loans company. The White Paper had assumed the private sector would take a leadership role both in providing the equity and in administering the system, an assumption that proved to be embarrassingly wrong. In fact, the only private company that could be found, and then just to manage the administrative system, was an American firm, EDS, which adapted its California student loans facilities management systems to the British context. While this development is ironic in the study of borrowing between America and Britain, it also suggests that there will be fundamental differences in the nature and willingness of different agencies and firms within a country to serve as administrative agents in borrowed programs. For, not only did banks balk at participating in the scheme, but universities also objected to their expected role of enrolling and processing students' applications. The final terms of the universities' involvement have been altered significantly, with the processing burden shifting more towards the Student Loans company, but disagreement on that point has continued to be quite heated. This is in contrast to American universities and proprietary schools that generally cooperate with banks and the government to help their students obtain loans; if anything, the cooperative trend increased with the 1990 formation of a student loans consortium in the United States involving the College Board, the Student Loan Marketing Association, and TIAA-CREF (the teachers' pension fund). Viewed primarily as an attempt to counter the US Government's administrative changes in the loan programs, the consortium set up a streamlined system that will draw the colleges into closer links with loan providers, and will encourage them to counsel students on their individual ability to handle debt repayments.

More subtle, but equally interesting from a comparative perspective, is the British government's tilt towards mortgage-style repayment in their final legislation. The Loan Act places almost everyone on a fixed repayment period of 5 years, with payments in equal monthly amounts, adjusted annually to take account of inflation. The Department of Education and Science's stated justification is that any other form, even its previously outlined income-contingent scheme, would be "far too complex and costly, particularly for employers." It appears likely that the American firms who bid for the loan system management contracts convinced the British Government that its original plans were too cumbersome and expensive to administer. Finally, there are some aspects of the loans Act that depart from American GSL characteristics, most notably the availability of loans to all interested students, and the absence of interest rates from loans. The absence of means-testing may reflect differing perceptions between the countries with respect to what take-up rates will be among upper-income students, or a more fundamental social view that means-testing is not appropriate for many social benefits. More simply, it may just reflect the infancy of the British loans program; in various stages of its development, the GSL program experimented with a more entitlement-oriented system (most notably in the late 1970s), but runaway costs led the American government back to stricter income eligibility guidelines.

In its implementation stage, the mortgage-style loan program has not proved to be very popular with students: in a Gallup poll conducted for the Confederation of British Industry, 66% of university-bound students surveyed favored income contingent repayments, while only 24% favored the present scheme. Interestingly though, only 13% said that loans had affected their postsecondary choices, so at least at this level, the concerns with occupational diversion have not been realized (Tysome, THES, November 1991).

Seven Problems of Appropriability

The transfer of American student loan models to the British case seems straightforward enough in the White Paper, but further analysis suggests that there are serious problems of "appropriability" – the ability to capture the attributes of the program and its benefits within a British context. This section will examine seven problems that British policy-makers face in adapting the American student loan model to the British context. Considered as a group, these seven problems suggest that the British government will not be able to adapt the American student loan program successfully. The fact that the British government is implementing it despite such difficulties means that there may be some severe consequences for Britain, both in educational policy, and in the wider political spheres of domestic policy and European labor market integration.

Cost-Reduction versus Cost-Benefit

The first problem of appropriability concerns differences in the two countries' fiscal philosophies. One of the strongest, and most ill-fated characteristics of the British government's view of higher education aid is the emphasis on cost-reduction rather than cost benefit. Cost reduction was a pervasive feature of Thatcher fiscal policy, but nowhere was the effect more poignant than in education and job training, where the early 1980s recession confronted young school leavers with a dismal labor market. The cheaper the program, the better. This emphasis on the PSBR over long run cost-effectiveness has led to the absurd result that the government hailed its loan initiative as a cost-saver, as one more advance in the relentless quest for a lower public sector borrowing requirement. Government ministers have argued that the program will actually break even by 2001. Early experience with the new loan program suggests that the high administrative costs and the low take-up rate of loans among eligible students will delay if not derail the Government's 2001 goal.[5]

This creates special problems in applying American designs like the GSL loan to the British case. If the principal test for policy enactment is its effect on the level of government debt, then a British version of the GSL is doomed to "failure".

Recent American statistics show the budgetary cost of Stafford loans has mushroomed in recent years. The number of loans has expanded, the amount per student has climbed, and the total default level has increased dramatically. The estimated cost to the government of defaults alone amounted to $1.6 billion in 1990.[6] Furthermore, the hidden cost of providing a loan guarantee can be substantial: initial cost of the guarantee may be quite low, but down the road defaults may raise the long-run cost of the guarantee significantly. With the passage of the 1990 Budget Reconciliation Act, Congress now requires that the expected "present value" cost of guaranteed loans be included in the budget year in which the guarantee is issued. Congressional Budget Office calculations suggest that this requirement will raise the Fiscal Year 1992 Stafford Loan obligation to $2.45 billion, or 28% of the $8.7 billion borrowed, and the total GSL budget entry in the US budget to more than $6 billion (CBO, 1991, p. 41). The political repercussions from these accounting changes remain to be seen.

Further analysis shows that default costs are just the tip of the iceberg. Other, less visible aspects of the program, including in-school interest subsidies, and a "special allowance" to the holders of student loan securities granting them an interest rate significantly above the Treasury Bill rate, comprise a huge fraction of the cost of the program. In 1990, The Pennsylvania Higher Education Assistance Agency studied a group of Pennsylvania students who began repaying their guaranteed student loans in 1989. Their longitudinal study found the government's actual subsidy costs for those students' loans to be distributed as follows:

2.4% to administrative cost allowance
33.6% to in-school interest subsidy
13.4% to the grace period interest subsidy
35.6% to the repayment period interest differential subsidy
15.0% to default payments.

They calculated the average total Federal cost per $1000 borrowed by Pennsylvania students at about $400, with students attaining the highest levels of education accruing the highest amount of Federal subsidy.

Thus, even though the costs associated with default are significant, they account for only a fraction of the total loan subsidy costs: more than 5/6 of the direct government outlays for the student loan program were in other categories than defaults, and after allowing for the indirect costs of supervising the financial intermediary and providing loan guarantees, defaults are probably under 10% of the government's costs (Davis and Greene, 1990).

Also, in the early 1990s, the difficulties of collection in a privately funded, publicly guaranteed loan program led to serious financial losses for some banks as well. Due to negligence in its sub-contracting of student loan monitoring, the Bank of America alone incurred a loss of $200 million, though they sought to shift some of the loss to the Federal Government. Private loan guarantee agencies, particularly those with high numbers of trade school students in their loan portfolios, have also suffered reverses. The Federal Government forced out the top management at one of these agencies, the Higher Education Assistance Foundation, and arranged for the student loan financial intermediary, the Student Loan Marketing Association ("Sallie Mae"), to take over its loan portfolio in the wake of a $1-2 billion government bail-out (Berg, 1990; Hilder, 1990). This could set a precedent for the government being liable for student loan expenses experienced by the private sector, increasing still further the total costs of the program.

Thus Britain would be well-advised to look beyond the potential default problem to a more complete picture of the long-term costs of a student loan program. Estimates in the U.S. have suggested that the true cost to the government of providing the GSL program runs about 35 to 50 cents for every dollar loaned out (depending on market interest rates, and the default rates) – a formidable fraction indeed. And, given the likelihood of higher administrative costs in Britain (due to the smaller loan volume and amounts, and to the start-up costs of the loan company) and the complete interest-rate subsidy and more flexible deferral policy, costs could run much higher. And if over time the Government does not curtail the availability of loans to upper-income students, the expenses may balloon even further, with the additional problem that a public subsidy would be going to some of society's least needy people.

If the Conservative Government defines success as the minimization of budgetary outlays, then the loan program will be politically viable only if borrowers are winnowed down to the lowest risk individuals and if the number of loans available is strictly controlled. This aspect of the current British political environment suggests two possible outcomes: either the program will be so restrictive that only those students needing the loans least will receive them, or else the program will suffer from runaway cost escalation. Barr (1989) has gambled on the latter: he has projected that even at the government's proposed level of provision, the White Paper seriously underestimates the costs. Barr's study suggests an annual cost of £250 million is more likely than the Government's estimate of £120 million per year, even if defaults are kept below 10%. If American experience with cost escalation is any guide, it is a mistake to implement a loan program as a cost-reducing gesture alone, particularly if the government has made any commitments to expanding access or increasing equity.

Student Loans and Manpower Planning

The second problem of appropriability concerns an important distinction that should be drawn between manpower planning in the two countries.

Despite the evolution in British government training bodies in the last ten years, from Industrial Training Boards and the Manpower Services Commission to Training and Enterprise Councils, planning is still more centralized in Britain than in the U.S., with the central government providing a substantial proportion of manual job training and placement. And, with respect to higher education, the British Government has been able to exercise highly effective control on numbers of new entrants in each field. As the only major source of funding for undergraduate education, the government has been able to prescribe almost exactly how many student places will be made available in the entire higher education system for each academic and professional discipline. The government has been quite open in its campaign to reduce the number of places in philosophy, for example, while increasing the number of places in high technology areas.

The prospect of student loans and the more distant specter of private sources of funding and increased access threaten this confidence in being able to exercise central manpower planning. The Chronicle of Higher Education has reported that

> ...officials in the Treasury have expressed concern about the loss of
> control over the number of students entering such subjects as
> medicine, law, and science that would results from the implementation
> of Mr Baker's plan (Walker, 1989).

The present bureaucratic structure in manpower planning represents a major obstacle to students becoming "free agents", able to circumvent the closely-linked education-labor market planning system in Whitehall by self-financing through loans or private funding. Given the existence of only one private university in Britain, students do not have the option of leaving the public university system. Even the failed 1990 attempt to establish a "guide price" bidding system (in which universities could obtain a certain number of student places by offering the lowest price per student to the central government) had an implicit manpower planning dimension to it. The Treasury and other departments are suspicious of an open-ended labor market policy, because budgetary control is more difficult, and employment policy more complex. Given these manpower planning considerations, the likely result of introducing an American student aid model will be continued Civil Service and Treasury pressure to restrict the number of loans granted to totals in line with their manpower goals. But the lesson of the American experience seems to have been lost on the authors of the White Paper: an entitlement approach to student aid, based on loans for anyone who wants one, would have reduced central planning control of university enrollments or areas of specialty. There is a fundamental conflict between the British Government's references to expanded educational access and its present manpower planning practices that an American-style program would only exacerbate.

Equitable Student Loans and British Income Distribution

The inclusion of an income-contingent repayment plan in Baker's top-up loan proposal (with its partial retention in the Student Loan Act) – and the absence of public criticism of this particular approach – provides an interesting counterpoint to American experience. It suggests that this approach may be more politically viable in the UK than a GSL-style program which has high initial repayments and the potential to reduce students' occupational choice. While there may be a variety of explanations for Britons' more pronounced preference for deferral and loan forgiveness options for low-income borrowers, it can probably be traced to income distribution, the typical life-time earnings profiles of British workers, and risk aversion. Some commentators have suggested that the British have a preference for a more egalitarian society than their American counterparts (Hochschild, 1981; Shapiro et al, 1989; Treagardh, 1990; Taylor-Gooby, 1985; deLone, 1979). While this point is highly debatable, it is true that the postwar pattern of more uniform income distribution in Great Britain means the probability of earning a vastly higher wage than other workers is quite low.[7] In Britain the variance of personal income is lower, as is the average income of British college graduates (O'Higgins, 1989). Finally, the lifetime earnings profile of British workers is flatter than that of their American counterparts, and tails off earlier. These characteristics may help to explain why the income contingent aspect of the Baker proposal drew little fire, though the generousness of the deferrals was curtailed in the final Act. Critics of the American STARS plan complained that it would be a veiled redistribution of wealth from high earners to low earners as long as a constant fraction of income-per-$1000 loaned were charged. There is actually an *ex post* risk to earning more than you expected when you agreed to the loan. A 20 or 25-year income contingent loan would wind up costing those with a steeply ascending income profile, or those with unusually high average salaries significantly more than a traditional 5-10 year loan with conventional amortized monthly payments.

So, the more homogeneous the borrowing population, the less important these objections become. Britain's potential borrowers would almost certainly be homogeneous, both because of the narrower socio-economic background of those qualifying for university places, and because of the likelihood of similar salary levels and lifetime income profiles.

Loan Repayments and the British Tax System

One more vital factor determining whether the American designs could be applied successfully in British higher education concerns the tax system. Income contingent loan programs require a means for monitoring and collecting graduates' incomes, a point which has raised serious objections in the United States. The centralized system of revenue collection in the UK would make that task easier. Information about low-income repayers requiring deferrals could be communicated to the student loan company accurately and efficiently. British people are subject to a more unitary tax structure, with almost no deductions and only two marginal tax brackets. For Americans accustomed to months-long budget wrangles between Congress and the Executive, and for tax codes bulging with special deductions, the curt announcement by the Chancellor of the Exchequer each March of the tax rate in Britain might seem a relief. It reflects a degree of central control unimagined in the United States, however, and the absence of many deduction or exemption categories allows little flexibility in adjusting tax bills to individual financial circumstances. Furthermore, the party in power has tremendous control over the tax system, and since a long-term student loan commitment might go through several changes of regime, individuals would face considerable uncertainty about how another party might treat the debt. The British tax system, therefore, would hypothetically provide a more reliable system of income verification than its American counterpart, but the political instability of tax codes would make long-term loan repayments a perennial political issue.

Furthermore, the Conservative Government made it clear throughout the loan planning period that they did not want to link loan repayments to Inland Revenue or the National Insurance schemes, principally because they want the loans program to resemble, if not become, a private-sector operation. To provide a justification for avoiding a publicly-administered program, the Government cited administrative complexity, invasions of privacy with respect to financial information, and the expense to employers of loan repayers–though they provided little evidence to support their position. Even after the collapse of the private bank consortium and the publication of studies pointing out the expense and difficulties of a government-run student loan agency, the Government held to its plan when it enacted the student loans bill. This decision led to an unexpected and significant outcome: ultimately an American firm was selected to administer a large part of the British loan program. EDS, a large American computer services firm specializing in computerized program management systems, is providing a beginning-to-end loan tracking and administration service to the British Government's Student Loans Company. Observers of the student loan planning process have drawn attention to the critical role American firms have played. American expertise in financial instruments and techniques, data processing, and administrative systems provided an important, perhaps decisive, impetus to the UK Government in deciding on the final shape of its loan program. From a policy borrowing perspective it is indeed noteworthy that an American firm is administering the program.

The Conservative Battle against Dependency

Another factor that limits the applicability of the American model is the Conservative Government's relentlessly ideological commitment to abolish "dependency". The Government has been concerned for a long time that the student grant for living expenses was too much like charity and was encouraging complacency and dependence on the welfare state. These views were reinforced by students' behavior when the real value of the grant declined significantly in the mid-1980s. They moved with great fluidity from student grants during term time to income support (welfare) in the summer. Students also became skilled in applying for housing benefit and other social security benefits. This development doubly alarmed the Thatcher government, first because the grant itself was viewed as a source of dependency, and second because students were becoming increasingly well integrated with the rest of the welfare system. Thus an important part of the student loan proposal is the assault on dependency, and making students ineligible for income support, housing benefit, and unemployment compensation. There is a very strong ideological assumption that loans will make students more responsible and independent than the present grant system. Many Americans share these sentiments too, but the *contiguousness* of student aid and welfare is a particularly British feature. In the U.S., the Pell Grant is generally not viewed as one step away from welfare dependency; the public generally sees the grant as empowerment, as a resource to enable students to participate in the higher education system. The British Government's concern with ending dependency might distort its perception of students' needs for assistance in completing their degrees, and it provides an additional complication to the adoption of an American-style loan program. The U.S. government has embedded its student loan program in a comprehensive package of student assistance: Pell grants, work-study, and student loans. If the British government is successful with its private agenda of stigmatizing student grants, the loan program could become the major source of student aid, a situation which would probably hinder some students' access to higher education.

Attitudes about Increased Access to Higher Education

British apathy about increasing access to higher education also represents an obstacle in the appropriation of American higher education models. Britain is anomalous in both the European Economic Community and OECD for its low proportion of young people in higher education. Depending on the definitions used, only about 13-20% of 18-20 year olds in Britain are enrolled in higher education.

Following the pro-expansion Robbins report in the early 1960s, the proportion did increase, nearly doubling from 7% in 1964 to 13% by 1971, but there was only a small increase during the 1980s, and a modest rise in the early 1990s.[8] While discussion of opening academe's doors wide has revived in the 1990s, young people themselves remain somewhat reluctant to stay on after age 16.[9] A 1991 White Paper proposed to increase participation of 18 year olds in education to 33% by 2000, but failed to provide the operating or capital expenditure needed to reach this goal (UK Gvt., 1991[b]; *The Financial Times*, January 13, 1992). The elitist image of higher education has remained in the public's mind, and the persistently upper middle-class profile of those who actually attend Britain's universities has done little to arrest that perception. Additional taxes on the working class to pay for the middle class's academic pursuits have not been a popular policy with the electorate. The Conservative Government may well have gained rather than lost votes when it cut funding to universities, abolished tenure, and capped the total number of student places – even in the face of increased applications. The new British loan system must be evaluated in that political context rather than an American one. If the price for expanded educational opportunity is a loan system for students and heavier government expenditure, the political system might drag its feet some on the path to expansion.

This is in sharp contrast to educational politics in the American system, where expanded educational access is one of the justifications for a loan system. The Congressional Research Service (1986), for example, has written:

> The purposes of the Federal student assistance programs in the Higher Education Act are to increase the 'access' for students from relatively low-income families to a college education.... and to provide limited assistance to students from families of more moderate means who have difficulty meeting rising college costs.

The reauthorization of the US Higher Education Act in 1992 brought changes in the relative importance of grants and loans in student aid, and concentrated federal grant resources more on the disadvantaged student population, and federal loan resources more on middle income students. Thus, while access will probably remain at the heart of the Stafford Student Loan Program, the British loan proposal is designed to help only those already enfranchised by the system, those who have survived the complex application process and been assigned a place.

Student Loans and British Political Culture

A final factor in Britain that limits the applicability of American designs is the different political culture. Though a thorough analysis is beyond the scope of this chapter, the British population has a different sense of what government should do. This difference in normative judgement between the two countries' electorates is best revealed by what features of the welfare state have been left unassailed by the Conservatives' ten year campaign: the core public provision of health care, the minimum child benefit payment, and "free" university tuition. The Education Act of 1944 established the last provision, and the Robbins Report confirmed and expanded the idea in the early 1960s. The Government made some preliminary incursions into reordering the public provision of higher education under Education Secretary Keith Joseph, exploring the possibility of loans to replace the grant system for middle-class students. They were stung by a back-bench revolt in Parliament which eventually forced Joseph to abandon the scheme. He resigned in 1986 and was replaced by a shrewder and more centrist Kenneth Baker.

Changes in British education policy are particularly worrying to the party in power, because education finance and governance are national political issues. In the United States, the federal government sets the tone and broad agenda of educational policy, but the curriculum and most of the school budget are debated at the state and local level. The unitary state structure in the UK ensures that the central government controls these matters, with the inevitable result that educational policy is a pawn in the national political debate over defense, social policy, employment policy, and taxation.

Thus, an issue like having students pay towards the costs of university strikes at deeply-held individual values and at the same time automatically ranks as a national political issue of great import. An American model assumes that students and their parents will bear some responsibility for tuition, while British public opinion remains steadfastly against it. In fact, the British Government's rhetoric promoting the loan proposal has stressed that loans would be introduced because the parents' required contribution to students' living expenses has risen. Statistics collected by the National Union of Students in 1987 provide some support for this government point: despite rising personal income among parents with children at university, parents have been unwilling to make up the gap opened by falling real levels of student grant (CVCP, 1990). The idea of a U.S.-style "Financial Aid Form", which assumes a parent's contribution based on a precise calculation of their ability to pay, would be completely alien. Until very recently, student support was viewed as the government's responsibility.

Implications for Policy Borrowing

Applied to the task of carrying lessons from the American student loan experience to Britain, the framework developed above suggests several key considerations for the process of policy borrowing. The private sector is influential in the American student loan system, and is likely to be influential in the borrowing process. The evidence bears this out: the American companies involved in bidding for the British student loans facilities management contract were vocal in criticizing the original British loan design. Two companies in particular, Wachovia and EDS, both argued that the original plans were too complex and unwieldy.[10] They pressed for fewer deferments, and Wachovia officials felt that Britain needed to look more closely at the National Direct Student loan program in the United States, and learn some lessons on how to link loan administration system with the universities. EDS pressed the British Government to pursue skip tracing of defaulters more aggressively, by collecting more information and by exploiting the national clearing bank system's direct debit for obtaining repayments. American businesspeople and bankers also pushed Britain to adopt a mortgage-style loan rather than an income-contingent one. In addition, they lobbied intensely for Britain to install more sophisticated data systems with more electronic interfaces. They also confidently predicted to their British counterparts that a financial intermediary would rapidly become a necessity if the loan program survived more than a couple of years.

While Britain debates its first experience with a student loan program, and decides whether the borrowed program will survive in a new environment, the United States is also at a crossroads. At the end of 1992, Congress reauthorized the Higher Education Act, as it must do every five years. In the discussions leading up to the Reauthorization, several themes emerged that may be relevant to British policy makers. First, the mature state of the American student loan program gives insight into the life cycle of any government loan scheme – why and how the program begins, changes in the terms and eligibility over time, and causes of breakdowns. Second, the effects of the private sector's involvement in the American loan program provides some evidence on how private firms' objectives and their profit motive exert influence on the government's loan programs.

The Reauthorization found the American student loan program at full maturity, but under great pressure. The GSL program has been through 25 years of tinkering. Policy makers have altered the interest rate subsidies, the eligible population, the maximum loan amount, the administrative systems, and the subsidies to banks. And again, in the 1991 round of Reauthorization hearings and drafts, a number of radical proposals, including a return to direct government-to-college lending, were debated.

The last 25 years have also witnessed the maturation of the institutions and institutional relationships involved in the student loan business: the banks, the universities, the proprietary schools, the state and national loan guarantee agencies, and the "multiple data entry" firms. In this $13 billion a year loan industry, the players conduct themselves with a level of sophistication that the 1960s authors of the first loan bill would have found staggering. It has become big business, a fact which has brought both increased efficiency and controversial levels of profit. The GSL's history provides a useful perspective for a country like Britain so new to the idea of student loans. Unfortunately, it also provides some warnings about the unavoidable problems created by a loan program: the degree of subsidy necessary to keep the private sector an integral part of the program, the necessity of means testing in a mature subsidized loan program, the inevitability of a financial intermediary, the tendency for the politically necessary financial "sweeteners" to diminish over the long run, and the dilemmas posed by galloping increases in the cost of education.

The Chances for Success

The analysis above points to several conclusions about the likelihood of the new top-up loan program being a success in Britain. The American loan models have been introduced to a somewhat hostile British public without much regard either for the realities of the American experience with student loans, or for the unique qualities of the British economic and political structure. The Americans have not been remotely successful in making the GSL program break even and have, in fact, failed to contain runaway costs. This is particularly noteworthy in light of the fact that the GSL program is now a seasoned, mature government program, one that has been altered and reshaped several times in its 25 year existence. Unless it restricts access to loans in Britain to able, affluent students, the Conservative Government cannot achieve its goal of cutting overall higher education costs by introducing loans. If cost reduction continues to be a central criterion of the success of the plan at the cabinet level, a loan program is quite likely to fail.

As for the British Government's other objective, reducing the welfare state, American models prove not to be a useful precedent. More Americans depend on the government for student loans than ever before, and in larger amounts per student. Yet there is little evidence that this increased indebtedness has decreased dependence on the American tripod of student grants, work-study, and loans, or that Americans feel any ideological attraction to a solely loan-based system to avoid "dependency". If the British Government has this goal in mind, the American models cannot serve as a precedent.

If Her Majesty's Government maintains a GSL-style program, it will also face the problem of occupational diversion that Americans have confronted. If the revived discussion of an income contingent repayment program leads to an alteration in the program, it may mitigate this possibility. The tax code and income distribution in Britain do provide support for this approach.

But American experiences with loan programs are only part of the story. The different political and economic factors in Britain, particularly the manpower planning concerns and the differing attitudes about equity and access, should be warnings to policy-makers that the program may have severe problems in implementation. It is more alarming, though, to consider the Department of Education and Science's call for expanded access to higher education through infusions of corporate and outside funds, rather than through combinations of public and private funding.

If both the student loan plan and the expansion of university places proposal are implemented, it will create an explosive policy situation. As discussed above, two Secretaries of Education have advocated using private money to expand places so that disadvantaged and minority students may have access to an education. But findings in America suggest that students from disadvantaged families and minorities have some of the highest default rates on student loans. (Daniels, 1988). The American experience suggests that the loan scheme cannot be both a tool for increased access and a method for reducing the PSBR.

Finally, from a broader perspective, Britain must expand its provision of higher education if it is to remain competitive within Europe, and internationally. *The Economist* has been a persistent critic of British policies in higher education, arguing that without more educational spending, British productivity growth will not be able to keep up with its European competitors in the new Single Market after 1992. Most of Britain's EC trading partners spend significantly more on education and training, and with the free flow of factors, including labor, Britain could suffer some severe dislocations from having a poorly skilled labor force. While a comprehensive student loan program, including allowances for defaults among high risk borrowers and reasonable repayment plans, may be an appropriate part of a larger UK bid for educational expansion, the current evidence suggests this is not what the Government has in mind. If it continues to cast a student loan program in the role of a cost-reducing, anti-dependency policy, it will underfund the initiative and target the wrong group of young people. And, unfortunately for Britain, an inadequately funded loan program will only exacerbate the problems it faces in remaining competitive in Europe and the world.

Notes

[1] The Brookings Institution, Washington, D.C. The author would like to thank Henry Aaron, Janet Hansen, and Lois Rice for their assistance during the preparation of the paper.

[2] To judge the appropriability of a program is to determine whether the program can be effectively and faithfully transferred from one country to another, without serious distortions in program substance or impacts.

[3] The "top-up" term used in the Government's proposals refers to their intention that loans would top-up the grants for living expenses. The White Paper anticipated that the grant would be fixed in nominal terms, so each year a loan would become a more and more important contribution to the students' living expenses.

[4] In addition to Stafford Loans (which were called "regular" guaranteed students loans until 1984), the Guaranteed Student Loan program includes Supplemental Loans for Students and Parent Loans to Undergraduate Students. Since 1984, GSL has been used to denote all three programs, with Stafford loans accounting for about three quarters for the real value of new guaranteed loans in 1990.

[5] In the first six months of the program's operation, the take up rate appeared to be about 10%, though the government had anticipated an 80% rate. By June 1991, about 180,000 students had applied for loans. Start-up costs were estimated by the government to be 15.25 million (Griffiths and Wojtas, Times Higher Education Supplement, 7/27/90; THES 10/12/90; Tysome, THES 6/28/91; Adonis, The Financial Times, 4/6/91).

[6] The $1.6 billion figure is from the U.S. Department of Education, "FY 1990 Guaranteed Student Loan Programs Data Book".

[7] Inequality in Britain is now as great as it has been since 1949, however: the top 20% in Britain receive about 42% of national income, with the bottom 20% receiving 8%. Still, this compares favorably with American figures of 47% and 3.9%, respectively. (Horwitz, 1992)

[8] The largest beneficiaries of the increased participation rates of 16-20 year olds in education and training in the early 1990s are the polytechnics and youth training schemes (UK Government White Paper, "Education and Training for the 21st Century", 1991).

[9] A recent Reader's Digest/BBC poll of 16-19 year olds found that only half of 16 year olds are staying on in full-time or part-time education. Sixty percent of the leavers said they left to earn money, and four out of ten said they left because they did not like school or see its relevance to the working world. (Tytler, The [London] Times, January 26, 1992)

[10] This information is based on telephone interviews with the individuals from these companies who were directly involved in the negotiation process.

References:

Adonis, Andrew, "Clarke Swots up on a Tory Academic Agenda", Financial Times, April 6-7, 1991

Barr, Nicholas, "Student Loans: The Next Steps", David Hume Institute Paper no. 15, August 1989

Barron's, "Credit Course: Student Loan Defaults hit Bank America Earnings", February 6, 1989

Berg, Eric, "Crisis at Top Loan Insurer: a $1.5 Billion 'F'", The New York Times, August 13, 1990

Blyska, Jeff, and Marie Hodge, "The Fault – and Default – in the Stars", New York Times, September 22, 1988

Congressional Budget Office, "The Experience of the Stafford Loan Program and Options for Change", CBO Papers, December, 1991

Congressional Research Service, "Reauthorization of the Higher Education Act: Program Descriptions, Issues and Options", Congressional Research Service for the Committee on Labor and Human Resources, US Senate, Senate Print, 99/8.

CVCP, "Distress and Uncertainty for Students," CVCP Press Release, 22 January, 1990.

Daniels, Lee, "Government Delays Tougher Loan Default Rules", New York Times, September 28, 1988.

Davis, Jerry, and Greene, Laura, "How Federal Subsidies to the Stafford Loan Program are Distributed among Pennsylvania Borrowers", Pennsylvania Higher Education Assistance Agency, 1990

De Lone, Richard, "Replication: A Strategy to Improve the Delivery of Education and Job Training Programmes", Public/Private Ventures, Philadelphia, Penn., 1990.

The Financial Times, "Mass Higher Education", January 13, 1992

Griffiths, Sian and Olga Wojtas, "1 Million Loans Ads Anger V-Cs", Times Higher Education Supplement, July 27, 1990

Hilder, David, "After Sallie Mae's Plunge, Some Analysts Say Fears Over HEAF Losses May be Overblown", Wall Street Journal, August 30, 1990

Hochschild, Jennifer, What's Fair?: America's Beliefs about Distributive Justice, 1981

Horwitz, Tony, "No Expectations: Working Class Culture Erodes Britain's Rank in a Unified Europe", The Wall Street Journal, February 1, 1992

O'Higgins, Michael, "Income Distribution and Redistribution: a Microdata Analysis for Seven Countries", Review of Income and Wealth, June 1989, 35, pp. 107-131.

Shapiro, Robert, "Public Opinion and the Welfare State: the United States in Comparative Perspective", Political Science Quarterly, Spring 1989, 104, pp. 59-89.

Taylor-Gooby, Peter, "Welfare, Hierarchy and the 'New Right': the impact of social policy changes in Britain, 1979-89", International Sociology, December 1989, 4, pp. 431-46.

Times Higher Education Supplement, "Student Loan Numbers 'Optimistic'", October 12, 1990

Treagardh, Lars, "Swedish Model or Swedish Culture?", Critical Review, Fall 1990, 4, pp. 569-590.

Tysome, Tony, "Lay-offs as Student Loan Operators head for Deficit", Times Higher Education Supplement, November 9, 1990

Tysome, Tony, "V-cs Shame DES over Loans Admin", Times Higher Education Supplement, June 28, 1991

Tysome, Tony, "Students Put Low Fees Above Bigger Grants", Times Higher Education Supplement, November 22, 1991

Tytler, David, "Pupils Reluctant to Stay on After 16", The [London] Times, January 26, 1992

UK Government White Paper, "Top-up Loans for Students", Department of Education and Science, HMSO, 1988

UK Government White Paper, "Education and Training for the 21st Century", Department of Education and Science, HMSO, 1991[a]

UK Government White Paper, "Higher Education– A Framework for Expansion", Department of Education and Science, HMSO, 1991[b]

U.S. Department of Education, "FY 1990 Guaranteed Student Loan Programs Data Book"

Walker, David, "British Cabinet Minister Calls for Reorganization", Chronicle of Higher Education, January 18, 1989, p.A37.

Magnet Schools, Choice and the Politics of Policy Borrowing

ANTHONY G. GREEN

Introduction

Late in 1987, Kenneth Baker, then the UK's Secretary of State for Education and Science, returned from a swift visit to the USA. He brought back a bright idea, an institutional innovation in education called 'magnet schools'. The term caught on, flourished briefly as a vehicle for educational policy controversy, lost energy, and had all but disappeared by late 1990. Although magnet schools have had a short and relatively unsuccessful career in Britain, their story can tell us much about the political process of policy borrowing.

This account will examine the phases of development of magnet schools in the US and then analyse the experience of borrowing the magnet school idea in Britain at local and national levels. The processes, meanings and purposes of international 'borrowing' of educational policies are also examined briefly. In particular, the chapter draws attention to the use of rhetoric in UK policy processes and compares the economic, cultural and demographic settings of magnet schools in the US and UK.

Magnets arrived in Britain during the second half of the 1980s.[1] This period was dominated by Thatcherite policies of educational restructuring which may be seen as part of a wider project to 'deconstruct' what remained of the British post-war social democratic settlement and its cultural and institutional forms (Department of Cultural Studies, 1991; Johnson, 1989; Jones, 1989). According to this analysis, the aim was to undermine state-sponsored equal opportunities policies, and to shift power decisively away from producers of state services such as teachers and LEAs, to clients and customers such as parents, employers and, to a lesser extent, young people themselves (Pring, 1987; Sexton, 1987).

The defining reference point for education policy change was and continues to be the 1988 Education Reform Act (ERA). Its ideological

n essentially liberal democratic idea of social efficiency and
equality of opportunity and outcome have a lower priority
ty and 'individual excellence', in both personal and
pects (Pirie, 1985). Customer choice and competition
ers are the recommended mechanisms for realising these
1989).

American magnet schools, as Kenneth Baker presented them during
the political run up to the ERA, at first seemed a promising model for the
UK. They were relatively differentiated and specialised, and therefore a
means to further diversify the public educational system. Some had a strong
vocational and technical bias, and hence were perceived to be filling a key
economic need. They were oversubscribed and appeared to deliver 'good'
education. The schools Baker had in mind were indeed magnetic, pulling in
their clients on the basis of parental choice rather than pupil allocation by
the local education authority. They seemed to represent all the benefits of a
system based on choice.

What Are Magnet Schools?

In 1987, few people in Britain had heard of magnet schools. Public
awareness, however, was soon 'informed' by the popular press, which drew
parallels with the 'Fame School' in New York. In addition, television
coverage featured magnet schools in educational documentaries and
analyses.

Intriguingly, in the US context it is difficult to define precisely what
constitutes a magnet school. This, no doubt, makes them useful as a
rhetorical device in educational politics. The common characteristics of
magnets are: that they are different from the 'comprehensive' neighbourhood
schools in that they have a distinctive educational identity or ethos; and that
entry is determined more by parental choice than by geographic location.
However only a minority of American magnet schools allow completely open
enrolment (Blank, 1983); 'controlled choice', based upon the ethnic
composition of the school district, is more common (Alves, 1983; Rossell
and Glenn, 1988).

Magnet schools can take many different institutional forms. They can
be found at each level of educational provision up to age eighteen, though
the tendency in Britain is to assume that they exist exclusively at the
secondary level. They may comprise whole schools or special programmes
within a school. Variety is the watchword. There are magnet schools
specialising in languages, mathematics, arts and humanities, computer
science and communications, and each may or may not be selective. Some
have a particular vocational focus, linking with occupations in the medical,
military, or aerospace industries; others are designed for the 'gifted and
talented', concentrating on academic, artistic or sporting activities and are
very selective. Some are specifically designed to attract students from families

which expect college and university entrance (such magnets may well be named 'academies'); others are 'opportunity' programmes for youngsters who are doing very poorly and in danger of dropping out before graduation. Some have an attractive location, such as the zoo (Buffalo, NY); others may follow a particular educational philosophy, such as Montessori schools. They constitute a rising proportion of US education – in the 350 largest school districts the average number of students in magnet schools rose from 3,100 to 10,300 between 1983 and 1989 (Wells, 1991).

Kenneth Baker's focus during his study trip to New York, however, was on a specific version of magnets. Some secondary schools he visited bore a marked similarity to the schools envisaged in Britain's City Technology Colleges initiative, announced some months earlier. Others resembled the selective British grammar school model. All the institutions visited were distinguished by strong scientific/technical or academic programmes which seemed to have the confidence of industry and higher education and were very attractive to parents. They represent a small and very particular aspect of magnet schooling, as a brief review of the development of magnet schools in the US will indicate.

The US Experience: from 'Magnets' to 'Choice'

The history of magnet schools in the US can be divided into two phases: phase one, from the late 1960s through the 1970s, was predominantly social democratic, while, during phase two in the 1980s, the balance of ideological forces swung toward a predominantly liberal democratic perspective.

The origins of the first phase of magnet schooling were largely in social rather than educational policy and this legacy is still important. US Magnets were born out of a concern for racial desegregation in the 1950s and 1960s, coupled with the growing significance of the black voice in the struggle for civil rights. They continued to spread and develop during the 1970s, primarily as part of a range of policies designed to improve the social conditions of poor inner city areas and the prospects of minority groups living in them (Levine and Havinghurst, 1977). This policy was a response to white resistance to desegregation through mandatory bussing, especially in the north and north-east, and took the form of voluntary, choice-determined integration through the school system (Klugar, 1975). In Britain, by contrast, the introduction of educational magnetism occurred in the 1980s in a context where the dominant political forces were far from sympathetic to policies which attempted this kind of social engineering.

In order to understand the novelty and significance of the early development of the magnet school concept in the US and, in turn, its significance for UK borrowing, it is important first to sketch in briefly some of the background of US public education provision.

There is a strong tradition in the US of a 'one best school' system, deriving from the 'progressive' era of the early twentieth century. During this period, business interests may be seen to have achieved a settlement in public education, which was codified and professionalised in order to insulate it from the dynamics of local democratic politics – a bureaucratic solution to the 'problem of democracy'. However, partly as a response to those very processes, educational administration became more or less conservative, often appearing to show little interest in educational innovation. In reality, the combination of a cultural silent majority and of business control left the educational bureaucracies with little room to manoeuvre, particularly across large tracts of middle America (Tyack, 1974).

In part this system arose as a response to a perceived need to establish a comprehensive system of schooling capable of dealing with social and cultural diversity as successive waves of immigrants entered the United States and presented a problem of 'nation building'. The 'one best school' approach to local, comprehensive education was intended to be an anti-elitist solution to the cultural and political complexities of managing public education while, at the same time, providing a disciplined and basically educated workforce for industrial production (Callahan, 1962). Fordist in form, it owed at least as much to Taylorism as to any subtleties of educational theory about the developing individual.[2]

Nationally, the politics of education became relatively low-key and largely symbolic, though periodically they were energised by crises such as Sputnik and the Cold War, social policy and the urban question during the civil rights struggles of the 1960s and early 1970s, and problems of declining economic competitiveness in the 1970s and 1980s. It was only in the 1970s that education in the US acquired a cabinet post at the national level and, in those terms, a significant profile and administrative base in Federal Government.

Magnet schools developed against this background, first appearing in Detroit in the late 1960s as a means of encouraging voluntary desegregation in a deprived urban area (Foster, 1973). The policy model adopted and widely followed elsewhere during the 1970s was to take individual, overwhelmingly minority schools in the inner city which were in deep trouble, and change them to such an extent that they would attract whites and retain socially mobile blacks. This involved both undertaking major refurbishments to the school, as well as the possibility of installing a new principal and the generation of a new public image and specific educational identity. Whilst designed to promote racial integration and assumed, by some, to be capable of positively readjusting opportunities in respect of race/ethnicity and social inequalities, this policy had little direct regard for the social class balance of the magnet schools' students. The political force behind it derived from a conjunction of social and economic trends: the growing success of the civil rights movement; the perceived failure of forced bussing as a desegregation measure; the ever-increasing suburbanisation of the US; and the flight of white and middle class (including minority) groups from the cities, driven by chronic urban decay associated with economic decline.

The Federal Government provided funds and political support to magnet schools. This was spurred by a series of court rulings that the racial imbalance of educational provision in several cities – Boston being the most prominent example – was unconstitutional and that bussing had failed to remedy this problem. What is especially striking to the British observer is the very active role of the courts in generating schooling policies and supervising the delivery of public education. There are indications, however, that by the end of the 1980s this influence had declined, as the pursuit of remedies for racial or ethnic inequalities became increasingly difficult in the face of neo-conservative opposition (Kushnick, 1990; Preger, 1987). Consequently, some of the focus has switched to economic remedies, possibly reflecting the growing political significance of the 'underclass' (Glasgow, 1981; Wilson, 1987).[3]

Significantly, in the light of subsequent British policy borrowing, the development of US magnet schools was not primarily concerned with open enrolment and the free play of market forces in education but, rather, the reverse. It was part of a numbers game in which city officials made strenuous efforts (in part, because much needed funding depended on it) to demonstrate to state and federal authorities that their school systems were reducing minority isolation which was, itself, a pernicious consequence of 'free choice' in the housing and education markets. Magnets were generally controlled by quota systems designed to achieve the best possible level of racial balance. So far as integration is concerned it may be argued that magnets have only been successful when coupled with schemes including a measure of mandatory desegregation in order to prevent overwhelming attendance by whites (Orfield, 1986).

The concern with racial integration did not disappear in the 1980s; nevertheless, national priorities shifted to focus on the US's declining economic competitiveness. This change was accompanied by a level of disillusionment with public education far more significant than that experienced in the UK. In Britain, polls have recorded relative satisfaction with schools and the teaching force until recently. British educational performance, as measured in exam pass-rates or staying-on rates, seems to be rising in contrast to reverse indications in the US.[4]

With this growing concern about efficiency and the restoration of American economic vitality, magnet schools have experienced a liberal democratic metamorphosis leading to a 'second phase' of development. They have come to connote the conservative modernist notion that diversity, choice and market mechanisms promote excellence (Chubb and Moe, 1990). This more recent phase of magnet schooling features a renewed commitment to 'standards' and 'excellence' as measured in international league tables of achievement, a key ingredient in the wider US educational reform movement of the 1980s (McNeil, 1988). This movement includes

217

renewed state-led reforms for controlling the curriculum, school resources and textbooks, as well as testing teacher competence, and the promotion of 'choice'. The education reform agenda, therefore, comprises apparently contradictory initiatives aimed both toward centralisation of control at the state level and decentralisation at the local level, a pattern which in general terms is not unlike that adopted in Britain.[5]

Evaluation of Magnet Schooling

What educational evaluation can be made of magnet school policy initiatives in the US? As they proliferated during the 1970s and 1980s, fragmentary evidence began to accumulate about the educational quality and effects of magnet schools (Dorgan, 1980; Estes and Waldrip, 1977; Rossell, 1985). They appeared to produce relatively good educational performance in some cases (Blank, 1983; Metz, 1986). The evidence is patchy, however, as in some respects, the magnet idea seems to have been carried along more on various waves of enthusiasm than respectable research and evaluation, as is often the case with highly politicised public policy. According to the one attempted national study, only a third of magnets were of 'high quality' and just 11% are non-selective (Blank, 1983).

More evidence is available about the differentiating effects of these institutions. Jackson's study of Cincinnati describes a 'camouflaged dual school system' in which magnets, whilst going some way towards a reduction of racial segregation, sharpen social-class segregation by disproportionately recruiting economically better off white and minority students (Jackson, 1988). A study of Boston, Chicago, Philadelphia and New York found that magnets syphon off students who are more likely to do well, leaving their comprehensive neighbourhood competitors in less favourable situations (Moore and Davenport, 1988).

Duax's study of Milwaukee schools compared selective and non-selective elementary magnets, [6] showing that the former tended to recruit more higher-income minority students than the latter and that the intake of non-selective magnets was much the same as for neighbourhood schools (Duax, 1988, 1989). The importance of Duax's study is that 'skimming' is relatively insignificant for non-selective magnets but of greater significance where selection is a factor as, for example, in the 'programme for the academically talented' in one neighbourhood school and for the 'early entrance' programme at another. Strenuous efforts continue to be made in Milwaukee's highly developed magnet school system to combine racial desegregation with a rising quality of education. In another Milwaukee study, Archibald reported that some 10 to 15% of the parents do not exercise their option of school choice (Archibald, 1988). These 'non-choosers' are ill-informed, hardly participate to the extent that they fall outside welfare safety-nets, are vulnerable to 'bureaucratic neglect' and are left with the least desired schooling options. Furthermore, a quarter of the city's black parents were unaware of magnets. Archibald concludes:

> magnet choosers seem to get the best schools; and those unaware of magnets or other school alternatives may choose schools they would avoid if they knew better.

In social terms, then, magnets may exacerbate already difficult situations and 'choice', far from improving the general quality of education in all schools by generating competition through market forces, may well either make little difference, or contribute to the educational deterioration of some schools. Thus, while many magnets may be "effective schools", this could be as much to do with differential recruitment of students and/or parents with commitment and enthusiasm, or to favourable resourcing, as it is a result of the educational value added by diversity and choice or, indeed, competition itself. It is not yet possible to tell from the available evidence.

In the current phase of US magnet school development, where it is being suggested that increasingly every school becomes a school of choice in a 'super-magnet' system, much attention has focused on Spanish Harlem, District 4 in New York. During the 1980s this case became an icon for the idea of successful choice-based educational improvement in the inner cities (Nathan, 1989), an idea appropriated by the Reagan and Bush Administrations. Not only is District 4 one of the most successful magnet experiments, it is also one of the most radical in terms of educational administration. It involves choice-based innovation which reflects both the social desperation of the situation and not a little charisma in educational leadership (Chubb and Moe, 1990).

With origins in the early 1970s, the leadership of District 4 encouraged teachers to form consortia and design schools which they believed would attract parents. Popularity was to be the key indicator of effectiveness. A variety of schools proliferated and, judging by improvements in educational achievement in this extremely poor area, the experiment has been a spectacular success (Domanico, 1989; *Education Week*, 1987; Kutner and Salganik, 1987).[7] District 4 attracts 11% of its elementary and 25% of its junior high school students from outside the district; this is both an index of success as well as a factor which may help explain the improvements in educational attainment levels.

Whilst such desperate situations as District 4 probably do not exist in contemporary Britain, nevertheless there may be lessons which can be drawn as to the possibilities of magnet schooling in inner-cities where social and economic decay is a continuing problem. To the neo-conservative wing of the choice movement, District 4 represents the effectiveness of market forces in action. However, an alternative explanation also exists, which stresses the positive value of power devolved to teachers in the Harlem experiment. Either way, this evidence provides powerful support to the moves towards local management of schools (LMS) in the UK as a means of releasing new staff energies and raising morale.

The variety, both in magnet development and in the evidence of its success, coupled with the different contexts of US and UK education reform creates varied opportunities and limitations for the successful borrowing of individual reform programmes. A crucial point to emerge about the borrowing of magnets from the US is the context of diversity in US educational provision, especially on a social/liberal democrat political continuum. This has led to a range of observations and interpretations from British policy makers as to the potential of magnets in the UK. Representatives of local education authorities (LEAs), the Association of Metropolitan Authorities (AMA) and HMI, have been able to emphasise aspects of US education policy evident in magnet schooling which differ from those championed by Mr Baker and others sympathetic to the Thatcherite agenda. Wandsworth's interest in magnet schools, discussed below, will provide a particular case in point.

Borrowing Magnet Schools

Britain's experience of borrowing magnet schools from the US at the national level is intimately connected to three institutional policy developments: the opting out of schools from LEA control, LMS and the development of City Technology Colleges (CTCs).[8] It is through these initiatives that the vocabulary of choice, institutional diversity and individual excellence, has assumed a prominent role in British educational reform. At the local level borrowing from the US has occurred in LEAs such as Bradford and Wandsworth, both of which have made moves to introduce magnet schools. In 1991, some three or four years into these initiatives, it is clear that British choice programmes have thus far failed to realise their expressed aims. Nevertheless, it is possible that the role they are playing in developing longer term, less overt objectives is moderately effective, and could even be spectacular regardless of whether the term 'magnet school' retains a place in popular education discourse.

City Technology Colleges

City Technology Colleges have been at the leading edge of educational controversy in Britain since they were launched at the Conservative Party Conference of 1986. These schools, as Roger Dale (1989) has observed, are emblematic of most of the key elements of the Thatcherite modernisation of secondary education. They bear close resemblance to certain kinds of magnet schools in the US with their enrolment through parental choice, their technical/scientific or vocational specialisation and, in theory, their association with urban renewal and extension of educational opportunities to children of working people who cannot afford private education. The selective magnet schools of New York – Bronx Science, Brooklyn Tech, Stuyvesant (more academic than vocational), the 'Fame' school and the Murry Bergstraum High School for business and commerce – provided Kenneth Baker with examples for CTC developments. All these magnets are successful, many times over-subscribed and offer excellent educational experiences, comparable to the higher reaches of the private sector for those who manage to get a place. They are at the élite end of the magnet school spectrum and, as such, are subject to critical scrutiny for their selectivity, which is achieved informally, firstly through parental initiative and subsequently by screening of candidates for aptitude, attitudes and past disciplinary and attendance records (Moore and Davenport, 1988).

The CTCs, like many US magnets, enjoy disproportionate funding, relative to other state schools.[9] Although they were set up as independent educational trusts with private funding, they receive 80% of their resources, in current expenditure and capital costs, from central government. Despite their generous funding, at the national level the CTC policy has been a dismal failure in several respects. It has been unable to attract the private funding in the form of commercial and industrial sponsorship, or come close to reaching the targets initially set for the number of schools to be established – by autumn 1991 only 13 of the 20 planned CTCs were in operation. From 1989 the government and CTC Trust amended their policy, withdrawing further central state funding for these schools and encouraging greater local involvement. This might take the form of local authority CTCs financed by LEAs, parents or private sponsorship. Such a situation parallels problems and criticisms made of magnets in the US, which receive extra funding-per-student (ranging from $200 on average to as much as $1,300 more per student in cities like Houston), much of it coming from local rather than federal sources (Wells, 1991).

Taken individually, the indications are that the CTCs, like many elite US magnet schools, are a success for those who gain access (Walford and Miller 1991). It would be surprising if they were not, given the generous resources and curricular flexibility CTCs offer to heads and teaching staff in a general climate of tight funding for public education. Interestingly, they do not seem to be particularly innovative, either in generating new vocationally-focused or scientific/technical interest in pedagogy or curriculum; Djanogly CTC, for example, has adopted a distinctly social orientation. Whilst it is early days, it is beginning to appear that the CTCs are delivering largely well-established forms of curriculum and pedagogy developed in British comprehensive education over recent years (Gewirtz, et al, 1991). They have been criticised, particularly at Kingshurst, Solihull, for failing to recruit inner city youngsters or to stimulate the least able; Kinghurst has also been judged as 'poor' by HMI in teaching craft, design and technology (HMI, 1991). If this pattern is sustained, then the significance of the inequity that CTCs represent will continue to be stark and their functions as models for other LEA schools will depend crucially on whether the majority of schools can achieve comparable funding levels.

In summary, at the national level the magnet school concept was selectively borrowed in the process of establishing CTCs to provide justification for the policy of decomprehensivisation, individual institutional excellence, diversity, selection and competition. In several respects it has become an embarrassment and a potential political liability in that the inequity of resourcing and relative meagreness of their distinctive achievements has raised serious doubts about the viability of the entire enterprise.

Local Authority Magnet Schools: Bradford and Wandsworth

At a local level, some authorities have borrowed the term 'magnet school' in constructing specific school reform proposals. Bradford and Wandsworth are the two LEAs most prominent in British magnet school policy and implementation. During the policy-formulation process each has been led by relatively enthusiastic Conservative leaderships with small political majorities. Both LEAs faced significantly falling school rolls and a surplus of school places, as well as possible difficulties, in justifying their record and even their continued existence if widespread opting out of schools from LEA control should take hold. In both, the resistance to the magnet proposals from parents, teachers and particularly headteachers has been fierce. Initial plans were scrapped in Bradford though tenaciously stuck to in Wandsworth. At various times in each authority, the leadership has denied that it is introducing 'American-style magnet schools', although both made study visits to the US before introducing their reforms.

At the centre of the opposition in both boroughs, mirroring national concerns with CTCs, is the question of equity and fairness in the distribution of resources. In Bradford, the initial plan involved financial inducements for six of the 24 schools to become magnets; some specialising in academic excellence, others in vocational studies. This proposal was subsequently modified in the face of demands by local headteachers and school governors that funding be spread evenly across institutions as required by LMS. Some extra resources were to have come from neighbouring authorities in payment for the education of their students attracted to Bradford by the magnets (a potential gain of £3.8m to Bradford LEA at the time). In addition, greater support from local business and more central government funding was expected and schools were to enter into competitive bidding for a proportion of magnet funds. However, Bradford was unable to convince its local educational critics that the package of changes would not result in greater selection and the plans are now, at best, on the back burner following the May 1990 local elections in which the Conservatives lost power.

Looking more specifically at borrowing at the local level, in October/November 1988 several education professionals from Bradford (three headteachers and one officer) visited New York and other cities. From the reports they produced (Flecknoe et al, 1988) it is clear that they drew very different lessons from the US than either Kenneth Baker or the local Conservative Party which backed the Bradford magnet scheme. Their report makes relatively little mention of magnets, and none at all of competition between schools or parental choice:

> We have seen schools given extra resources to mount magnet programmes, selecting students who demonstrate enthusiasm for such programmes. They appear to fulfil their purposes well. We have also seen the schools left behind in the allocation of resources, which receive the students who have not been accepted in the magnet schools. The depressing effects were visible in the teachers, students, fabric and resources (p. 3).

> There is a great inequality in the allocation of finance to schools. Three of the most prestigious – taking the most motivated and able students by selection – have huge amounts of money for equipment and for extra teaching programmes. Neighbourhood schools are definitely poor unless a particular Superintendent or Principal has manipulated the system to secure a larger slice of the cake from State, Federal or Corporate sources (p. 9).

The Bradford Report remarked upon the different cultural and social contexts (language, poverty, drugs, safety, teenage pregnancy) of education in the US and the UK, as well as the poverty of imagination in American elementary education, the drabness of classrooms and the 'testing imperative' (p. 22). The study-team also noticed the relatively active involvement of private sector companies in education, and the emphasis being put upon parental involvement in their children's education. Apart from more effective training for school management and the general concept of specialized schools, there appears little that they wished to borrow.

In Wandsworth, magnet schools appeared on the local agenda against a background of financial and administrative problems at least as severe as those in Bradford. Some 35% of Wandsworth youngsters travel to schools outside the LEA or attend private schools, leaving 3,500 spare school places. Magnets were proposed as a kind of educational salvation from school closures, redundancies and other drastic measures.

During a phase of consultation, seven possible types of magnet schools were proposed in a controversial pamphlet made available to all parents. Magnets were suggested in: sports and leisure studies; travel and tourism; visual and performing arts; catering, marketing and fashion; science, technology and the technology of the arts; language, law and administration; and music and mathematics.

While describing what to expect from magnets in much the same terms as Bradford's plans, the pamphlet also went into more graphic detail about the social and educational future of the Borough. It did so by prominently featuring a decontextualised quotation from Stuart Maclure, former editor of *The Times Educational Supplement*, which had appeared in *The Sunday Times* on 18 June, 1989:

> "Schools...could eventually fall into three groups. First the high performing schools – city technology colleges, opted-out schools and local authority magnet schools – such as those planned by Wandsworth; then a larger group of run-of-the-mill institutions delivering the standard national curriculum; and finally the deprived sink schools, mostly in the inner cities with large numbers of people who speak English as a second language".

The mixed message of the quotation (is it a threat, a promise or a prediction?) and the final reference to non-native English speakers, which some read as a racist remark in the social and educational context of Wandsworth (though not in Maclure's original article), did not smooth the public consultation process. Some readers no doubt interpreted the quotation as a lesson about education in the US and a direct reference to what should be avoided in Britain by way of urban decline, and deepening social and racial differentiation.

Like Bradford, the borrowing process in Wandsworth entailed both an education official – the Chief Education Officer (CEO) – and a group of headteachers visiting the USA in early 1989 specifically to examine magnet schools. Two contrasting reports were produced on their return (Wandsworth Borough Council, 1989a; 1989b). While the CEO, Donald Naismith, produced a positive assessment of lessons learned from the New York and Florida school systems, the heads' report was more circumspect, pointing out quite sharply the negative side of US magnet experience and drawing some alternative lessons for Wandsworth to those identified by Naismith.

Naismith's report acknowledged the problems of definition: magnets can involve whole school programmes or particular and specialised programmes within any one school which made them, in many respects, 'indistinguishable from specific grant projects, the Technical and Vocational Educational Initiative and conventional vocational courses found in this country' (p. 2). Most US magnet programmes, he asserted, provided a strong vocational focus and offered employment links. He stressed student rather than parental choice as an important feature of US 'educational ownership' (p. 2). This was seen as especially important in reducing truancy and early leaving ('dropping-out') in the US, and in improving basic skills such as reading.

Naismith also located magnets within a wider movement for choice which he saw as having a British counterpart in educational 'free trade', open enrolment and LMS. He remarked that the American system of schooling was 'astonishingly comprehensive', with no state denominational schools, and very few special or single-sex schools. Magnet schools, 'by raising standards', were aiming at halting the 'bright white flight' (p. 4) from the public system of education, and so contributed to reduced social differentiation. His report went on to stress, however, that it was impossible to judge the success of the magnet school concept. Among the concerns raised were the tension within and between schools created by magnets' privileged funding and doubts over magnets' sustainability: 'How long can you keep up this level of funding of expanding investment in a growing state programme and what happens when the money runs out?' (p. 5).

Such questions were left unanswered in the report. Clearly, Naismith recognised the issue of 'less preferred schools' in the US choice system but remarked that given that schools were rather larger, on average, in the US than the UK, they were 'less numbers sensitive' (p. 6). Following the lead of US administrators, he cited the extraordinary popularity of the magnets as shown, for example, by the queueing (sometimes overnight) at first-come, first-served magnets.

The positive lessons Naismith highlighted were about student motivation based on choice, interest and 'a strong relationship to the world of work and the prospect of employment', (p. 6) and he pondered upon whether magnets could be part of a response to skill shortages in the 1990s. The weakness of magnets, as Naismith perceived it, was a matter of 'philosophy' in that the idea compounded the 'confusion which exists in American and English systems between 'education' and 'training' and thus deciding where the right balance was to be struck between 'liberal education [and] the acquisition of useful skills and competences' (p. 7). The report indicated that any general solution fell outside the power of one authority but that a coherent approach could be attempted through local curricular policies. Before proceeding to recommend that magnets be accepted as a 'possible means of school organisation inside the borough' (p. 7), Naismith reaffirmed what to him was Wandsworth's key problem: recruitment. The solution was simple – magnets will attract.

Accompanying this report was one submitted by the six headteachers who also went on the visit. Their account was somewhat different, not so much in what was seen, but in its interpretation and emphasis. The major differences relate to their concerns about: resources and support services (both identified as superior in the US); conditions of service; social selection and differentiation; and whether what they had seen in the US indicated that, on the whole, public education was at present superior in Britain. The heads specifically mentioned equality of opportunity, a theme not found explicitly in the CEO's report, and inter-school co-operation which, while mentioned by him, was noted without drawing conclusions. They identified a tension that seemed to exist between the requirements of the National Curriculum (more extensive than any state-mandated curriculum in the US) and the choice and diversity promised in magnet programmes. They also expressed a concern that 'magnets carry with them the considerable danger of too early specialisation based on superficial information and rather random choice procedures which, in the long run, deny equality of opportunity', (p. 2) and retard teachers' professional responsibilities.

Despite reservations over magnets, the heads viewed the trip to the US as a useful stimulant to thinking further about curriculum specialisation and its effects on student motivation. The visit had not only given them a valuable opportunity to observe another education system but also the chance to develop their own network, strengthening the possibility of more co-operation in the future. By implication, inter-school competition and educational entrepreneurialism were not high on their agenda. They also made little of school-based management, stressed by Naismith in connection with observations about educational reform in Dade County, Florida.

The clear differences of emphasis in the two Wandsworth reports reflect the different perspectives and interests of the CEO and the headteachers. The concerns of the latter are about managing their schools with least disruption in a context in which successive educational policy changes appear rapidly. Many of these they regarded as wrong-headed and a challenge to their cherished beliefs about education as a social service. They tended to rally round a commitment to comprehensive education and to maintain a spirit of professional co-operation rather than competition. To the CEO the priority was to move ahead towards a free market with consumers being offered a choice of distinct specialisms rather than generic neighbourhood comprehensives. In such political contexts, borrowing is evidently a process of selective presentation, as analysis of a series of other reports and assessments of US magnet ideas and broader aspects of US education indicates (see AMA, 1989; DES, 1990).

By late 1990, Wandsworth was less sanguine about magnets while maintaining official enthusiasm for them. At the same time a 'mixed economy' of local education provision was emerging through CTCs, opted out schools and the continuing attraction of the private sector. The Borough proposed to close three or four schools to alleviate the problem of excess capacity while embracing the new concept of the local authority CTC (not unlike US vocational magnet schools), and continuing to express support for private and voluntary-aided educational provision as part of its commitment to diversity and choice.

In addition, the LEA put up a fund of £10m. to attract bids by secondary schools to encourage magnets. There appears to have been very little enthusiasm from secondary school heads and governors to engage in competition for these resources. Even in the context of two schools having closed and the threat of more school closures, only one of the remaining schools has made a bid (to provide the new LEA technology CTC as a magnet) while two schools have applied to opt out of LEA control and another appears to be moving in that direction. Their rationales for opting out are to preserve comprehensive education and to remove themselves from the interference and heavy-handedness of the local authority.

The term 'magnet' is now hardly used in education discussion, though in professional and political discourse it is found in Wandsworth's official publications, along with the terminology of 'centres of excellence' in the service of 'diversity', 'choice' and a 'mixed economy' in education. It is also used in a notable recent pamphlet by the chair of the education committee (Lister, 1991). In this document, the most distinctly radical local voice is heard in proposals which envisage a minimal role for the LEA, rather as Chubb and Moe have suggested for the US. Lister sees the LEA as an 'educator of last resort' which should encourage opting out. Interpreted in an unflattering light, in the context of policy-borrowing, this view is not dissimilar to the attitude of many consumers and avoiders of public education in US inner cities, where public education commands very little respect. The market solution clearly echoes the perspectives of the 'libertarian' wing of the Conservative Party nationally.

Lister's proposals include an endorsement of magnets as mechanisms to motivate students via specialisation and to reintroduce selection in which the criterion of admission will be 'solely the demonstrable ability by [students] to benefit from the education being offered'. Meanwhile, the financial pressure to 'specialise' (the new term for 'magnetise') continues to be kept up through the capital funding for building and maintenance which, along with the virtually inevitable drift towards intensification of competition between schools consequent upon LMS and open enrolment, means that the remaining LEA schools find the policy of differentiation and diversity difficult to resist.

Concluding Remarks: Something Blue?

In the mid 1980s, magnets were 'discovered' by British ministers and have been presented largely for the purposes of legitimising various aspects of Conservative educational reforms. That discovery and its presentation tended to overlook the complex history of US magnet schooling from which a range of diverse 'lessons' could have been drawn.

How they are interpreted depends, of course, upon the perspective brought to bear on that history. To the extent that there is a progressive social democratic dimension to magnet schooling in the US, it is, perhaps, surprising that some British Conservative politicians should have shown such enthusiasm for it. To those in the US with social democratic interests, magnets evoke what is wrong with a 'free' choice system (Arons, 1989; Willie, 1989); most American magnet schools currently operate under 'controlled' choice in order to counteract the effects of self-selected ethnic segregation and act as a proxy for social-class segregation. They require very careful monitoring so as not inadvertently to play a role in stratifying public education. Equity is the issue constantly returned to by America's magnet critics, the simple point being that opportunities to 'choose' and the differential benefits of 'choice' are not fairly distributed.

Since Baker's visit in 1987, the political issue in US education has increasingly shifted to empowering parents and teachers to challenge bureaucracies of local educational administrations. The cultural significance of this is different on either side of the Atlantic, particularly for teachers. From a lower level of morale and status, US teachers' organisations and interests have seen the movement for 'choice' and renewal of interest in alternative education policies as an opportunity to improve their collective position. In Britain, meanwhile, the politics of magnet schooling have been interpreted by teacher organisations as a subtle (or not so subtle) ploy to weaken their collective position.

At the national level in Britain, US magnet schools provided a distinctive, if ephemeral, vehicle for supporting the Thatcher Government's broad policies of educational diversification and consumerism, and for the specific policy of CTCs. The attractiveness of magnets, however, has been adversely affected by the faltering progress of CTCs. Nevertheless, the concept did its work in that it initially helped to deflect opposition to, and provide a positive articulation for, elements of Conservative policy. It contributed to the politics of deconstructing commitment to 'system thinking' lodged in the social democratic ideology of entitlement and public service. By the same token, it legitimised 'individual thinking', in both personal and institutional terms, and promised the systematic benefits of competition.

At the local level, magnet schooling as a specific policy has only had a significant effect in Wandsworth LEA. There it was significant that the term quickly became positively interpreted by the LEA leadership and negatively by the teachers' organisations, as they struggled to control and define the agenda for specialisation and the place of vocational education and selection in education, while simultaneously developing and maintaining the confidence of the parents and students.

This chapter has illustrated the view that policy-borrowing at every level in education is a complex political process. In the case of magnet schooling, the rhetorical possibilities of the term and the opportunities for selective interpretation of its educational and social reality in the US, were thoroughly exploited in Britain by advocates of 'new right' education policy. The initiative was short-lived, however. Opposition to the concept emerged which stressed the negative effects of magnet schools on the social conditions of American inner-city education, through the process of selection and differentiation of status and resources (Green, 1991).

When related to the wider concept of policy-borrowing, the significance of the magnet schools case stems from the differences in conditions and policy objectives on the part of borrower and lender. In this account policy-borrowing has been shown to be essentially controversial because policies such as magnet schools are, themselves, contested locally.

Nevertheless, effective cross-national policy-borrowing can be seen to have little to do with the success (however defined) of the institutional realisation of the idea in its native context. Moreover, the effectiveness of borrowing in political terms should not solely be measured by the widespread implementation of the idea in its new home. Success for the politician may be at least as much a matter of the role the idea plays in influencing policy and practice in the short term. In this light, the history of magnet schooling is of less significance than its role in political discourse and legitimating other related policies (Edleman, 1977).

Notes

[1] In fact this was a second coming and there is, perhaps, a certain historical irony in the fact that the Inner London Education Authority (ILEA), abolished by the Conservatives, had taken an interest in magnets in the mid-'70s. It had sent a delegation to New York in 1976 to observe magnets within the broader context of urban education policy and the workings of the New York Urban Coalition (ILEA, 1976).

[2] For a discussion of Fordism, see David Finegold's article in part 2 of this volume.

[3] Large financial inequalities have always existed in the resources of school districts. For instance, in the Milwaukee metropolitan area the most affluent school districts spent about 30% more per pupil than the least affluent; in New Jersey the size of the gap was $10,000, and in Texas the most extreme difference between districts was $17,000 per student per year (Karp, 1990; Public Policy Forum, 1990).

[4] It is extremely difficult to substantiate fully the extent of satisfaction and/or acquiescence with the provision of public education in Britain during the 1980s. An indication is found in an *The Independent*/Mori poll where 74% favoured comprehensive schools compared to 24% preferring selective education (*The Independent*, 4 May, 1989). The generally high level of support that teachers received during the long industrial dispute of 1984, where blame tended to be attributed to the government, adds weight to this view. In the US, the linking of comprehensive public urban education with a wave of alarming reports and invidious international comparisons (National Commission on Excellence in Education, 1983) apparently came as no surprise in the 1980s, whereas in Britain there was relatively little disquiet about education. Indeed, it might be suggested that Britain was approaching the point where it could begin to demonstrate the first achievements of a predominantly comprehensive system. The first cohort of 'really comprehensive' youngsters had gone through the schools (Chitty, 1989) and evidence was becoming available from Scotland of the benefits of a more comprehensive system (McPherson and Wilms, 1987). It may be argued that the middle and aspirant working class were broadly satisfied with comprehensive schooling but developed a scepticism about government policy and feared disruption and reduction in resourcing. Responsibility for problems with the efficiency of educational performance was thus seen to rest at least as much with central government, probably more so, than with either the local education authorities or with teaching staff.

This is not to overlook a steady flow of criticism of public education from the Black Papers, the National Council for Educational Standards, the Hillgate Group, etc. Rather, it is to suggest that their impact upon the mainstream of popular opinion has been felt only relatively recently, following the 1988 Education Reform Act. There are signs that disquiet about public education has become more widespread in the 1990s alongside the apparent availability of and concern for 'choice' in the newly consumer orientated educational marketplace. A marker may be the rise in appeals (more than doubled, 1988) by parents unable to get their children into the school of their choice (*The Times Educational Supplement*, 2.8.1991).

[5] This question is discussed in more detail by W.L. Boyd in this volume.

[6] Non-selective magnet schools have open enrolment for students throughout the school district and do not deny entry on the basis of students' academic, attendance or behaviour record. Enrolment is on a first-come, first-served or lottery basis (Duax, 1988, p.1).

[7] The school population is 60% Hispanic, 35% Black, 4% White, 1% Asian; almost 80% of the students are eligible for the free lunch programme. In 1974 only 15% of students were reading above grade level; by 1988 62% were reading at or above grade level, roughly the City-wide average (Domanico, 1989).

[8] Little space will be devoted here to opting out and LMS since they are policies more likely to be transferred or legitimised from Britain to the US than vice versa. In this context, it is interesting that the controversial work of Chubb and Moe (1990), which argues for the necessity to deconstruct the local education authorities, bases its conclusions primarily on comparison of the private and public sectors in the US. It could be mobilised in the UK in the service of opting out and LMS but, at the time of writing (Autumn, 1991), this work has yet to be discovered, let alone borrowed, though no doubt, by the time of publication it will have been used in endorsement of freedom of choice for parents, students and, less prominently, for teachers. As a policy initiative in Britain, opting out has had at best a sluggish though growing response, despite financial inducements by government. Given the greater party political polarisation about both education and local government finances in the UK compared to the US, opting out is likely to continue to be highly controversial.

Wholesale opting out would mean taking centralisation in the interest of freedom to further extremes. Yet for a government committed to modifying collectivist orientations, it is a path fraught with immense political dangers, possibly even ushering in the administrative basis for greater equalisation in resourcing than is available currently. At the same time, it could begin to open up the possibility of further social democratic borrowing from the US by collectivist interests here, particularly in the use of litigation to obtain equal resourcing between areas, perhaps as part of a more extensive political drive for a Bill of Rights and renewed interest in citizenship.

[9] Capital spending per pupil at CTCs is almost 50 times greater than for other local authority schools – £7,450 per pupil compared with £94 per pupil. While, in great measure, this reflects start-up capital expenditure for CTCs, few doubt the relative generosity CTCs enjoy compared with the long delays in vital repair and capital expenditure faced by many of their local authority 'competitors' (Straw, 1991, Ramsden, 1991)

In the US, the Bush administration is trying to make federal magnet funding available to schools other than those connected with desegregation initiatives, but this policy is powerfully resisted in Congress, which sees no need to subsidise better-off residential areas in a time of large budget deficits.

References

Alves, M J (1983). "Cambridge Desegregation Succeeding", Integrated Education, Vol.12, January/December.

AMA (Association of Metropolitan Authorities) (1989). "Coming to America", Study Visit to the United States of America by the Association of Metropolitan Authorities, December 1988.

Archibald, D A (1988). "Magnet Schools, Voluntary Desegregation and Public Choice Theory: Limits and Possibilities in a Big City School System", Doctoral Thesis, University of Wisconsin, Madison.

Arons, S (1989). "Educational Choice as a Civil Rights Strategy", in Devins, N E (ed). Public Values, Private Schools, London, Falmer.

Blank, R K et al (1983). Survey of Magnet Schools: Analysing a Model of Quality Integrated Education, ABT Associates for US Department of Education, Washington, DC.

Callahan, R E (1962). Education and the Cult of Efficiency: A Study of the Forces that have Shaped the Administration of the Public Schools, Chicago, University of Chicago Press.

Chitty, C (1989). Towards a New Education System: The Victory of the New Right?, London, Falmer.

Chubb, J E and Moe, T M (1990). Politics, Markets and America's Schools, Washington DC, Brookings Institution.

Dale, R (1981). "Education and the State: Contributions and Contradictions", in Apple M (ed.), Cultural and Economic Reproduction in Education, London, Routledge and Kegan Paul.

Dale, R (1989). "The Thatcherite Project in Education: The Case of the City Technology Colleges", Critical Social Policy, Issue 27, Winter.

Department of Cultural Studies (1991). Education Unlimited: Schooling and Training and the New Right Since 1979, London, Unwin Hyman.

DES (Department of Education and Science) (1990). Aspects of Education in the USA: Teaching and Learning in New York City Schools, London, HMSO.

Domanico, R J (1989). Model For Choice: A Report on Manhattan's District 4, New York, Manhattan Institute.

Dorgan, M (1980). "Integration Through Magnet Schools: Goals and Limitations", Integrated Education, No 18, January.

Duax, T (1988). The Impact of Magnet Schools on a Predominantly Black Community, Doctoral Thesis, University of Wisconsin, Madison.

Duax, T (1989). "Attrition at a Non-selective Magnet School: A Case Study of a Milwaukee Public School", Equity and Choice, Winter.

Edleman, M (1977). Political Language, London, Academic Press.

Education Week (1987). "The Call for Choice: A Special Report", June 24.

Estes, N and Waldrip, D (eds) (1977). Magnet Schools: Legal and Practical Implications, Piscatawasy, New Jersey, New Century.

Flecknoe et al (1988). Teaching in the City, Directorate of Education, City of Bradford Metropolitan Council.

Foster, G (1973). "Desegregating Urban Schools: A Review of Techniques", Harvard Educational Review, Vol 43.

Gewirtz, S et al (1991). "Parents' Individualistic and Collectivist Strategies at the City Technology College, Kinghurst", Paper presented at the International Sociology of Education Conference, Westhill College, Birmingham.

Glasgow, D (1981). The Black Underclass, New York, Random House

Green, A G (1991). 'Magnet Schools : Not so Attractive After All?', Forum, Vol 32, No. 2, Spring

HMI (1991). 'The City Technology College, Kingshurst, Solihull : A Report by HMI', Department of Education and Science.

ILEA (1976). "New York City Schools", Report of the Education Officer to the Policy Co-ordinating Sub-Committee of the Education Committee.

Jackson, C C (1988). "The Struggle for Quality Desegregated Education Beyond the Alternative School Program: Cincinnati, Ohio, 1974-1988". Doctoral Thesis, University of Cincinnati.

Johnson, R (1989). "Thatcherism and English Education: Breaking the Mould or Confirming the Pattern?", History of Education, Vol 18, No 2.

Jones, K (1989). Right Turn: The Conservative Revolution In Education, London, Hutchinson.

Karp, S (1990). "Rich Schools, Poor Schools & The Courts", Rethinking Education, Vol 5, No 2 Jan/Feb.

Klugar, R (1975). Simple Justice: The History of Brown v. Board of Education and Black America's Struggle for Equality, New York, Vintage.

Kushnick L (1990). 'US : The Revocation of Civil Rights', Race and Class, Vol. 32, No. 1, July/September.

Kutner, M A and Salganik, L H (1987). Educational Choice in New York District 4, Pelavin Associates, Inc.

Lawton, D (ed.) (1989). The Education Reform Act: Choice and Control, London, Hodder and Stoughton.

Levine, D U and Havinghurst, R J (eds.) (1977). The Future of Big-City Schools: Desegregation Policies and Magnet Alternatives, Berkley, McCutchan.

Lister E (1991). LEAs – Old and New : A View from Wandsworth, Centre for Policy Studies, October.

McNeil, L M (1988). "The Politics of School Reform"', in Boyd, W L and Kerchner, C T (eds.) (1988). The Politics of Excellence and Choice in Education, London, Falmer.

McPherson, A and Wilms, J D (1987). "Equalisation and Improvement: Some Effects of Comprehensive Reorganisation in Scotland", Sociology Vol 21, No 4.

Metz, M H (1986). Different By Design: The Context and Character of Three Magnet Schools, New York, Routledge and Kegan Paul.

Moore, D R and Davenport, S (1988). "The New Improved Sorting Machine", Presentation to the Eastern Writers Association, New Orleans, Louisiana, April.

Moore Johnson S (1990). 'Teachers, Power and School Change', in Clune W H and Witte J F (eds.) (1990) Choice and Control in American Education, Vol. 2, London, Falmer Press

Nathan, J (ed) (1989). Public Schools By Choice, St Paul, Minn., The Institute For Learning And Teaching.

National Commission of Excellence in Education (1983). A Nation at Risk: The Imperative for Educational Reform, Washington D.C., US Department of Education.

Orfield G (1986). 'Knowledge, Ideology and School Desegregation : Views Through Different Prisms', Metropolitan Education, No. 1, Spring.

Pirie, M (1985). Privatisation, London, Adam Smith Institute.

Preger J (1987). 'American Political Culture and the Shifting Meaning of Race', Ethnic and Racial Studies, Vol. 10, No. 1, January.

Pring, R (1987). 'Privatisation in Education', Journal of Education Policy, Vol 2, No 4.

Public Policy Forum (1990). Public Schooling in the Milwaukee Metropolitan Area 1990, Milwaukee WI, Public Policy Forum.

Ramsden J (1991). 'Exposing a Valueless CTC Claim', The Times Educational Supplement, 25th October.

Raywid M (1986). 'Family Choice Arrangements in Public Schools', Review of Educational Research, Vol. 55, pp 435–467

Rossell, C (1985). "What is attractive about Magnet Schools?", Urban Education, Vol 20, No 1.

Rossell, C H and Glenn, C L (1988). "The Cambridge Controlled Choice Plan", Urban Review, Vol 20, Summer.

Sexton, S (1987). Our Schools: A Radical Policy, Warlingham, IEA, Education Unit.

Spring, J (1988). Conflict of Interest: The Politics of American Education, New York, Longman.

Straw J (1991). 'Halt CTC Programme Now', Labour Party News Release, PR1291, October 15th.

The Times Educational Supplement (2.8.91). 'Appeals Soar Over Choice of School'.

Tyack, D B (1974). The One Best System: A History of American Urban Education, Cambridge, MA, Harvard University Press.

Walford G and Miller H (1991). City Technology College, Milton Keynes, Open University Press

Wandsworth Borough Council (1989a). Report of the director of Education on the Study Visit to the USA, February 1989, Paper No. 5879.

Wandsworth Borough Council (1989b). Report of Principles and Heads: The Future of Education in Wandsworth: Post American Study Tour Position, Paper No 5879A.

Wells, A S (1991). "Once a Desegregation Tool, Magnet School Becoming School of Choice", New York Times, 9 January 1991.

Willie, C V (1989). "Diversity, School Improvement and Choice: Research Agenda Items in School Desegregation for the Next Decade", Paper presented at the American Educational Research Association Conference, March 1989.

Wilson, W J (1987). The Truly Disadvantaged: The Inner City, The Underclass and Public Policy, Chicago, University of Chicago.

Choice and Market Forces in American Education: A Revolution or a Non-event?

WILLIAM LOWE BOYD

Is choice of schools "an idea whose time has come" in American education? Or is the growing ferment about choice and market forces really "much ado about nothing"? Are Americans witnessing a revolution or a non-event in education policy? This chapter considers the evidence on this topic, the place of choice in the American education reform movement, how this compares with the more revolutionary British experience, and the prospects for choice initiatives in the US in the future.

At first blush, choice seems to have made amazing strides, not only toward respectability, but even toward ascendance in American reform policy debates. Until the mid-1980s, few Americans took seriously the idea that parents should be able to choose freely – without financial penalty – between public (i.e. state) schools, let alone between public and private schools. Indeed, the very idea of choice of schools for parents conflicts with a cherished American idea: the ideology of the comprehensive, "common school" as a public institution for the promotion of democracy.[1] According to this ideology, American children from all social classes and all cultural backgrounds should have the unifying experience of attending a common and undifferentiated, state-supported and state-operated school. Ideally, they should experience a common curriculum in what was designed to be the "one best system" of schooling (Tyack, 1974). By this means, immigrants could be "Americanized" and social divisions minimized. To even question this egalitarian ideal was to risk being branded an elitist.

Of course, economists, who are impervious to such considerations, have long argued that schooling can be provided more efficiently through markets than by government monopolies. From Adam Smith to Milton Friedman (1955) and his disciples, ideas have been advanced for government-supported "voucher plans" to enable parents to select the state or private school of their choice for their children. In the 1970s, the Nixon Administration for a time advocated and provided support (rarely accepted) for experimentation with education voucher plans. Interestingly, the key intellectual leadership in this effort was provided by Christopher Jencks (1966; see also Center for the Study of Public Policy, 1970), who has a long record of concern for the poor and disadvantaged. Later, John Coons and Stephen Sugerman (1978) championed a similar effort, trying unsuccessfully to get a referendum for a state-level education voucher plan on the ballot in California.

The main upshot of these efforts, which triggered vehement opposition from education interest groups, was to make the term, "voucher plan", a bad or at least controversial word. Opponents claimed voucher plans inevitably would benefit the rich and hurt the poor, would be divisive and destructive, and would generally undermine democratic public education.

Times have changed. During the Reagan era, the semantics and agenda of education policy shifted radically, from a focus on equality to one on excellence and diversity (Clark & Astuto, 1986). It no longer is un-American to advocate school choice for parents. In part, this shift in public opinion can be credited to a decision by most reformers to focus only on parent choice among public schools. By avoiding the divisive question of public subsidies for private and sectarian schools, this formula won bipartisan support and helped open the policy debate. Readiness to consider formerly taboo measures has also been fostered by a broad and growing dissatisfaction with the performance of American public schools. Neither Democrats nor Republicans claim the existing system is satisfactory.

The first major breakthrough for the choice movement came in 1986, with the publication of the National Governors Association (1986) report, *Time for Results*, which endorsed choice among public schools. Since that time, state governors from both parties have backed plans to expand options for choice. This has included not only free choice of public schools within school districts (rather than automatic assignment to a school within an attendance or 'catchment area'), but increasingly choice among schools in adjacent school districts. The key laboratory for choice innovations has been Minnesota, which pioneered the first statewide choice plan (Mazzoni & Sullivan, 1990). By September 1989, more than twenty states had passed or were considering legislation to expand school choice (Boyd and Walberg, 1990, p. ix).

In this context, President George Bush called choice "perhaps the single most promising idea in American Education" and Lauro Cavazos, his first Secretary of Education, asserted that "parental choice is the cornerstone of restructuring elementary and secondary education" (*Education Week*, January 18, 1989, p. 24). Not surprisingly, business leaders (Kearns & Doyle, 1986) and major business publications are also advocating choice and market forces as solutions for what ails American schools. *Forbes* magazine (Brimelow, 1990) and the *Wall Street Journal* (1990; Bacon, 1990; Gigot, 1990) are now calling US public schools a 'socialist education system', 'America's collective farm' with predictable failure built in. In a society where conservatives, over the last few years, have managed to make the term "liberal" an insult and an obscenity – the "L-Word" they call it – the idea that we have a "socialist" education system might just catch on and get not only the attention of business people, but even the attention of educators.

Yet, despite the swell of support for choice, and a variety of choice initiatives and experiments, many observers still doubt that choice will become a truly significant part of the US education reform movement. It continues to face strong opposition from educators and their associations and unions. Moreover, public education, as a vast and ponderous American institution, is notoriously difficult to change (Cuban, 1979). Real choice initiatives, as opposed to small, symbolic efforts, challenge the whole basis on which public education is organized and governed. Until now, the US reform movement has been content to seek less fundamental changes. Nevertheless, recent developments suggest that a turning point may be approaching in this debate.

American School Reform in the 1980s

The "excellence" school reform movement of the 1980s was triggered, and continues to be fuelled, by a concern for declining student achievement and a belief (rightly or wrongly) that inadequate American education has much to do with our "crisis" in economic competitiveness. By the late 1980s, demographic trends with serious implications for the American workforce added a further sense of urgency to the reform movement.

Developments in US education have been widely characterized as dividing into two "waves" of reform. Ironically, these two "waves" have been driven by competing impulses. The first wave emphasized control over school; the second, autonomy for teachers and schools. The conflict between the standardization and centralization embodied in the first, and the emphasis on teacher autonomy and professionalism embodied in the second, has commonly been called the "San Andreas fault" in the reform movement.

Prompted by the remarkably influential, federally sponsored, report *A Nation at Risk* (National Commission on Excellence in Education, 1983), the first wave of reform efforts centralized control at the state level. "Excellence" was pursued through state mandates intensifying much of what already was being done – e.g., higher graduation requirements for teachers and students, more testing, a more standardized curriculum, competency-based teacher education. When carried to the extreme, this approach has tended to "de-skill" teachers by reducing opportunities for professional discretion (McNeill 1986, 1988).

By contrast, and coming somewhat as a reaction, the second wave of reform built upon the notion of professionalizing teaching and restructuring schools. Epitomized in the Carnegie report, *A Nation Prepared* (Carnegie Forum, 1986), and the National Governors Association (1986) report, *Time for Results*, the second wave argued that decentralization, flexibility, and autonomy are essential, both to foster engagement in teaching and learning, and to meet the diverse needs of an increasingly heterogeneous student population. As noted above, part of the means for school restructuring emphasized in the Governors' report was "parental choice" (ie, autonomy for the consumers: parents and students). When initially proposed, this idea was dismissed by many observers. But, as we have seen, it has been gaining support rather dramatically.

Still, there is little doubt that the conflicting "undertow" from the first wave of reform has impeded the progress of the second wave reforms (Hawley, 1988), which have mainly focused on restructuring schools via school-based management plans and an enhanced decision-making role for teachers. There is talk of the coming of a "third wave", but its character is still unclear. One candidate might be choice, but another might be even more pronounced "nationalizing" and centralizing forces. Certainly, the momentum behind the state curriculum alignment and national-level testing movement is growing (Kirst, 1989). With the first agreement on national goals for education in American history – between President Bush and state governors – some see the US moving toward a de facto national curriculum (Doyle, 1988), a development being pursued de jure in the United Kingdom.

Thus, it is significant that, at the first annual meeting of the Business Roundtable to be devoted to a single topic – education – "a recurring theme in both (President) Bush's speech and the panel discussion was the need for an overarching national strategy for reform" (Walker, 1989, pp 1 & 17). Corporate leaders at the meeting agreed that fundamental reforms and restructuring were needed, not incremental improvements. But as one of the reform leaders, Ernest Boyer, emphasized, the challenge in developing a national strategy is balancing "this need for co-ordination with the need for more school-based innovations" (Walker, 1989, p 17).

Even though it is unclear how to ensure a balance between control and autonomy, simultaneous efforts in the United States already exist to increase both the centralization (to the state level) and decentralization (to the school level) of governance arrangements in education. In fact, this is a worldwide phenomenon. An international expert on school-based management, Brian Caldwell writes that;

> In general, governments in many countries are adopting a more
> powerful and focused role in terms of setting goals, establishing
> priorities and building frameworks for accountability – all constituting a
> centralizing trend in the centralization-decentralization continuum – at
> the same time as authority and responsibility for key functions are being
> shifted to the school level – a decentralizing trend. Much uncertainty
> arises because these trends, almost paradoxically, are occurring
> simultaneously or in rapid succession (Caldwell, 1989, p.3).

Enter Chubb and Moe

Even if the "third wave" of US reform tips toward choice among public schools, rather than an emphasis on nationalizing forces or pursuit of a new balance of bureaucratic forces, will the strategy selected be sufficient for the challenges the country faces? In an important and controversial book that has intensified the debate on choice, John Chubb and Terry Moe (1990, p.228) say the answer is likely to be "no":

> [We] can only believe that the current "revolution" in American public education will prove a disappointment. It might have succeeded had it actually been a revolution, but it was not and was never intended to be, despite the lofty rhetoric. Revolutions dismember old institutions and replace them with new ones. The 1980s reform movement never seriously thought about the old institutions, and certainly never considered them part of the problem.

Chubb and Moe's response, in *Politics, Markets and America's Schools*, is an attempt to plant the bomb that will blow up the existing school system. They report research that purports to demonstrate that, unlike private schools, American public schools are enmeshed in bureaucratic politics and regulations that usually impede their effectiveness. As a solution, they advocate removing the public schools from political governance and placing them in market-driven, statewide choice systems involving both public and private schools. Although they say they have no illusions that their recommendation will be adopted in any state, they nevertheless "are cautiously optimistic" that a coalition of reformers might grow that could overcome the power of the education establishment and install something resembling their proposals in the next decade (pp.226-227).

Because Chubb and Moe's analysis has changed, as well as intensified, the debate on choice, we need to briefly describe and discuss their book. Moreover, since their analysis places previous reform efforts, including those involving choice plans, in a new light, their discussion provides a framework in which to review American choice efforts to date. Whatever one thinks of their book, it does have the virtue of forcing us to re-examine how fundamental aspects of the American school system work.

Chubb and Moe's book has been taken far more seriously than earlier calls for choice because it was published by a respected liberal think-tank (The Brookings Institution), rather than a conservative one, and because it is an empirical study presenting data which the authors claim support their analysis and recommendations. Their data are drawn from the well-known, national survey data base, 'High School and Beyond' (HSB). In 1984 an 'Administrator and Teacher Survey' was developed to supplement the HSB data set. The authors' "multivariate analyses are based on the sample of 389 [public and private] schools with valid data on schools, principals, teachers, and students" (Chubb & Moe, 1990, p 231). Their study covers the years 1980-1984 and assesses student performance via achievement tests administered in 1980 and 1983. The authors summarize their three key findings as follows:

One, schools do indeed perform better [when]... they possess the
effective school syndrome of organizational characteristics – to the
extent, in other words, that they have such general qualities as clear
goals, an ambitious academic program, strong educational leadership,
and high levels of teacher professionalism.

Two, the most important prerequisite for the emergence of effective
school characteristics is school autonomy, especially from external
bureaucratic influence.

Three, America's existing system of public education inhibits the
emergence of effective organisations. This occurs, most fundamentally,
because its institutions of democratic control function naturally to limit
and undermine school autonomy (Chubb and Moe, 1990, p 23).

In other words, Chubb and Moe conclude that the attitudes and attributes
associated with what researchers have called "instructionally effective"
schools are found much more frequently in private schools than in public
schools. Unlike private schools' educators, who can pursue a clear
instructional mission, they believe that public school educators are hampered
and distracted by the politics, contending interest groups and bureaucratic
regulations which surround the governance of public schools. This political
and bureaucratic "hash", they contend, prevents the professional autonomy
needed to design and maintain distinctive and unencumbered educational
programs.

Although their book has captured a great deal of public attention and
support, it is being subjected to increasing academic criticism about its
methodological limitations.[2] For example, John Witte (as reported in
Rothman, 1990) has argued that the study is seriously flawed and that,
indeed, the 'High School and Beyond' data set itself is suspect. Glass and
Matthews (1991) present a sweeping critique of the study and particularly
emphasize two points: ambiguity about the direction of causality and a tiny
difference in the dependent variable of student achievement:

> [P]recisely the finding on which Chubb and Moe hang their entire
> proposal for school reform – that organizational autonomy is related to
> high achievement – is likely to arise from a causal influence of
> achievement on organization: Low-achieving schools prompt managers
> at all levels to intervene to solve the problem of poor performance; high
> achieving schools are spared the kind of meddling that well-intentioned
> persons from the state agency to the school building are prone to offer
> (p.25).

> [Their] sweeping recommendations are based on statistical results in
> which the model only accounts for 5% of the variance in the dependent
> variable of student achievement...One implication of this result is that
> enormous changes in a school's position on the organization variable
> will be predicted to yield very small changes on the achievement

240

variable. A school that moves from the 5th percentile to the 95th percentile on autonomous organization would be expected... to climb a month or so in grade equivalent units on a standardized achievement test (p.26).

Whatever the resolution of the debate about the methodological problems of Chubb and Moe's study, their book makes an important contribution in its critical assessment of the piecemeal approach to contemporary school reform in the United States. Despite the importance and attention that have been attached to the reform movement, there is no coherent overall approach, in sharp contrast to the comprehensive British school reform effort embodied in the 1988 Education Reform Act in which choice, through open enrollment and schools "opting out" of local government control, were central features. Thus, Chubb and Moe decry the melange of measures being pursued in various US states, arguing that they are essentially grab-bags of reforms pursued by policy makers with no overall theory of what is wrong or how to correct it. They assess the most popular of the reform initiatives currently being pursued and conclude that all of them fail to deal with what, in their view, is the fundamental problem: the democratic, governance structure of public schools which ensures the perpetuation of encumbering politics and bureaucracy. Although desirable, choice among public schools does not go nearly far enough, in their view, because it is still embedded in a structure that will limit the range of choices that is available and prevent the liberating dynamics of real choice:

> Most of the choice plans that get put into effect (or, for that matter, even gain serious attention) are grafted onto the traditional system and make only marginal changes in it. Choice becomes part of a big compromise among contending political powers – no one loses jobs, no bad schools are closed down, vested interests remain securely vested, the basic structure of the system stays the same. In a nutshell, this is why reforms always focus on giving parents and students choice, but never free up the supply and governance of schools. Parent-student choice is popular, and it can be accomplished with minimal disruption to traditional structures, while real change on the supply side is fundamentally threatening to established interests and hence never gains political acceptance. The reality, therefore, is that choice plans fail to take advantage of what choice really has to offer – and they leave intact the crippling institutional causes of the schools' past problems (Chubb & Moe, 1990, p.208).[3]

In sum, Chubb and Moe argue that what they view as the partial or "pseudo" choice plans now being pursued could result in little more than a non-event. In this critical light, we can turn to a brief discussion of the pros and cons of the main options for choice now being implemented in the United States.

Options for Choice

Despite its increasing popularity, choice in education stirs strong feelings on both sides of the Atlantic. Advocates of parental choice believe that it can create powerful incentives for school improvement. When consumers can "vote with their feet", educators get clear signals about their performance. Without such signals, advocates say, performance incentives are weak and monopolistic indifference thrives. Choice, it is argued, also can benefit educators. When teachers have more choice and control over what they teach, and the kind of school or program with which they are affiliated, this enhances their professionalism, creativity, and commitment to their work. Moreover, choice for both teachers and students can create communities of shared values, which foster effective schooling. Thus, on the basis of a review of more than a hundred studies of various public school choice plans, Mary Anne Raywid (1989a, 1989b) concluded that when families can choose among public schools, students achieve more, like school and themselves better, parents have better attitudes toward school, and educators feel more like professionals.

Clearly, proposals for choice hold exciting potential for both consumers and producers of education. But, like other fundamental reforms, choice threatens the status quo and introduces some unpredictable elements. Critics of choice say that it will exacerbate inequality. For example, they contend that magnet schools have negative side-effects on non-selective schools: students who remain in ordinary neighbourhood schools may lose the stimulation of bright classmates or those with special interests who choose to attend magnet schools. And teachers in ordinary schools may lack the stimulation of entrepreneurial colleagues who choose or are recruited to teach in the magnet schools.

Choice clearly raises provocative questions and stimulating policy issues. In assessing the principal options for choice and the issues surrounding them, it is essential to recognize that a variety of plans exists and that the potential advantages and disadvantages of plans vary according to their specifics, which deserve close scrutiny. The main types of public school choice plans are: open enrollment; "controlled choice"; interdistrict choice; "schools within schools"; and magnet schools. Some of these plans can be combined, so there are more variations and associated details than can be covered in this brief discussion.

Open Enrollment and "Controlled Choice"

The simplest plan is the idea of open enrollment within school districts, enabling children to attend any public school in the district and not just their neighbourhood school. Some of the issues surrounding open enrollment plans are generic to choice plans generally. Thus, advocates argue that open enrollment spurs school performance and increases consumer satisfaction by enhancing market forces and allowing parents to pick the school that best meets the needs of their child.

Critics reply that, rather than improving performance, open enrollment will weaken less favoured schools and ones in less desirable neighbourhoods by facilitating the exodus of students and leaving those left behind worse off. Moreover, they contend that the sorting process that open enrollment encourages will exacerbate the segregation of children by race and social class. Market dynamics, they argue, always produce winners and losers and favour those who already are advantaged. For example, better educated parents will be better able to obtain and interpret the information needed to make a wise choice of schools for their children.

Advocates respond that market dynamics already exist in public school systems and cannot be eliminated: affluent families already can afford to choose where they live in order to gain access to better schools.[4] Rather than increasing inequality, choice plans can promote equality by giving less affluent families access to a range of schools without the prohibitive cost of moving their place of residence. Informed access can be facilitated by school performance reports and by school counsellors who can help less well educated parents weigh the choices open to them. Further, open enrollment plans can be designed to provide what Michael Alves and Charles Willie (1987) have called controlled choice i.e., the use of quotas within voluntary, open enrollment plans to enhance racial and social class balance in schools or, at least, to see that segregation is not increased. Finally, advocates argue that schools that lose enrollment get a clear and desirable signal to improve their programs or to begin again with new management.

Interdistrict Choice

Many advocates of choice believe that choice of public schools within school district does not go far enough. They are concerned about families living in school districts whose schools do not satisfy their children's needs. These include, for example, less affluent families who cannot afford to move to other districts and families living in districts that lack adequate high schools or specialized schools for gifted children. Beginning in 1987, Minnesota has pioneered an interdistrict plan. It has a kindergarten through grade 12, statewide choice scheme in which state funds follow students wherever they choose to go, regardless of where they live in the state. Governor Perpich and educational reformers in Minnesota argued that such a plan was needed to stimulate the fundamental improvements they sought for their state's schools.

Interdistrict choice plans raise substantial implementation issues that have to be dealt with carefully. One problem is to avoid discrimination in admitting non-resident students to schools, while at the same time permitting schools to set space limits. Another problem is transportation costs, especially for low-income students. Additional problems encountered in Minnesota have included desegregation regulations; "the transfer for athletic, social, and other nonacademic reasons of students into the selected schools; disrupted district planning due to the ease of student choice; and the undermining of the "left behind" schools and districts – especially small, poor ones – that lack resources to compete" (Mazzoni and Sullivan, 1990, pp. 154, 167).

Initially, the number of students taking advantage of the interdistrict choice option in Minnesota was quite small, so the effects of the plan were neither as sweeping nor as harmful as advocates and opponents, respectively, expected. In a related reform, Minnesota has also pioneered a Post-Secondary Enrollment Options Act (1985), which gives eleventh and twelfth-graders the option to seek to attend any public or eligible private post-secondary institution at state expense, on a part or full-time basis.

Schools within Schools

One of the objections to choice plans is that in sparsely populated areas there may not be enough schools in reasonable proximity to enable a choice of schools. This is a real problem but advocates of choice suggest that the schools within schools approach may be a feasible solution, except in very small schools. In this approach, which was employed in the Alum Rock, California voucher experiment in the 1970s, schools can develop and offer a choice of programs or pedagogical approaches within a single building. Parents then can choose, for example, between more traditional or more "progressive" classroom teaching or between programs emphasizing science, math, or the arts.

The schools within schools plan can be applied in urban as well as sparsely populated areas. Indeed, perhaps the best known "success" story in the choice movement builds on the approach. In Community District 4, the low-income, East Harlem school district in New York City, administrators have encouraged teachers to develop a variety of programs for students to pick from at the middle school level. In this district, teachers as well as students and parents are empowered by the ability to make program choices. The names of some of the junior high programs that have been created suggest the range of interesting programs available: the East Harlem Maritime School, the East Harlem School for Health and Bio-Medical Studies, the Jose Feliciano Performing Arts School, and the Northview Tech for Communication Arts and Computer Science.

The results have been impressive given the District's economic and demographic situation over the lifetime of the experiment. Because of low income, almost 80 percent of the students qualify for the free-lunch program. Over half the families are single-parent families. And nearly all students are minorities; 60 percent are Hispanic and 35 percent are black. When the program began fifteen years ago, only about 15 percent of the district's students read at grade level or above and it ranked last among the thirty-two school districts in New York City. Now, however, about 65 percent of its students read at or above grade level and the district ranks fifteenth or sixteenth depending upon which test is used.[5]

Magnet Schools

Magnet schools are one of the oldest mechanisms for choice. They have been used extensively, especially at the high school level and in large urban districts, both to provide specialized, high quality programs to attract and retain students with special interests and to foster voluntary racial desegregation. The Bronx School of Science and New York's Performing Arts High School are famous and long-established examples. If demand for admission to these schools is a measure of success, then there is no doubt that they are successful. Advocates of choice emphasize magnet schools' success in contributing to desegregation and curbing the exodus of able and middle-class students from large urban school districts. In the absence of a wide selection of magnet schools, such as is found in New York City, it is claimed that the exodus of the middle-class student population would have been much more severe. Evidence in support of this claim can be found in comparison with cities that have not developed a highly regarded set of magnet schools.

Critics of magnet schools contend that they cream off the more able students and leave regular schools, and the students they serve, worse off. They argue that students and staff in the regular, "non-special" schools suffer morale problems and feel that magnet schools unfairly get special attention and resources. Further, they claim that admissions practices and access to admissions information favour middle-class students rather than disadvantaged students. Rather than seeing high demand for admissions as a measure of success, they worry about those who are not admitted to magnet schools. To the critics, magnet schools are the manifestation of a "new improved sorting machine" in education, sifting out those who will be the winners and losers in society (Moore & Davenport, 1990).

Again there is some merit to both sides of the issue. Magnet schools can have many beneficial effects. But, it is also true that they usually have not been designed to serve the interests of at-risk youth, although they can be so designed. As one researcher has concluded, "Most magnet schools are not academically selective, and there is some evidence that the use of criteria for admission which are selective is decreasing. However, from the evidence available, the "self-selection" of students through voluntary applications for magnet schools results in most magnet schools serving very few at-risk students" (Blank, 1989). The evidence does suggest, however, that magnet schools can and do improve performance for students with varying levels of ability and prior achievement. And, it is possible to design, as New York City has done, admissions arrangements for magnet schools that insure a degree of balance of ethnic and ability groups in their membership.

Does Choice Work?

As noted above, Raywid concluded from her extensive review of studies of public school choice that it contributes to better student achievement and improved attitudes among parents and teachers. Moreover, the District 4 story in East Harlem, New York shows that choice can be a vital part of a school improvement effort that dramatically raises the performance of poor, disadvantaged children. It is true, though, that choice challenges fundamental aspects of public schools as they have existed, and it indisputably raises perplexing questions about equity and has its full share of implementation problems.

Advocates of choice will respond that perplexing questions about equity, not to mention effectiveness, already abound in our present system. They believe that measures can be built into choice plans that will foster equity and that choice plans can be designed specifically to help disadvantaged children. They question whether fine-tuning or intensifying the existing system, which is largely governed by equity considerations, will generate necessary improvements. And they point out that all innovations bring implementation problems.

Critics of choice caution, correctly, that it is not a "magic bullet" or panacea that will produce dramatic improvements overnight. In a thoughtful critique of choice plans, Ann Bastian (1990) emphasizes that choice in District 4's success in East Harlem was part of a larger, sustained school improvement effort. She also notes that in it teachers collaborated more than they competed, and that their empowerment was an important ingredient in the success. This is a point that deserves special attention. For choice to be meaningful, there must be a range of real choices, not a smorgasbord of bureaucratic monotony. Consequently, as noted earlier, analysts agree that "demand side" choice for consumers (i.e., parents and students) needs to be complemented by "supply side" choice for producers (i.e., teachers and school administrators). Without freedom and encouragement for educators to develop new and distinctive programs, choice will be largely restricted to minor variations on the same dull theme. Moreover, without this sort of empowerment, educators are likely to feel frustrated and may not achieve their potential.

If critics argue that choice is not enough by itself (and that indeed it can be dangerous by itself), other reformers argue that choice among public schools may not be enough, that we must go much further in the direction of choice. As we have seen, Chubb and Moe (1990) contend that the current US school reform movement will not succeed, even if all of its "bell and whistles" are installed, including choice among public schools. Thus, although Chubb and Moe praise the East Harlem experience as the best example of choice in the public school sector, they also caution that the creative local leadership that made this success possible is vulnerable to the hierarchy of democratic control in which it is lodged. These local leaders:

not only [provided] parents and students with choice, but also
[liberated] the supply and governance of schools from district control.
This freeing up of the supply side is what makes the East Harlem
system so bold and unique. But its creation is entirely dependent on the
visionaries themselves and their hold on power. The structures of
democratic authority remain in place, and, if they become occupied by
people with different beliefs or constituencies, the same public
authority that liberated the schools could then be used to regain control
over them (Chubb & Moe, 1990, pp.214-215).[6]

Despite Chubb and Moe's pessimism about the abilities and tendencies of
public schools, there is positive evidence besides that provided by East
Harlem. Kenneth Wong (1989) observes that urban school districts have
developed an array of "mediated choice" programs within public schools to
meet the policy challenges they face under fiscal constraints. By "mediated
choice" programs, he means that student choice is not completely
market-driven, but is regulated by a complex selection process which, in
part, serves school district purposes:

> Choice programs are designed to address the pressing policy challenges
> in the urban context. They are used to promote racial desegregation in
> a voluntary manner, retain middle class families in the city's public
> school system, attract intergovernmental grants for innovative activities,
> and encourage localized educational reform that yields good academic
> performance (p. 1).

While recognizing the functions that choice plans serve, Wong is sensitive to
the criticism that they may have inequitable side-effects. Consequently, he
studied the distributive equity in resource allocation to schools with and
without choice programs in the city of Chicago:

> Our preliminary findings suggest very little difference in per-pupil
> spending and pupil-teacher ratio among types of schools. Choice
> programs have not fundamentally altered the district's budgetary
> decisions. Resource equity among schools, as illuminated by the
> Chicago case, seems to offer a crucial explanation for the increasing
> popularity of choice programs. In other words, much of the internal
> discontent with choice has been tempered by the fairly even
> distribution of resources to all schools. Once the political support for
> choice programs from within the system is secured, urban school
> districts can use these programs to perform important institutional
> functions (p.2).

Wong then asks a key question, the answer to which relates to Chubb and
Moe's thesis:

> If choice programs do not benefit from the budgetary allocation, what
> accounts for their ability to accomplish the difficult tasks listed earlier?

247

The answer seems to lie in their relative autonomy from the central office direction. Using the Chicago case, [it appears] that choice programs generally operate in a loosely-coupled vertical authority structure to the extent that schools enjoy substantial discretion on admissions, curricular development, and staff hiring. While resource equity tempers opposition to choice programs, the latter's governing structure seems to have contributed to their institutional vitality (pp.2-3).

No Renaissance Without Revolution?

By the end of 1990, there was a growing sense in the United States that, despite undeniable progress, the school reform movement was falling well short of the level of improvements needed to protect and advance the national interest. Thus, despite the second wave's calls for fundamental restructuring of schools, progress in "restructuring" seemed slow and ambiguous, in part because of a lack of agreement about exactly how schools should be restructured. In this context, calls for more revolutionary reforms began to be heard with increasing frequency.

A number of developments suggested that we might be moving into a time of more fundamental and radical reforms. President Bush's appointment of a new Secretary of Education, Lamar Alexander, brought a much more dynamic thrust to federal education policy (see Gigot, 1991). As governor of Tennessee, Alexander gained a national reputation as a leading educational reformer. Upon becoming Secretary, he surrounded himself with market-oriented reformers and critics of the status quo (David Kearns, the former Xerox chairman; Diane Ravich, neo-conservative historian of education) and like-minded informal advisers (Denis Doyle, Saul Cooperman, and Chester Finn, author of a new book entitled *We Must Take Charge: Our Schools and Our Future*).

Alexander has said that, "One of the lessons of education reform in the 1980s is that we've been too slow and too timid. What we need is a populist uprising" (as quoted in Gigot, 1991, p 6). Consistent with this view, in unveiling the new federal education plan developed by Alexander, President Bush said, "To those who want to see real improvement in American education, I say: 'There will be no renaissance without revolution'" (as quoted in Norris, 1991, p 11). Yet, as Norris (1991) observes, Bush aspires to revolutionize American education with an expenditure of no more than $820 million over five years, less than the cost of one Stealth bomber. Moreover, no new money is involved since funds will be drawn from the Education Department's existing budget.

The new plan provides for $550 million to build 535 new schools – presumably one for each Congressional district – designed to be "national models of excellence". In a proposal reminiscent of the City Technology Colleges in Britain, American industry will be asked to contribute $150 million toward the construction of these schools and, in turn, will have a voice in their design and curriculum. This new school scheme, Norris (1991) suggests, may be a "sweetener" to help gain acceptance of companion proposals to increase parental choice. Here, Bush proposes to spend $230 million to encourage school districts to adopt choice schemes and is again advancing the controversial idea that federal 'Chapter 1' monies for disadvantaged students should be allowed to follow them to private and even parochial schools.

Republicans have proposed this idea for 'Chapter 1' funding before, but have been beaten back by liberal Democrats in Congress, who fear, as do many urban educators, that an exodus to private schools might be imminent and further jeopardize the already precarious finances and standing of embattled urban schools. Indeed, one of the most surprising developments in early 1991 was the revival of interest in public funding for private school choice. In February, *Education Week* carried a front-page story (Olson, 1991) proclaiming that "proposals for private school choice [were] reviving at all levels of government". The article highlighted:

(1) President Bush's proposal for financial incentives for school districts adopting choice policies for public and private schools;
(2) a proposal before the Detroit Board of Education to permit some private schools to become public schools eligible for public funding;
(3) a decision by officials in Epsom, New Hampshire to provide tax abatements for property owners who sponsor a high school student's private education;
(4) Milwaukee's much publicised experiment with a publicly funded plan enabling low-income students to attend private non-sectarian schools (in effect, a local version of the federal voucher idea).

Together with campaigns for similar ventures in Pennsylvania and Michigan, these developments suggested an unexpected breakdown of the recent political consensus that publicly funded choice plans should be restricted to public schools.

This shift in opinion seemed attributable mainly to a combination of impatience with the pace of reform and the effects of Chubb and Moe's book and Polly Williams' leadership in the Milwaukee venture (Olson, 1991). Ms Williams is a black, inner-city leader and former welfare mother who has become a state representative in Wisconsin. She is an articulate and dynamic speaker and her advocacy for private school choice for inner-city families has brought legitimacy to the choice concept beyond right-wing circles. With black, inner-city leaders in Detroit as well as Milwaukee supporting private school choice, and some liberal Democrats beginning to re-examine their positions on the subject, there could be a sea change in the making.

However, since parochial schools comprise by far the largest portion of US private schools, the future of private school choice really depends on the Supreme Court's position on the Constitution's First Amendment "wall of separation between church and state". Always in the past, the Court has held that the First Amendment prohibits any public funds going for church-related activities. But the Court now has a conservative majority as a result of appointments during the Reagan era. As happened in Australia in a similar situation (Boyd, 1987), the Court might in the future interpret the First Amendment to permit public monies going to religious organizations, so long as all faiths are treated equally and none are favoured. If this should eventually happen, there will indeed be a sea change in education policy. For the present however, the organized political opposition, as well as legal barriers, to private school choice will remain imposing. So, the future is very much in doubt.

"Be Bold, Be British"

As Lamar Alexander was preparing to unveil the new federal education policy, *The Economist* (March 23-29, 1991, pp. 19-20) published a leader challenging him to learn from the English experience, to "be bold, be British". Clearly, British school reform under the Conservative government is bold. But, from a mainstream American point of view, it also seems unbalanced. Mainstream Americans have to be concerned about equality as well as excellence. Equity concerns are built into their system through the legal guarantees embodied in the Bill of Rights and the 14th Amendment. US policy makers have to think about these things as they craft legislation. No similar provisions distract Conservative politicians from their goal of efficiency in Britain. With a strong majority in Parliament, Tory ministers pursue their objectives with an unhampered zeal that American Congressmen can only envy.

Although the Conservative government is more moderate under John Major than it was under Margaret Thatcher, it nevertheless continues to pursue a market-orientated, Thatcherite education policy largely unadulterated by concerns for equity.[7] In the United States, even advocates of choice systems, such as Coons and Sugarman (1978) and Chubb and Moe, tend to wrestle with, and try to build in, safeguards against the obvious inegalitarian consequences of completely unregulated systems. The same does not seem to be the case in Britain. There are, however, some striking similarities as well as differences between the British and American reform experiences:

- In both countries, reform efforts are driven to a large extent by pressures for a better educated workforce to enhance economic competitiveness.
- Both countries are increasing both the degree of centralization and the degree of decentralization of school governance. Thus, on both sides of the Atlantic more decision-making authority is being shifted to the school level ("School Based Management" in the US; "Local Management of Schools" in Britain). But at the same time there are new centralizing forces: the National Curriculum in Britain and the new National Goals in

the US (a surprising and unprecedented development, given the tradition of local control of education).

- Both countries have magnet schools and programs for school choice. In a strange turn of events, the City Technology Colleges in Britain, which were patterned after American magnet schools, now may have been the inspiration for the Bush Administration's proposal to ask for industry funding for its proposed new "models of excellence" schools. Similarly, the "Assisted Places" scheme in Britain provides a working model of the proposed 'Chapter 1' voucher plan permitting choice of private schools.[8]

Important differences between the two nations include not only legal provisions affecting equality but also differences in political culture:

- In Britain, market choice in education tends to be associated with privilege and the tradition of private, independent schools, and the re-establishment of selective grammar schools.
- In the absence of a feudal and aristocratic past, and with a long history of comprehensive, non-selective high schools, choice of schools has a less elitist connotation in the United States.
- The individualist, rather than collectivist, tradition in America makes a shift toward market-oriented social policies less threatening than in Britain. Contemporary American school reform has enjoyed widespread bipartisan consensus; British education reform has been ideologically charged, highly politicized, and divisive.[9]
- The question of racial integration or segregation has been of much greater importance in the US and formed a context for the early development of magnet schools.

As noted earlier, in contrast to the piecemeal, decentralized approach in the United States, education reform in Britain has been centrally directed and, with the passage of the 1988 Education Reform Act (ERA), comprehensive and systematic. Many commentators have noted that market-oriented competition was the central theme of the ERA, with the notable exception of the (somewhat counterbalancing) National Curriculum component. This centrally-imposed curriculum, however, will provide an instrument for universal inter-school comparison through the testing of pupils at the ages of 7, 11, and 14, and will establish in Britain the kind of comprehensive, centralised control which eluded the first wave of U.S. reformers. Two other key choice components of the ERA are what Hywel Thomas (forthcoming) calls the "pupil as voucher scheme" (open enrollment with funds following students), and the provision for state schools to "opt out" of their local education authority (LEA) through a vote of parents, thus becoming "grant maintained" schools directly funded by the national government. Both components expose the LEAs to competitive pressures.

Although there is nothing quite like the grant maintained scheme in America, Chubb and Moe are, in effect, advocating a gigantic "opting out" scheme for American schools. In contrast to Britain, where individual schools decide whether to opt out or not, Chubb and Moe's proposal would have US state-level policy makers opting all of their schools from existing state systems of democratically controlled, school district governance in favour of a market-driven system of state-funded public and private schools. Nevertheless, the likely effects of Chubb and Moe's scheme and of the British grant maintained scheme are similar. In both cases, schools are removed from democratic, community governance, and community-wide planning is replaced by the "invisible hand" of the marketplace. What is especially worrying in the British context is a possible revival of the inegalitarian, two-tiered system of selective grammar schools and secondary modern schools. The Secretary of State for Education, Kenneth Clarke, is not only urging all schools to opt out (and offering attractive financial incentives to do so), but has also decided to relax the earlier regulation preventing newly opted out schools from changing their character (most likely from comprehensive to selective grammar school) for five years. The fear among egalitarians is that this is creeping privatisation of state schools and a possible reintroduction of selection and elitism. The response from defenders of Government policy is that opting out is a key means for freeing schools from bureaucracy and making them more efficient, effective and responsive.

Policy makers on both sides of the Atlantic would be well advised to look closely at the empirical studies of school choice that are beginning to accumulate in Britain. They give us, for the first time, some systematic, large scale data on what happens when choice schemes with particular features are implemented. Parental choice policies similar to those in the ERA for England and Wales have been in effect in Scotland since 1982. Studies there (Adler, Petch & Tweedie, 1989; Echols, McPherson & Willms, 1990) provide an important test of the assumptions undergirding the ERA. Some of Adler, Petch and Tweedie's main findings challenge these assumptions:

- For a majority of these parents, choice involved finding a satisfactory alternative to the district school rather than making an optimal choice from a wide range of possible schools.
- In requesting schools for their children, parents have been influenced much more by geographical and social factors, e.g., proximity and discipline, and by the general reputation of the school, than by educational considerations.
- On the whole, the schools that have gained the most pupils have been the formerly selective schools in middle class areas, while the schools that have lost most pupils have been those that serve local authority housing schemes in deprived peripheral areas.

■ There is considerable evidence of "band-wagon" effects, and little evidence of the market functioning as a self-correcting mechanism. (Adler, 1990, pp.4-5).

A key feature in Adler's findings is that the strong motivators of parental choice are often not related to wider issues of institutional reform and pedagogy but may, rather, be based on more prosaic considerations such as proximity and social status of the school. He concludes (1990) that the outcomes of parental choice policies in Scotland also have included less efficient use of resources, a widening of inequalities between schools, and the re-emergence of a two-tier system of secondary schooling in the big cities. Nevertheless, he argues that parental choice between schools should not be abandoned; rather, the policy should be modified as needed to ameliorate these undesirable outcomes.

Conclusion

Despite their important differences, both Britain and the United States are experimenting with similar market-orientated policies as means fundamentally to restructure and improve their schools. Sentiment in the United States is becoming more supportive for bold and even revolutionary measures for school improvement. But the array of political forces and the constitutional checks and balances in the American system favour incremental rather than radical change and have, thus far, prevented the development of policies as radical as those in Britain. However, the American Supreme Court holds the "wild card" with the possibility of a reinterpretation of the First Amendment separation of church and state. Should this card ever be played, it will redefine the game and American education policy might begin to look "bold and British".

Epilogue – 1993

Since the writing of this paper in 1991, the following developments have occurred: the Democrats in Congress were able to prevent passage of most of the proposed features of President Bush's "America 2000" education plan, including the highly controversial provisions for tax-supported choice of private and parochial schools. As with the City Technology Colleges in Britain, the proposal for the creation of 535 new model schools, with significant funding from private industry, gained little support. Under the Clinton administration, the America 2000 plan was revamped and repackaged as the "Goals 2000" plan, with the significant omission of the controversial choice provisions. National education goals and some form of national or state-level testing in pursuit of these goals continue to receive support. Despite lack of support for school choice by the Clinton administration, choice continues to receive considerable attention at the state level. A major voucher plan initiative, affecting private as well as public schools, will be put before the voters of California in November 1993. And voucher proposals are pending before a number of other states' legislatures. Finally, several states (e.g., Minnesota, California, Colorado) have passed legislation for "charter schools" and many states have such proposals before them. With the hope of promoting excellence and a wider range of choice, charter school legislation enables the creation of public schools *independent* of local school districts. Thus, this American trend roughly parallels British provisions allowing schools to "opt out" of local education authorities.

Notes

[1] There was even an attempt in one state (Oregon) to outlaw private schools in the 1920s. This effort was declared unconstitutional by the Supreme Court in the Pierce vs. the Society of Sisters decision.

[2] Not surprisingly, Chubb and Moe's analysis is also being criticized on empirical, conceptual and philosophical grounds. See, for example, the important paper by Bryk, Lee and Smith (1990).

[3] On the importance of supply-side as well as demand-side choice for effective choice systems, see Elmore (1988)

[4] On the complex and often inequitable system of school financing in the US, see Coons, Clune and Sugarman (1970) and Wise (1967).

[5] This description of the Community District 4 experience is drawn from Chubb and Moe (1990, pp.212-214) and Nathan (1990, 279-280). A G Green, in this volume, also discusses the District 4 experiment in his wider analysis of magnet schools.

[6] For a detailed discussion of the East Harlem experience, the dangers of recentralization, and the "creative non-compliance" that made this innovation successful, see Fliegel (1990)

[7] For support of this statement, see Ball (1990), Ball and Whitty (1990) and Whitty and Menter (forthcoming).

[8] For an evaluation of the Assisted Places Scheme, see Edwards, Fitz and Whitty (1989).

[9] Most of the British school reform literature is combative. Contrast, for example, the description of British reform in Ball and Whitty (1990) and Francis (1990) with that of American reform in Murphy (1990) or Boyd and Kerchner (1988).

References

Adler, M (1990) "Parental choice and the enhancement of children's interest". Paper presented at Seminar on Public and Private Choice in Education, Centre for Educational Sociology, University of Edinburgh, March 4.

Adler M, Petch A, & Tweedie J (1989) Parental Choice and Educational Policy, Edinburgh: Edinburgh University Press

Alves Michael J, & Willie Charles V (1987) "Controlled Choice Assignments: A New Approach to Desegregation", Urban Review, Vol.19 pp. 67-86.

Bacon K H (1990) "Liberals are joining conservatives in urging use of free-market philosophy to reform schools", Wall Street Journal, June 5, p. A24.

Ball S J (1990) Politics and Policy Making in Education: Explorations in Policy Sociology, London:Routledge.

Ball S J & Whitty G (eds) (1990, June) "English Education in a new ERA: Urban schooling after the Education Reform Act", Special issue of The Urban Review Vol.22 P. 2.

Bastian Ann (1990) "School Choice: Unwrapping the Package", in W L Boyd & H J Walberg (eds.), Choice in Education: Potential and Problems, Berkeley, CA:McCutchan.

Blank, Rolf K (1989) "Educational Effects of Magnet High Schools". Paper presented at Conference on Choice and Control in American Education, University of Wisconsin-Madison, May 17-19.

Boyd W L (1987, Fall) "Balancing public and private schools: The Australian approach and American implications", Educational Evaluation and Policy Analysis, Vol.9, Pt.3, pp. 183-198.

Boyd W L & Kerchner C T. (1988) The Politics of Excellence and Choice in Education, London: Falmer Press.

Boyd W L & Walberg H (eds) (1990) Choice in Education: Potential and Problems, Berkley, CA: McCutchan Publishing Corp.

Brimelow P. (1990) "American Perestroika," Forbes, May 14, pp. 82-86.

Bryk A S, Lee V E, & Smith J B (1990) "High School Organization and its Effects on Teachers and Students: An Interpretive Summary of the Research", in W H Clune & J F Witte (eds.), Choice and Control in American Education, Vol 1, New York: Falmer Press, pp. 135-226.

Caldwell B J (1989) "Paradox and Uncertainty in the Governance of Education". Paper presented at the annual meeting of the American Educational Research Association, San Francisco, March 29.

Carnegie Forum on Education and the Economy (1986) A Nation Prepared: Teachers for the 21st Century, Report of the Task Force on Teaching as a Profession. New York:Author.

Centre for the Study of Public Policy (1970, December) Education Vouchers: A Report on Financing Elementary Education by Grants to Parents, Cambridge, MA: Author.

Chubb J E & Moe T M (1990) Politics, Markets and America's Schools, Washington DC: The Brookings Institution.

Clark D L & Astuto T A (1986, October) "The significance and permanence of changes in federal education policy", Educational Researcher, pp 4-13.

Coons J E, Clune W H, and Sugarman S D (1970) Private Wealth and Public Education (Cambridge MA: Harvard University Press).

Coons J E & Sugarman S D (1978) Education by Choice: The Case for Family Control, Berkley, CA: University of California Press.

Cuban L (1979) "Determinants of curriculum change and stability, 1870-1970", in J Schaffarzick & G Sykes (eds) Value Conflicts and Curriculum Issues, Berkley, CA: McCutchan.

Doyle D P (1988) "The Excellence Movement, Academic Standards, a Core Curriculum, and Choice: How do they connect?", in W L Boyd & C T Kerchner (eds), The Politics of Excellence and Choice in Education, New York:Falmer Press.

Echols F, McPherson A & Willms J. "Parental Choice in Scotland", Journal of Education Policy, Vol. 5, Pt. 3, pp. 207-222.

Economist (1991, March 23) "Be Bold, Be British: A Lesson for America's Schools'", Vol. 318, No. 7699, pp. 19-20.

Education Week (1989, January 18) "Perhaps the single most promising reform idea" p. 24.

Edwards T, Fitz J, & Whitty G (1989) The State and Private Education: An Evaluation of the Assisted Places Scheme, London:Falmer Press.

Elmore R F (1988) "Choice in Public Education," in W L Boyd & C T Kerchner (eds), The Politics of Excellence and Choice in Education, London:Falmer Press.

Fliegel S (1990) "Creative Non-compliance," in W H Clune and J F Witte (eds), Choice and Control in American Education, Vol. 1, London:Falmer Press.

Friedman M (1955) "The Role of Government in Education", in R A Solo (ed), Economics and the Public Interest, New Brunswick, N J:Rutgers University Press.

Francis M (1990, June) "Race and the Education Reform Act", The Urban Review, Vol. 22, Pt. 2, pp. 115-129.

Gigot P A (1990) "Bush team fails the test on school choice", Wall Street Journal, June 8, p. A12.

Gigot P A (1991), "School reform now turns to revolution", Wall Street Journal, April 8, p. 6.

Glass G V & Matthews D A (1991, April) "Are data enough?", Educational Researcher, Vol. 20, Pt. 3, pp. 24-27.

Hawley W D (1988) "Missing Pieces of the Educational Reform Agenda," Educational Administration Quarterly, Vol. 24, pt. 4, pp.416-437.

Jencks C (1966, Winter) "Is the public school obsolete?", The Public Interest, Vol. 2, pp.18-27.

Kearns D & Doyle D (1988) Winning the Brain Race: A bold new plan to make our schools competitive, San Francisco: Institute for Contemporary Studies.

Kirst M W (1989) "Who should control the schools? Reassessing current policies", in T Sergiovanni & J Moore (eds), Schooling for Tomorrow, Boston:Allyn & Bacon, pp.62-89.

Mazzoni T & Sullivan B (1990) "Legislating Educational Choice in Minnesota: Politics and Prospects", in W L Boyd & H J Walberg (eds), Choice in Education: Potential and Problems, Berkley, CA:McCutchan.

McNeil L M (1986) Contradictions of Control: School Structure and School Knowledge, New York and London: Routledge and Kegan Paul/Metheun.

McNeil L M (1988) "The Politics of Texas School Reform", in W L Boyd & C T Kerchner (eds), The Politics of Excellence and Choice in Education, New York: Falmer Press.

Moore Donald, & Davenport Suzanne (1990) "School Choice: The New Improved Sorting Machine", in W L Boyd & H J Walberg (eds.), Choice in Education: Potential and Problems, Berkely CA:McCutchan.

Murphy J (ed) (1990) The Education Reform Movement of the 1980s, Berkley CA: McCutchan.

Nathan Joe (1990) "Progress, Problems, and Prospects of State Educational Choice Plans", in W L Boyd & H J Walberg (eds), Choice in Education: Potential and Problems, Berkley, CA:McCutchan.

National Commission on Excellence in Education (1983) A Nation at Risk: The Imperative for Educational Reform, Washington DC: US Government Printing Office.

National Governors Association (1986) Time for Results: The Governors' 1991 Report on Education, Washington DC, Author.

Norris B (1991) "A revolution starts with small change", Times Educational Supplement, May 3, p. 11.

Olson L. (1991) "Proposals for private-school choice reviving at all levels of government", Education Week, Vol. 10, No. 22, February 20, pp. 1, 10-11.

Raywid, Mary Anne (1989a) The Case for Public Schools of Choice, Bloomington, IN: Phi Delta Kappa.

Raywid, Mary Anne (1989b) "The Mounting Case for Schools of Choice", in Nathan (1989).

Rothman R (1990) "Paper launches academic attack on Chubb-Moe book on education", Education Week, Vol 10, No 11, November 14 pp. 1, 20.

Thomas, Hywel (forthcoming) "The Education Reform Movement in England and Wales", in H Beare and W Boyd (eds.), Restructuring Schools: An international Perspective, London:Falmer Press.

Tyack D (1974) The One Best System, Cambridge, Mass: Harvard University Press.

Walker R (1989) "Bush to appoint group to proffer education ideas", Education Week, June 14, pp. 1 & 17.

Wall Street Journal (1990) "Review & Outlook: Teachers vs kids", June 6, p. A16.

Whitty G & Menter I (forthcoming) "The Progress of Restructuring", in D Coulby and L Bash (eds), The 1988 Education Reform Act: Conflict and Contradiction, London:Cassell.

Wise A C (1967) Rich Schools, Poor Schools, Chicago: University of Chicago Press.

Wong K K (1989) "Choice in Public Schools: Their Insitutional Functions and Distributive Consequences". Paper presented at Annual Meeting of the American Political Science Association, Atlanta, August 31- September 3.

Notes on Contributors

Thomas Bailey is Director of the Institute on Education and the Economy, Teachers College, Columbia University. He is the author of numerous articles and case studies including "Market Forces and Private Sector Processes in Government Policy: The Job Training *Partnership* Act," *Journal of Policy Analysis and Management* (Winter, 1988), and "Primary, Secondary and Enclave Labour Markets: A Training Systems Approach," *American Sociology Review* (1991). He has completed one of the largest independent studies of the Private Sector Industry Council in the USA.

William Lowe Boyd is Distinguished Professor of Education at Pennsylvania State University and in 1990-91 was a visiting Fulbright Scholar at the University of Liverpool. His research speciality is education policy and politics, and he is co-author of *Private Schools and Public Policy: International Perspectives* (with James Cibulka) and *Choice in Education: Potential and Problems* (with Herbert Walberg).

Sarah H. Cleveland is a 1992 Yale Law School graduate and is currently clerking for a Federal district judge in Washington, DC. She has worked as a consultant for the US Commission on the Skills of the American Workforce and contributed to the 1990 National Commission on Education and the Economy report, *America's Choice: High Skills or Low Wages.*

David Finegold is a policy analyst at RAND, specializing in international comparisons of countries' education and training and industrial systems. He is the author of *Education, Training and Economic Competitiveness* (Oxford University Press, forthcoming) as well as a contributor to proposals for reforming British post-compulsory and higher education.

Anthony G. Green is Fellow in the Policy Studies Centre at the Institute of Education, University of London. He has conducted a three-year study of the development of magnet schools in the USA and Britain.

Laurel McFarland co-edited this volume while an economist at the Brookings Institution in Washington, DC. She has written several articles on the economics of post-secondary education and has contributed to comparative education projects at the National Academy of Sciences and the Organization for Economic Cooperation and Development. She is currently writing a book on the relationship between community colleges and labor markets.

Christine Peterson is a senior research analyst at RAND. Her research interests include the economics of household behavior, labor markets, health, and military manpower issues. She has co-authored numerous publications in those areas, using large micro datasets.

David Phillips is a Fellow of St Edmund Hall, Oxford, and Lecturer in Educational Studies, and Director of the Centre for Comparative Studies in Education, based at the Department of Educational Studies, University of Oxford. The author of many books and articles on comparative education, educational policy, and modern language teaching, he is also Editor of the *Oxford Review of Education* and serves on the Editorial Board of *Comparative Education*.

David Raffe is Professor of Sociology of Education at the University of Edinburgh, and co-Director of the Centre for Educational Sociology. His research interests include education and the youth labor market, with a particular interest in vocational and post-compulsory education and comparative studies. His publications include *Fourteen to Eighteen* (1984) and *Education and the Youth Labor Market* (1988).

William Richardson is Senior Research Fellow at the Centre for Education and Industry, University of Warwick. His research interests are divided between sixteenth-century political studies and education and labor policy in twentieth-century national economies. His most recent book, co-edited with David Finegold and John Woolhouse, is on the reform of post-16 education and training in England and Wales.

David Brian Robertson is Associate Professor of Political Science at the University of Missouri, St Louis. He is the Associate Editor of *Journal of Policy History* and the co-author (with Dennis R. Judd) of *The Development of American Public Policy: The Structure of Policy Restraint* (1989). He is currently writing a book on the role of federalism and business in the development of American labor market policy.

Russell W. Rumberger is Associate Professor of Education, University of California, Santa Barbara. His research interests include education and work, school dropouts, and education policy.

Hong W. Tan is Senior Economist in the Private Sector Development Department at the World Bank in Washington, DC. His recent publications include "Private Sector Training in the US," and "Youth Training in the US, Great Britain, and Australia," in *Research in Labor Economics*, volume 13,

1992 (Ronald Ehrenberg, editor). His current research interest is the cross-national study of determinants and outcomes of enterprise-based training in seven countries.

Jerold L. Waltman obtained his PhD at Indiana University and is professor of political science at the University of Southern Mississippi. His works include *Copying Other Nation's Policies* (1980) and *The Political Origins of the US Income Tax* (1985); he has also co-edited three other volumes, *Dilemmas of Change in British Politics* (1984), *Political Economy: Public Policies in the United States and Britain* (1987), and *The Political Role of Law Courts in Modern Democracies* (1988). At the moment, he is completing a text in American politics which will be published in 1993.